Jeannie Morgan has done
understand healing both for
recommend this book to you

Robby Dawkins, International Sp
What Jesus Did"

Jeannie Morgan is the real deal. She exemplifies the very subject
she writes about as a compelling witness, a fruitful practitioner,
and an effective trainer in healing prayer. Our faith and our
churches need both the message and the ministry Jeannie
brings in such a thoughtful and heartfelt way.

David Parker, Senior Pastor, Desert Vineyard California

Jeannie has many years of experience in the healing ministry.
This is a very useful handbook for any who feel called to be
involved – it is very readable, very practical, and very informative
with fascinating accounts of how people have been wonderfully
blessed through this ministry. We warmly recommend this book.

David and Mary Pytches, Speakers and authors

Jeannie's new book is a down-to-earth, practical and useful book
for anyone wanting to be involved in Jesus' healing ministry. Buy
it, read it and put it into practice!

Debby Wright, Senior Pastor Trent Vineyard Nottingham

If you want to see the ministry of Jesus more fully embedded in
the life of your church, then this highly readable and practical
book is a must! Jeannie shares with us deep insights forged on
the anvil of experience.

Mark Bailey, Lead Pastor Trinity Cheltenham, New Wine Leadership Team

By the same author
Encounter the Holy Spirit
Let the Healing Begin

www.ourhandshishealing.co.uk

OUR HANDS
HIS HEALING

A PRACTICAL GUIDE TO
Prayer Ministry and Inner Healing

JEANNIE MORGAN

MONARCH
BOOKS

Oxford, UK & Grand Rapids, Michigan, USA

Published by Monarch Books (an imprint of Lion Hudson plc)
Wilkinson House, Jordan Hill Road, Oxford OX2 8DR, England
Email: monarch@lionhudson.com www.lionhudson.com/monarch
and by Elevation (an imprint of the Memralife Group)
Memralife Group, 14 Horsted Square, Uckfield, East Sussex TN22 1QG
Tel: +44 (0)1825 746530; Fax +44 (0)1825 748899;
www.elevationmusic.com

ISBN 978 0 85721 491 1
e-ISBN 978 0 85721 492 8

First edition 2014

Acknowledgments

Unless otherwise stated, Scripture quotations taken from the Holy Bible, New
International Version Anglicised. Copyright © 1979, 1984, 2011 Biblica, formerly
International Bible Society. Used by permission of Hodder & Stoughton Ltd, an Hachette
UK company. All rights reserved. "NIV" is a registered trademark of Biblica. UK
trademark number 1448790.
Scripture quotations marked NCV taken from the New Century Version. Copyright © by
Thomas Nelson, Inc. Used by permission. All rights reserved.
Scripture quotations marked NLT are taken from the Holy Bible, New Living Translation,
copyright © 1996, 2004, 2007 by Tyndale House Foundation. Used by permission of
Tyndale House Publishers, Inc., Carol Stream, Illinois 60188. All rights reserved.
Scripture quotations marked The Message taken from The Message. Copyright © by
Eugene H. Peterson 1993, 1994, 1995, 1996, 2000, 2001, 2002. Used by permission of
NavPress Publishing Group.
Scripture quotations marked NRSV are from The New Revised Standard Version of the
Bible copyright © 1989 by the Division of Christian Education of the National Council of
Churches in the USA. Used by permission. All rights reserved.
Scripture quotations marked NKJV taken from the New King James Version. Copyright
© 1982 by Thomas Nelson, Inc. Used by permission. All rights reserved.
Scripture quotations marked KJV taken from The Authorized (King James) Version.
Rights in the Authorized Version are vested in the Crown. Reproduced by permission of
the Crown's patentee, Cambridge University Press.

A catalogue record for this book is available from the British Library

Printed and bound in the UK, April 2014, LH26

Readers may photocopy Chapter 18 and up to ten further pages free of charge for use in
training.

Note: Some names have been changed for the sake of privacy.

To my dear friends David Pytches, Mary Pytches
and Mike Pilavachi
You have enriched my life. I have been loved, taught,
challenged, encouraged, impassioned, and inspired by
you all for the last thirty-plus years. Thank you for so
generously imparting to me, and a multitude of others,
the treasure you have received from Jesus, particularly:

Freely you have received; freely give.

*"'The kingdom of heaven has come near.' Heal those
who are ill, raise the dead, cleanse those who have
leprosy, drive out demons. Freely you have received;
freely give."*

Matthew 10:8

CONTENTS

SPECIAL DEDICATION

David Pytches

David, a big THANK YOU that all those years ago you "stepped out of the boat" and encouraged many others of us to do likewise.

You risked so much all those years ago as you led many of us in St Andrew's Church to minister in the power of the Holy Spirit. We made mistakes as we were learning but you taught us and pointed the way. Your passion was, and still is, infectious. My time at St Andrew's Church under your leadership was a huge training ground. You are an amazing leader and I thank God for you. Because of the many risks you took under the anointing of the Holy Spirit, many ministries have been birthed.

Through the past thirty plus years you have encouraged me in so many ways. Thank you for not giving up on me, especially in those early days before I became a Christian, when I was rejecting many things you were showing me about Jesus. Your input was key to my conversion, along with visits from another dear friend, Barry Kissell.

I love you very much and want to thank you for not only reading the manuscript to this book but giving me your helpful and wise comments. Thank you so much for not using a red pen!

Mary Pytches

Mary, your passion for Jesus and His healing ministry has been an inspiration to me. In those early days your quest to go deeper and seek the Lord for models of ministry that you could share and equip others with was truly pioneering. Your desire to bring healing to the broken-hearted has been a role model to me. Many times in those early days I was at the receiving end of your tender prayer ministry when I was fragile and hurting. I am so thankful to the Lord for you: as you ministered to me you also encouraged me to minister to others.

Mary, you have imparted much wisdom to so many, including me. On behalf of those who have been at the receiving end of your teaching, equipping, or hands laid on... thank you for the legacy. You have a wealth of understanding and compassion for the broken-hearted and such a big desire for people to be the best that they can be.

Your sincerity and integrity in ministry is something I seek to emulate. I love you, Mary, and value our chats; I always leave feeling encouraged. I look forward to seeing what the Lord does through you in the years ahead.

Mike Pilavachi

Mike, my friend, you never cease to amaze me. I have adopted your statement that prayer ministry is for everyone no matter what age they are or who they are as long as they have a pulse and love Jesus! Your refreshing approach draws everyone in. Many times over the years, without you probably realising, you have imparted to me permission to go forward, stepping up the risk factor in prayer ministry. Your love and passion for Jesus is infectious. I love the way you disperse hype, intensity, and fear during times of ministry in the power of the Holy Spirit. The way you are always concerned for the "one" among the crowds, your constant pushing through to see more of Jesus, and your passion and love for the desperate, the hurting, and the marginalised is truly inspirational.

Thank you for your honesty and transparency as a leader. It has been wonderful watching the Lord growing Soul Survivor Watford Church under your leadership.

The many years we have worked together have been invaluable to me. Ken and I have had many adventures with you following Jesus and we look forward to many more. We both love you, Mike. Thank you, my friend, for encouraging me more than you can imagine.

ACKNOWLEDGMENTS

Thank you to all those who have allowed me to be part of their healing journey through prayer ministry. I have changed your name if your story is mentioned in this book.

Thanks also go to my husband Ken, the love of my life: you are the "chalk to my cheese"! I value your comments and your wisdom. Thank you for not complaining this past year when I have been shut away in my office for many hours typing, when we could have spent more time together. Thank you for the reminders of the time, getting me to stop and eat as it was usually way past lunchtime!

I am grateful for the help of Tony Collins of Lion Hudson, for once more guiding me through getting this book into print. Your timely comments and advice have been much appreciated. I valued your encouragements during the editing process.

To Penelope Wilcock: thank you for such a speedy, well thought through edit. I valued your detail and care.

To Jenny Ward and everyone else at Lion Hudson/Monarch: a big thank you for the part you played along the way.

To Phil Loose and everyone at Elevation: thank you for everything you have done too.

Most importantly, thank you, my Jesus, for Your ministry that You allow me to be part of sometimes, as You release prisoners and set the captives free.

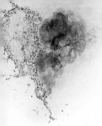

FOREWORD

I have known Jeannie and her husband Ken for nearly thirty years, and throughout that time I have witnessed her praying for people and seeing God do the most remarkable things. Jeannie has both known God's incredible healing first-hand and ministered His healing power to people's hearts, minds and bodies, week in and week out, year in and year out, at our local church, in her everyday life, at our festivals, and during her travels around the country and the world.

Jeannie has an incredible gift for listening to God and has learned much over the years about the ways God sets people free from physical and emotional pain. She is no armchair theologian but an anointed and gifted practitioner who grounds her teaching in examples and stories from the many things she has seen God do. Jeannie also has an extraordinary gift for releasing others into ministry and imparting what she's learned to encourage and equip the church. Her heart is clear that God wants to use every single one of us to minister His love and healing, and this book deals with the questions, doubts and fears that would hinder many of us from sharing in this ministry.

If you would like to learn how to pray for physical healing and for broken hearts to be mended, and if you want to cooperate with God in seeing people restored and set free, I cannot recommend this book highly enough. Whether you want to pray for friends who don't yet know Jesus, be involved in ministry at church, or are looking to train and equip others in ministry, this will be an invaluable resource for you.

Jeannie's compassionate heart, wisdom, humility, practical nature, integrity, and her love for Jesus and for people, all shine through in this book. I strongly and warmly commend *Our Hands, His Healing* to you with my heartfelt endorsement.

Mike Pilavachi
Soul Survivor

PREFACE

The fact that many churches are starting to have a ministry of prayer for physical, spiritual, and mental healing is something that is to be greatly welcomed. If we do genuinely believe in a God who answers prayer today, then there is no more obvious way of practising that belief than by having a ministry of prayer for those who need help. To fail to pray is, in effect, to deny the faith.

Yet the reality is that prayer ministry in the church context raises many issues. Some of these issues are theological: How do we pray? How do we know what we should pray for? What's going on when nothing seems to happen? Other issues are practical: Where should prayer ministry occur? What qualifications should those involved have? Should I pray for someone of the opposite sex? Where, exactly, on someone's body should I place my hands when I pray for them?

These issues do not have easy answers and it is all too possible to stumble forward with enthusiastic experimentation in the pious hope that "it will all work out fine". Well, God is gracious and in the area of prayer ministry (as elsewhere) He no doubt often works through our mistakes and lets things "work out fine". Yet if we mishandle prayer ministry it is all too easy for what should be a rich blessing to turn into something that causes hurt, confusion, and division.

It is in the light of these challenges that I very much welcome this stimulating handbook on the ministry of prayer healing by my friend and veteran of Soul Survivor, Jeannie Morgan. A long-term practitioner of healing, whether physical, emotional, mental or spiritual, Jeannie here presents some very helpful guidelines on how to conduct prayer ministry.

I seem to remember describing Jeannie's previous book, *Encounter the Holy Spirit*, as being perceptive, practical, and powerful. Well, those qualities are here too, but there are also other virtues, not least the fact that this book balances things that might be seen as opposites. So, for instance, it is both *spiritual* and *practical*. It looks warmly to Jesus and the work of His Holy Spirit, but also covers what we now call "best practice". You will find references to holiness and halitosis, to angels and to a recipe for anointing oil. Jeannie has managed the rare achievement of having her head in heaven with her feet firmly on the ground.

It is also both *optimistic* and *realistic*. Jeannie firmly believes that physical and spiritual or inner healing occurs, yet she is a wise enough practitioner to know that healing comes as the gift of a sovereign God and cannot be commanded by prayer. We ask the Lord that healing will occur but accept equally (He *is* Lord) that He may withhold it. A particular strength here are those places where she acknowledges the role of medicine, hospitals, and psychiatry in helping the hurting.

It is *sane* and *stimulating*. Jeannie is careful enough to make no false promises and no exaggerated claims. Yet she is challenging and encouraging, particularly in helping us to consider the possibilities of healing of those festering mental wounds that may go back decades. We are reminded that God has the power to heal wounds – whether they be mental or spiritual – that we may have long considered incurable.

Finally this book is, at the same time, both *authoritative* and *humble*. With her years of experience in prayer ministry, Jeannie could easily have delivered rules on how things must be done. Instead, she protests – with genuine humility – that she is not an authority in this area. I am afraid I beg to differ: she knows what she is talking about. Nevertheless, it is both refreshing and challenging to see how she wishes Jesus to take all the glory.

This is a how-to book. Go and do it.

J.John (Revd Canon)
www.philotrust.com

SETTING THE SCENE

I do not consider myself to be an authority on the subjects spelt out in this book. My aim is to share my experience of seeing Jesus, in His powerful love, using an ordinary person to set others free. I want to share with you things I have discovered on my journey of ministering to broken people in the hope that you too will be encouraged in your journey of healing and grow in prayer ministry. I too am still learning and hope that it will always be so.

One of the things I love about Jesus showing the disciples how to heal the sick is that they only did what He showed them to do; they didn't drag a big trolley of reference books behind them to consult on how to do it! There is no ABC for healing the sick or casting out demons – no fixed formulae. This book is not a reference-type text book. It's for your guidance: a collection of practical ways for seeing more happening when we pray for people who are "broken-hearted" or struggling with past hurts. It also explores hard questions like "What do I do when I lay hands on someone and nothing seems to be happening?" There are also plenty of accounts of people receiving healing and how that seemed to happen.

The book is in three parts and includes notes to leaders:

1. Prayer Ministry
2. Inner Healing Ministry
3. Pastoral Prayer Ministry

There are many books written on the subject of the Holy Spirit and gifts of the Holy Spirit. Because of this I have not covered these important aspects in this book. I have assumed that the reader will already have a knowledge and experience of the Holy

Spirit. (I have recommended some particular titles at the end.)

We can't rely on the visiting speaker at our churches or the person on the stage at a conference to be the one who does and sees "the healing miracles". We are all meant to be involved in one kind of ministry or another (1 Corinthians 12:5). Clearly some are called to heal the sick. It doesn't take intelligence, just an available willing heart. It is certainly an area of great need.

In the Bible Jesus ministered wholeness, not just healing of the body. He healed people spiritually and emotionally. I am excited at seeing people made whole through the process of healing.

If someone receives emotional, mental, or spiritual healing, the effect is far reaching. As people are freed from their past, becoming the person God intended them to be, the knock-on effect for their whole church is that increasing numbers are available for God to use in advancing His Kingdom. Their friends and family may also be challenged by their attitude, commitment, and choices.

It is for freedom that Christ has set us free.

Galatians 5:1

I want to see freedom in the body of Christ. Many churches are full of people held captive to their own and others' sin. Many people have never known affirmation or what it is to feel safe. Some have experienced so little love that they cannot receive any of the wholeness that Jesus wants to give them. Some hate themselves and believe no one could ever love what they see as hateful.

I want to see those who don't know Jesus receive His love into their brokenness.

Ministering to broken people should carry with it a warning. You will get addicted! You can't get enough of watching Jesus changing lives, bringing restoration and healing.

I passionately want to set captives free, enabling them in their turn to set others free. As we are set free it will draw our eyes to those outside the church, taking the healing and freedom of Jesus to a hurting world.

I believe that after just one session of prayer ministry, people who don't know Jesus cannot help but be drawn closer to Him. We need to have this ministry in our churches but also to take it beyond the churches out into the world.

That is why we have to get more involved in "doing the stuff" that Jesus taught the disciples to do.

Are you up for it?

PART 1
PRAYER MINISTRY

Chapter 1

OUR HANDS

CONTROL

What comes into your mind when you think of the word "control"?

If you are a man, then maybe it's a "remote control".

If you are a fashion model, then probably it's "weight control".

If you are a youth, then it might be "zit control".

If you are an engaged Christian couple, then it's probably "self-control".

If you are a married woman, then possibly "birth control".

If you are on *X Factor*, then it could be "voice control".

If you are an airline pilot, then it's probably "air traffic control".

And if you are an elderly person, then it is probably "bladder control".

As you can see, the word "control" is part of our everyday language.

Most of us like being "in control". Sometimes when we can't *be* in control we can feel very uncomfortable. This is an important aspect of prayer ministry because we *can never* control the Holy Spirit.

MINISTERING OUT OF LOVE AND COMPASSION

When we are ministering the love and healing of Jesus in the power of the Holy Spirit, our spirit has to be tracking and interacting with Him. We give control over to *Him*, asking Him what *He* is doing as, like Jesus, we can do only what we see the Father doing (John 5:19) if we are to minister faithfully.

Before continuing to read why don't you join me in praying?

Dear Holy Spirit, I choose to give over control to You now. I want You to use me and guide me into truth. Please fill me with Your power. Show me as I read this book those things You want me to know. Encourage me to launch out in prayer ministry, bringing the healing of Jesus. For His glory. Amen!

Almost thirty years ago I started ministering to broken people. Jesus had brought so much healing into my own life that I longed to see others receive from Him too. After ministering for a few years, I was prompted by the Holy Spirit to ask for more of Him. Then some years later I said to Jesus, "Show me how to love people." I made this my daily prayer for about a year. Just those six words. Prayers don't have to be long. On a few other occasions, at key times when the Holy Spirit was moving in power in our church or at conferences, I have asked Jesus, "Give me Your heart for the broken." Also I have asked Him, "Jesus, show me what You see; break my heart with the things that break Yours." Believe me, Jesus will take you at your word! Don't pray these words unless you mean it.

Why not do that now? If you are serious about ministering to the broken, pray along with me:

Dear Holy Spirit, please come and fill me now with the love of Jesus. Give me Your heart for the broken. Show me what You see. Break my heart with the things that break Your heart, Jesus. I want to love people like You do. Take me on a journey of learning how to minister in the power of the Holy Spirit, bringing Your healing, hope, deliverance, and freedom. Fill me with Your love and compassion for Your broken people. Amen.

Having your heart broken for those with emotional pain isn't pleasant; it is uncomfortable. It may mean that you will start weeping at unexpected times. Many times I have walked into our lounge catching the last ten minutes of a documentary showing acts of injustice and have started to weep as my heart has been wrenched for those displaying pain. Don't get me wrong: it's not a girlie weepy thing. It's seeing people who need the love of Jesus and experiencing His love for them and His desire to set them free from inner pain.

Hearing another's story of hurt during prayer ministry may cause us to feel emotional. It may even remind us of our own story of inner emotional pain. Feelings of empathy may rise within us for the one we are praying for. It is easy to minister out of this place, and indeed outside of prayer ministry times it is useful for launching us into action to comfort and provide practical help for the person suffering. However, during prayer ministry, we could easily get worn out and emotionally drained by ministering to a lot of people using empathy. Practising prayer ministry with the compassion of Jesus (as well as His power) means that we can (if necessary) pray for one person after another without feeling emotionally drained. Also our empathy shows that we care, but it is the powerful love, compassion, and mercy of Jesus that brings forgiveness, healing, freedom, and restoration.

Praying for the broken-hearted is addictive. At times you may experience the tremendous love of Jesus – His compassion for those that have been abused or taken advantage of in some way. At times this may feel like righteous anger. Our reward in doing prayer ministry is seeing Jesus set people free. But it also costs us. It takes time. It means a ministry in the background. No one else sees what you are doing. It offers little status or recognition. In spiritual terms, though, there is an awareness that the enemy's territory is being plundered as you see the person you are praying for being set free and able to receive more from Jesus. Are you ready for the journey of a lifetime?

If we start ministering to the broken-hearted with just our own sympathy or empathy, we will soon get discouraged, tired, and worn out. If we try to minister without the love of Jesus, then the Bible tells us that we will just be an ugly noise, a clanging cymbal (1 Corinthians 13:1). After speaking of various gifts Paul tells us that the greatest gift is love (1 Corinthians 13). Ministering to the broken is a ministry of love. Without the power of the Holy Spirit we would be at a loss as to how to proceed. A good starting point is to ask the Holy Spirit for "gifts of healing". It is okay to ask God for spiritual gifts. The Bible tells us to "eagerly desire gifts of the Spirit" (1 Corinthians 14:1). As God's children He wants us to be as a child – not childish but child-like in our asking. A young child doesn't stop and wonder whether it's okay to ask for things.

MINISTERING IN THE GIFTS

I remember when my grandson Ted was eight years old, his parents asked him what gifts he wanted for his next birthday. He didn't hold back in his asking. After searching through a very large catalogue of *Star Wars* Lego sets Ted covered two sides of A4 paper with his list of what he would like to receive! We are meant to be like that with our heavenly Father. He wants to give good gifts to His children and He gives the Holy Spirit to those who ask (Luke 11:13).

I am presuming that you already know about gifts of the Holy Spirit. If not, I suggest you read one of the many books that cover this subject. Using these gifts is an important part of prayer ministry. Two books that might help you learn more about the Holy Spirit are: *Come Holy Spirit*, by David Pytches, and *Encounter the Holy Spirit*, by Jeannie Morgan.

As the Bible shows us, each one of us gets to receive at least one of these gifts and all the gifts of the Holy Spirit are available to us all of the time as and when the Holy Spirit chooses to use them through us.

> **Now to each one the manifestation of the Spirit is given for the common good.**
>
> 1 Corinthians 12:7

As we start and continue to use these gifts we are given more and more opportunities to use them. We gain in confidence and often these gifts develop and grow. Other gifts may then be added to complement and interact with each other.

Some people manifest a particular gift so frequently that it develops into a recognisable "ministry". The ownership of both gift and ministry as always belongs to the Holy Spirit. It is His ministry, not ours.

We are all commanded by Jesus to heal the sick and cast out demons. He can empower and use each one of us to do this. As Paul tells us, *all* the gifts are available to *all* of us, as and when the Holy Spirit decides (1 Corinthians 14). Not everyone is given "gifts of healing" to use as a permanent gifting but that doesn't mean that we can't ask for them – "eagerly ask for spiritual gifts..." – or that the Holy Spirit will not use this gift through us when He chooses to. We know we have received this gift if we see people regularly receiving healing. The offer is plural, *"gifts* of healing". My theory is that this means physical, emotional, spiritual, and mental healing. Some people seem to operate more often in one or the other. This doesn't mean that if your *thing* is inner healing then you will not see physical healing taking place, as healing is about wholeness. It may be that your passion will be for one or the other. All those praying for healing should want wholeness for themselves and for others and be praying for this when ministering.

If we know that our motive in the healing ministry is a love for people, then with confidence we can ask for gifts of healing. Also if you know someone who already prays for the broken-hearted then you could ask them to pray for you to receive this gift. If you already operate in gifts of healing, ask for other gifts to complement them – prophecy, words of knowledge, discerning of spirits, tongues, or miracles.

Let us just pray about that now:

Jesus, I thank You that You send Your Holy Spirit, the power from on high, to be our Counsellor and Comforter. Thank You that I can ask for these gifts of the Holy Spirit to build up the church and bring people into the Kingdom. Please cleanse me now so that I may receive what You want to give me. Thank You for everything You did on the cross for me. Thank You that You want to use me to bring healing and wholeness in Your name. I eagerly ask also for spiritual gifts, especially prophecy, words of knowledge, gifts of healing, discernment, and miracles. I ask that You will release these gifts to me and through me as I lay hands on those who need Your healing and wholeness. Glorify Your name through me, Lord. Amen.

As already mentioned I started to pray for others after receiving a lot of healing from past hurts myself. In the church where I became a Christian (St Andrew's Church, Chorleywood, under the leadership of Bishop David Pytches), we were taught that we had freely received and so we were to freely give (Matthew 10:8). One week I would be screaming out with my own inner pain and receiving prayer ministry and the following week I would be laying hands on others as they received freedom from their pain. We were like a family, not embarrassed at seeing each other fall apart. It brought us closer together. We were all the same: the walking wounded. Our vicar David Pytches would say, "The nursery may become disorderly, because that's life. The cemetery is very orderly, but that's because it is a place of death."

Some times during prayer ministry were definitely more like being in a nursery!

I have a passion to see the body of Christ, whether in a children's group, a youth group, or an older congregation, empowered to be the Healing Church – Jesus bringing healing through His people. "Bring us the lost!" should be our cry. We are meant to be ministering healing and wholeness to believers inside the church and taking this ministry beyond the building into the streets and homes of those "outside" the church. That might mean ministering to strangers or to our friends and family. Jesus and the disciples ministered to strangers, friends, and family and we are meant to do the same.

HEALING ON THE STREETS

A few years ago our church (Soul Survivor Watford) started something called WHOTS (Watford Healing On The Streets). Every month a group of people set up a row of five chairs and a vertical banner with the word "HEALING" on it and ask passers-by if they would like prayer. Some amazing things have happened. We were encouraged to start doing this by a group from Causeway Coast Vineyard in Northern Ireland who have been doing it since 2005. They have seen many people healed on the streets. Sometimes when people just walked past those praying, the Holy Spirit came upon them and healed them! How easy is that? On the two occasions I personally went out with the team, I saw Jesus bring healing. It is embarrassing at first, as passers-by don't always want to know, so gradually we learnt some tactics. To help people feel at ease members of our team who wanted to receive healing would occupy two of the seats so that passers-by could see them receiving prayer and understand what might be involved if they came forward. This gave them confidence to come up when we invited them to come for prayer for healing.

Many significant healings have taken place and we have seen people come along to church as a result of the healing they received.

In the past I have also ministered healing to strangers in the street when I have been on my own as and when prompted by the Holy Spirit. I have ministered to a stranger outside a hospital, on a hospital ward, on the street where I live, outside my local supermarket, as well as on holiday abroad. Each time something worthwhile has happened. Those I prayed for seemed to really appreciate being ministered to and were visibly moved often to tears as they sensed the love of Jesus. Healing has occurred for some while others have received partial healing. Although no miracles so far, one person in hospital gave her life to Jesus on my second visit, which I count as a miracle.

I want to encourage you to try this for yourself. The more we risk the more we see.

An inspiring book to read that includes ministering to those who don't know Jesus is *Do What Jesus Did*, by Robby Dawkins – a real-life field guide to healing the sick, routing demons, and changing lives forever.

HEALING IN THE CHURCH

Our churches may include people who have been abused, whether physically, emotionally, sexually, mentally, or spiritually. Some may even have suffered the whole lot. They could have been bullied or raped, lied to or taken advantage of in some way. Others live with secrets festering away or consciences riddled with guilt.

No wonder numerous churches exhibit powerlessness instead of advancing the Kingdom! There are vast numbers of people who are tied up by past pain. The good news is that it doesn't have to remain this way. We can all be used by God to set captives free and release prisoners (Isaiah 61:1). A lot of people lack courage or have not known the means to be used as channels for the powerful love of Jesus. He can come and visit those imprisoned by pain. I have experienced Him do this for me personally, and seen Him set free countless others over many years of prayer ministry.

Let us make ourselves available to the Holy Spirit to use, learning from each other, and of course from the Comforter and Counsellor the Holy Spirit, how to minister to the broken-hearted. It doesn't take superior intelligence. It's just being a willing, open, and available child of God. The great news is we don't have to be all healed up and made totally whole before He can begin to use us.

If we waited for that we might have to wait until we get to heaven! I was healed, I am being healed, I will be healed – but I'm not letting imperfection hold me back.

RECEIVING A VISION

In the 1980s at a John Wimber conference (the founder of the Vineyard Churches) I saw a horrific scene in my mind's eye while praying – a vision of row after row of dead people stretching miles into the distance. It was very dark with no light except for a small glimmer the size of a ten-pence piece on the nose of one of the dead bodies. I heard the words, "These are the casualties of war." I knew this meant they had lived in darkness and died in the same way. Then I heard the words, "How much of My light have you shone in that darkness?"

The voice wasn't condemning me, just asking the question. As I watched that small piece of light shining on just a tiny part of one person I sobbed and sobbed for about an hour. I felt mortified as I realised I'd had the opportunity but not taken it, to shine the light of the love of Jesus into someone else's life. As I repented, the Holy Spirit came upon me with such joy. Then I realised that in the past I had felt powerless to do anything but now all I needed was to be available to Him. *He* would be the Teacher, Enabler, Comforter, and Counsellor. All I had to do was wait, watch, listen, and speak only the words He gave me when ministering. This took off all the pressure: it was His work, not mine; not *my* ministry but *His* and *His alone*. The only one to get the glory would be Jesus.

Let us pray about that now:

> *Jesus, I know I haven't the means, ability, or strength to make anything happen – to bring healing to the broken-hearted. But I do know that You can do all things. All You want is for me to be an empty vessel. I ask now that You would forgive me and cleanse me from anything that would prevent me from doing that. Forgive me my pride for thinking that I can do anything in my own power. Forgive me my fear that has kept me from stepping out in Your name to heal the sick and broken, and cast out demons. I offer myself to*

*You, to do with as **You** will. Please give me Your heart of mercy. Shine Your light on those You are calling me to see. I want to see with Your eyes. Give me many opportunities to lay hands on those who need You. Empower me now, Holy Spirit. Amen.*

MODEL OF MINISTRY

At Soul Survivor Watford Church we use the model of ministry we learned at St Andrew's Church Chorleywood under the leadership of David Pytches. This was demonstrated to us by John Wimber and his team. Over the years we have found this format to work really well. It has safeguards built in for those being prayed for as well as for the prayer team itself. This doesn't mean all other practices of prayer ministry are wrong, but when we gather a ministry team for one of the festivals or at our church, we make sure that people joining our team are willing to lay down their own expression of ministry and accept ours for the occasion, so that we are all "singing the same tune".

UNDER AUTHORITY

We all need to be under authority. If we are part of a ministry team at our church then we need to be under the authority and leadership of the ministry team leaders. They in turn will need to be under the authority of the pastor/minister. This is good practice, as we all need to be accountable, teachable, and open to correction. We can't join and then insist on our own agenda. If we have a need to be needed or in control, as we pray for others they will sense that. As they open themselves up to the Holy Spirit they will also be sensitive to the spirit of the person who is praying for them. People who have been at the receiving end of ministry from someone bringing their own needs into the healing dynamic have described to me a feeling as if all the blood were being drained from their body – very uncomfortable. They just want the prayer time to be over as the sensation prevents them from receiving. Unfortunately prayer ministry sometimes attracts needy people who do not have the maturity to refrain from imposing their own emotional condition upon the situation.

So it is vital to establish a set of values, guidelines, and character requirements as we approach prayer ministry for healing. We have found the guidelines and principles outlined in the following pages to be important in helping us keep a sense of propriety and a safeguard for both those praying and those being prayed for.

For ease of reference, throughout the rest of this book "ministry in the power of the Holy Spirit" will be referred to as "prayer ministry".

For want of a better word, those ministering will be referred to as "Pray-ers" and those receiving prayer ministry will be referred to as "Receivers".

VALUES OF PRAYER MINISTRY

Isaiah prophesied the coming of such ministry:

> The Spirit of the Sovereign Lord is upon me because he has anointed me to preach good news to the poor. He has sent me to bind up the brokenhearted, to proclaim freedom for the captives and release from darkness for the prisoners, to proclaim the year of the Lord's favour... to comfort all who mourn and provide for those who grieve... to bestow on them a crown of beauty instead of ashes, the oil of joy instead of mourning, and a garment of praise instead of a spirit of despair. They will be called oaks of righteousness, a planting of the Lord for the display of his splendour.
>
> Isaiah 61:1–3

This is a very rich passage of Scripture. I would encourage you to meditate on the whole of Isaiah 61 and let the Holy Spirit speak to you through it. Then just wait in the stillness for Jesus to come close.

JESUS

Obviously our model for ministry is Jesus. Everything we do is done in His name. We are to honour Him and to bring glory to His name, not ours. He didn't heal people because He wanted to be famous or look good; He was moved by divine commission and compassion. He ministered to outcasts and the lowly. We need to realise that we are ministering as a channel of His love: no more, no less. He has all power and authority. Nothing can separate us from the love of God that is in Christ Jesus.

In our prayer ministry we want Jesus to look good, not us. So we don't draw attention to ourselves in any way by having an inappropriate dress code – not wearing anything too revealing or showing too much flesh. We also need to be aware of our personal hygiene as well as keeping our breath fresh, especially after eating garlic or heavily spiced foods.

If we are engaged in prayer ministry at the front of our church after a service we focus on the Receiver as the most important person in the world at that moment to us. We must not get distracted by seeing a friend in the congregation and let our mind wander or start thinking about what we are going to have for lunch!

The Receiver should leave the prayer time knowing above all that Jesus loves them. The Receiver may not think that they have received what they wanted, but Jesus usually gives what is needed, not necessarily what is wanted. We respect people's dignity and minister to them as if we were ministering to Jesus, and as we would like to be ministered to ourselves.

We emulate Him by being patient, showing His grace and mercy regardless of what our opinion may be of the Receiver or their situation. We assume an unshockable expression, not burdening the Receiver with any judgments of our own: this is the Lord's time, not ours.

We don't share our own story or that of someone else who may have suffered something similar. When we minister to people we don't hug or stroke them.[1] They don't need our comfort; at that moment they need Jesus. If we stroke or hug them they will be receiving from us, not Him.

In everything we do during prayer ministry we want to point to Jesus and not to ourselves. This means He gets all the glory for everything done during this time.

THE BIBLE

The Scriptures are to teach, inspire, and equip us. We don't want to do anything contrary to God's word. He will not contradict Himself. We uphold the word of God as "God-breathed" (2 Timothy 3:16). If we are worried about the source of anything we are experiencing in the Spirit then we can test it against God's word.

So it's vital for us to read the word of God regularly, observing how Jesus healed people and using that as our own model. But there is no need to keep quoting the Bible as we minister to people. It is enough that the teaching of the Scriptures has sunk right in, and is the foundation for everything we do.

THE CROSS

Jesus has opened the way back to the Father for us through His sacrifice for us on the cross. His death was the time and place where the enemy was defeated (Colossians 2:13–15) who will one day be destroyed. Death is swallowed up in victory (1 Corinthians 15:54). We benefit from acknowledging that we can come to Jesus, standing at the foot of the cross to receive our forgiveness and healing. This is the place we can encourage others to come. No one will ever be turned away.

> When you were dead in your sins and in the uncircumcision of your sinful nature, God made you alive with Christ. He forgave us all our sins, having cancelled the written code, with its regulations, that was against us... he took it away, nailing it to the cross. And having disarmed the powers and authorities, he made a public spectacle of them, triumphing over them by the cross.
>
> Colossians 2:13–15

> **For the message of the cross is foolishness to those who are perishing, but to us who are being saved it is the power of God.**
>
> 1 Corinthians 1:18

Our ministry is to lead others to Jesus on the cross to receive forgiveness and in turn to offer their own forgiveness to those that have hurt them, however long ago, whether they have asked for forgiveness or not. During prayer ministry, as pain from the past begins to surface, they should be encouraged to admit the pain and forgive those who have inflicted it. This area will be addressed later in another chapter. Forgiveness releases power, so this is very important.

THE HOLY SPIRIT

When Jesus came to earth He set aside some of His divine attributes, not knowing everything and not being physically able to be everywhere at the same time. He relied on the empowering of the Holy Spirit. The Holy Spirit is God, not part of God. All of God is in the Holy Spirit just as we encounter all of God in Jesus and worship all of God in the Father. We too need the empowering of the Holy Spirit to do the works that Jesus did and still does. The Holy Spirit brings glory to Jesus and the Father. The Holy Spirit glorifies Jesus during prayer ministry. He is Comforter and Counsellor *to* us in our personal walk of faith, but also *through* us during prayer ministry.

We honour the ministry and work of the Holy Spirit. We interact with Him as we minister, acknowledging that it is His ministry, not ours. It is impossible to over-emphasise that Jesus must get the glory, not us. To minister in the name of Jesus we must be filled to overflowing with the Holy Spirit (Acts 1, 4), and continually be re-filled as we give away in ministry the love and power He is giving us. If we just keep being filled with the Holy Spirit without passing on His gift we may soon become like a stagnant pond. We should instead be like a river-fed lake, continually being filled and flowing out, with what the Holy Spirit is pouring in. There is always more and more of Him!

CHARACTER CHECKLIST

One of the principles we have learnt at Soul Survivor is that even though a person has the most amazing gifting and anointing, if they lack integrity and good character they can bring the whole ministry into disrepute. It is important that those involved in prayer ministry do the following:

- We are to regularly confess our sins to God.
- We must remain open to receiving healing and wholeness.
- We try not to let the sun go down on our anger but release it in a way that doesn't harm others.
- We do our best to remain open and teachable to those who are in authority over us.
- We are to be accountable for our actions.
- We are not looking for a way to get our own needs met when ministering to others, though we may feel a sense of fulfilment.
- We should not minister to someone of the opposite sex alone.
- If married we must always remain faithful to our partner.
- We must realise that sometimes we will get things wrong and not be afraid to admit it.
- We should have a humble, teachable heart.
- We always give God all the glory for any healing received, as it is in every case entirely of His doing.

POWER AND AUTHORITY

When we utter the name of Jesus we evoke the most powerful name:

> ... that at the name of Jesus every knee should bow, in heaven and on earth and under the earth.
>
> Philippians 2:10–11

Without even thinking, and often at times of extreme stress, I have called upon His name and He has saved and delivered me from danger. For instance, at times when I pull out too soon into the flow of traffic on a roundabout, I realise my mistake, and seeing the approaching car about to mow me down, I will shout out "JESUS!" So many times I have been saved from impending disaster.

If we are a Christian we have His name upon us. We are clothed with Christ (Galatians 3:26–28). It's as if we wear the uniform of His name. If you have a job that requires you to wear a uniform, you represent that company while you wear it – you have the logo of the company you work for on your uniform. If you work for Marks and Spencer you will have their name on your badge. If you work for John Lewis you are one of their partners. When you work for Jesus you wear His badge of power and authority.

All power and authority belong to Jesus (Matthew 28:18), but He allows us, His followers, to use that power and authority in His name.

> When Jesus called the Twelve together, he gave them power and authority to drive out all demons and to cure diseases, and he sent them out to proclaim the kingdom of God and to heal the sick.
>
> Luke 9:1–2

Guess what? He hasn't changed His mind! He still wants to give that same power and authority to us. The problem is we don't often *take hold* of what He is giving us. It needs to be an *active, eager embracing*, not a passive waiting. We always think we have to receive more, but He has already given it. It's up to us to use it.

A policeman wears a uniform of authority. He *knows* he has authority and he uses it. When others look at him they instantly know that he has that too; yes, the uniform gives them the clue, but it is the way he acts while wearing the uniform that shows them he has it. We too need to be like the policeman, not just *knowing* we have been given it but by *using* the authority given to us in the name of Jesus. During prayer ministry the enemy recognises that we have taken hold of this authority in the name of Jesus.

There is a difference between authority and power. For the policeman his authority enables him to step out into the path of an oncoming vehicle and signal "stop in the name of the law". He has *authority* to do that, but the policeman doesn't have the power to physically stop the moving vehicle from mowing him down. He isn't Superman!

To help clarify the distinction, consider when a prison officer takes a bunch of keys: these keys can open all the doors of a cellblock. He has the *power* to do this because he holds the keys. But he cannot release the prisoners from the prison because he hasn't got the *authority* for that. He is a warder not a judge.

But we can have *both* for God's ministry through us – both power and authority, to heal the sick, cast out demons, and set the captives free.

In the Bible many people recognised that Jesus had both power and authority and were amazed (Mark 1:21–28).

Before starting to pray for someone I acknowledge the fact that all power and authority belongs to Jesus but He is using me as a channel. It all belongs to Him but I am clothed with Christ. I am aware that I have all power and authority in His name. The same power that raised Jesus from the dead clothes me. Therefore, although I feel weak in my own strength and can do nothing on my own, I can use this power and authority in Jesus' name. At His name the enemy is running scared. Knowing this releases me to trust the leading of the Holy Spirit and helps me not to fear what might happen during the prayer ministry time. I don't have to come up with the answers to others' needs. It is not my responsibility for the Receiver to get healed. I am just being obedient to Jesus' command to heal the sick and cast out demons.

Let's take time now to receive that power and authority from Jesus and pray:

> *Heavenly Father, may Your Holy Spirit please come upon me now in power. I believe that all power and authority belongs to Your Son. I believe that Your name is the most powerful name on earth and in heaven. I ask now that You will impart to me power and authority in Your name to preach the gospel, heal the sick, cast out demons, and at Your command raise the dead. For the glory of Jesus: I receive from You now. Thank You, Lord. Amen.*

And now take time to be a Receiver yourself!

Offer up your hands to Jesus and receive power and authority in His name.

EXPECTANCY

I am usually expectant when I pray for someone that the Holy Spirit will come upon them in power.

Jesus has promised in the Bible that "... your heavenly Father will give the Holy Spirit to those who ask Him" (Luke 11:13 NCV). I realise that the Holy Spirit really wants the person I am praying for to receive healing and wholeness. He wants it far more than I do. Our attitude sometimes can be "What if Jesus doesn't heal...?" My thought is, "Why *wouldn't* He want to heal?"

Sometimes we can talk ourselves out of listening to the leading of the Holy Spirit in prayer ministry because we are too busy inwardly debating with ourselves or doubting that anything will happen.

We really need to open our spiritual ears and spiritual eyes so that we can be ready to receive whatever God is saying to us or showing us.

I believe that every time we lay hands on someone while ministering in the power of the Holy Spirit, *something* will be happening. It might not be the thing that we are expecting but something will take place.

There is a huge amount of evidence that Jesus still heals today. New Testament theologians examine the healing stories in the Bible so that we can study what is known about the healing ministry of Jesus. I want to encourage you to study such books, alongside the Bible, asking the Holy Spirit for fresh revelation. If I were to include lots of biblical stories and more theological arguments, this book would have to be twice as thick!

There are also books on prayer ministry and inner healing that contain in-depth biblical accounts of Jesus healing, or make the case for why Jesus still heals today. My assumption is that the reader of this book does not need persuading that Jesus heals people.

I have also assumed that the reader will have been filled with the Holy Spirit and continues to keep being filled. This is crucial for powerful prayer ministry. Otherwise you will be ministering in your own strength and wonder why nothing much is happening.

The following story illustrates for me how sometimes our Father God lets us do prayer ministry in the name of Jesus, and we think we are doing something – but it's really Him doing it!

HE ORCHESTRATES IT!

My daughter and her four-year-old daughter Marybeth were playing virtual sports on the Nintendo Wii. They were running a race with some others on the screen. Marybeth was running on the spot in front of her mum who was holding the Wii controller. Marybeth got very excited as she kept overtaking people in the race. Her excitement was extreme. What she didn't realise was that the person she was watching on the screen wasn't her, but her mother, as Marybeth didn't have a controller in her hand. When Marybeth won the race her face was priceless. At this point her older brother started to say, "No, Marybeth, you didn't –" Just in time his mother clamped a hand across his mouth! That day Marybeth carried herself a little taller. She had competed and won. It was an important day for her, as usually her older brother beats her at everything.

Our heavenly Father allows us to be part of the race and win. We sometimes forget that He stands behind us orchestrating every move. He loves to see our pleasure, joining in, because He loves us and takes pleasure in us; He wants us to be confident, to stand tall.

Are you ready for the adventure?

Notes

1. During pastoral prayer ministry there may be occasions when the Holy Spirit prompts the Pray-er to engage in a ministry of "holding" (this is very different to hugging); this will be explained in a later chapter.

Chapter 2

GETTING STARTED

*They will place their hands on people who are
ill, and they will get well.*

Mark 16:18

WHAT IS PRAYER MINISTRY?

Prayer ministry is not praying for someone *at a distance*. When we pray this way, we are praying *about* someone, not ministering the love and power of Jesus *to* them; we would normally call this intercession. Prayer ministry is prayer that is up close and personal. It is allowing ourselves to be used by God as a vessel or a channel of His love to work in someone's life in the power of the Holy Spirit. It is a power ministry of the Holy Spirit, not a time for wordy prayers. It is offering ourselves to the Lord as a way for the flowing of the Holy Spirit; facilitating a way for the Receiver to open up to God; encouraging the Receiver to bring their worries, sickness, and past hurts to God. It is our spirit interacting with His Spirit as He gives direction and revelation bringing the healing love of Jesus. When we are involved in prayer ministry we don't have to try to persuade Jesus to heal people. In the verse above, Jesus told His disciples to "heal the sick" or "lay hands on the sick and they will get well". It was God's power and might that would change people's lives, not the words of man. I am so thankful that this is still the case today.

There is something really heartening in seeing people minister to each other in the body of Christ, and I am certain that it pleases God too. Of course, it is an essential part of ministry within the church, but how it must please Him when He sees us doing it *outside* the church, just like Jesus and the disciples did! In fact it is a lot easier to pray for those outside the church, as people often seem very thankful that we care enough to minister to them.

In Jesus' time, there were no manuals on the "ABCs of Prayer Ministry"! Jesus had modelled it and all the disciples (after Pentecost) relied on the empowering and prompting of the Holy Spirit. So we too are not following a formula. The following chapters in this book are not prescriptive. They contain some hints and suggestions plus some aspects of prayer ministry that I like to think of as a tool kit that can be useful – but only at the prompting and direction of the Holy Spirit.

If we follow formulae we are using our minds and not tracking the directing of the Holy Spirit. He knows what, how, and when. We need to be in tune with Him, following His lead – not suggesting but facilitating whatever He is doing.

So do not worry if you feel "under-qualified" in the area of prayer ministry. You do not need to be experienced to start laying hands on people, because it is the Holy Spirit who is ministering healing through you. It is advisable to partner with someone more experienced, as not only will you be able to learn more about prayer ministry but you will be able to pray with one another after the prayer time if you feel out of your depth.

MIND ISSUES

When a leader or speaker at a meeting invites people to come forward to receive prayer, it is helpful to understand what may be going through the minds of those people needing prayer. There are hundreds of different reasons why someone reaches out for ministry at any given time and it may be a battle for them to even rise up out of their chair. At other times, the Holy Spirit can propel them forward as the anointing falls on them to receive healing. Whatever the reason, be aware of the following battle that can rage in the minds of people as they come forward for prayer ministry. They may be thinking:

- It's me again! I am always coming up for prayer. Everyone will think I have terrible problems.
- God may be too busy with the needs of others to give me any attention.
- What if nothing happens? I'm not expecting it to – nothing ever seems to work.
- I don't want to fall over!
- I feel vulnerable and hope I am not ambushed by one of those prophetic people who will tell me what I have to do.
- I know what I need and I do not want God to speak to me about anything else.
- I just want to be free. Will I ever be free?

In fact, you may have thought some or all of these things yourself, prior to receiving ministry. So much can swirl around our heads at times like this that often we need to dial down a bit and relax to experience the presence of Jesus. More than anything it is Jesus we want. It's not just about a "power encounter" for its own sake, but about meeting with Jesus.

BE STILL AND KNOW

Would you like to practise that right now? Maybe your mind is so full today that you are finding it difficult to concentrate as you read this book.

Why don't you invite His Holy Spirit to come to you and then just be still? Focus your thoughts on Jesus, without saying anything, simply being aware of Him. Sense Him standing near you. If you find this difficult then imagine Jesus on the cross, dying for you. Now repent of anything you may have said or done to grieve Him. Or maybe imagine Jesus standing at the foot of the cross ready to interact with you. Offer your whole being – emotions, intellect, hopes and dreams, disappointments and pains – to His care. You do not need to struggle with this; instead do it from a place of stillness, calm, and trust. Some people find it difficult to be still and do nothing. It can take time and practice, especially if life is busy and you live with a lot of stress. It is tempting to think of all the prayers we *should* pray and all the things we *should* do, rather than taking time just being with Him.

So now, just enjoy His closeness for a while. The Bible tells us to "Be still, and know that I am God" (Psalm 46:10) and it is enough to do just that. Just BE!

You will find that your soul, mind, body, and spirit all feel refreshed by being in His presence. It is wonderful!

This is how we want others to encounter the presence of Jesus when we minister to them. It is important that we have experienced it ourselves on a regular basis so that we can discern whether others are encountering God or not. If they are not, you will need to lead them into stillness. You can do this by suggesting how you practise the presence of God personally by the ways I have suggested or some alternative method.

ISSUES OF CONFIDENCE

When we are praying for people we might be distracted by so many undermining thoughts buzzing round in our heads, such as:

- What if nothing happens?
- What if something happens and I don't know what to do?
- What if the person thinks I am no good at praying?
- What if there is an evil spirit present?
- I am really not very good at this!
- I wish so-and-so were here instead of me!
- What if it's not God's will to heal this person?
- Jesus will not use me because I am not a very good Christian.

Let me answer these concerns in order to encourage you and impart hope to you.

What if nothing happens?

Something always happens! It might not be what the person has asked for or what you wanted to happen, but that is not your responsibility, it is the Lord's. He wants that person to be whole much more than you do, so all you have to do is be obedient to His word and lay hands on them.

What if something happens and I don't know what to do?

This is not an exam! It is good to remember how weak you really are, because it is God's power that is made perfect in weakness (2 Corinthians 12:9). You can only help if you follow what the Father wants to do, so ask Him. Be willing to be a fool for Christ's sake. You do not have to have all the answers. Recognise that sometimes you may get it wrong, but there is grace to cover it all. God will show you what to do at the time. Try not to panic, but learn to be still in His presence.

What if the person thinks I am no good at praying?

Lay your reputation on the line. Do not be afraid of what other people think; just be obedient to the Lord. The person has come forward for healing, not to judge you and your prayers! It is an encounter with God they need, so be faithful in leading them towards Him.

What if there is an evil spirit present?

"The one who is in you is greater than the one who is in the world" (1 John 4:4). If there is no one more experienced to call on, you can pronounce the following command: "In the name of Jesus, with His authority, I bind anything contrary to the Holy Spirit" and then pray the peace of Jesus on the Receiver. Speak to your leader, who may take over or tell you of someone else with more experience who could meet with the person at another time.

I am really not very good at this!

You might not be good at it, but the Holy Spirit is! When your mind speaks negatively tell yourself to stop it and begin to ask the Holy Spirit what He wants you to do next. Remember, the truth is that with Him all things are possible and nothing is too difficult (Matthew 19:26).

I wish so-and-so were here instead of me!

God can use anyone for anything. Remember in the Bible we are shown that He even used a donkey to speak His words (Numbers 22:28). The reality is we often learn more by being flung in at the deep end than by taking years to learn a formula. Think of Peter walking on the water. Jesus soon rescued him when he thought he was sinking. All the gifts of the Holy Spirit are available to all of us all the time. He will determine as and when we need them. So bring any sense of inferiority to Jesus and surrender it to Him. Don't allow the enemy to undermine you with accusations or lies such as "you are useless at prayer" or "everyone else is better than you". He doesn't want you to be involved in prayer ministry.

What if it's not God's will to heal this person?

Healing has always been and always will be in the heart of God. The fact that we don't always see people healed shouldn't rob us of this truth. When we are doing His will and His work, we must be content to leave the outcome with Him. "I am the Lord, who heals you" (Exodus 15:26).

Jesus will not use me because I am not a very good Christian.

Compared to Jesus no one is good enough! Jesus knows every part of you and He loves you. He has given you this chance to be involved in this amazing ministry. We are all like "jars of clay" in His hands (2 Corinthians 4:7). He uses us as His vessels, but sometimes our feelings of inferiority can get in the way. Come to the foot of the cross now and surrender it to Jesus. Being humble does not mean putting ourselves down; it means being ready to give all the glory to God. Often the Holy Spirit will work through us powerfully when we are feeling the least spiritual. It is His work, remember!

For God, who said "Let light shine out of darkness", made His light shine in our hearts to give us the light of the knowledge of God's glory displayed in the face of Christ.

> **But we have this treasure in jars of clay to show that this all-surpassing power is from God and not from us.**
>
> 2 Corinthians 4:6

HOW DO I PREPARE?

Before going up to pray for someone at the end of a church service, I usually go through the following little checklist in my head. After ministering to people for a while, you will find that you do this almost automatically in a matter of seconds. It is as if these points become a way of life in ministry.

1. *I ask for cleansing from sin.* I want to be a clean vessel for Jesus to use.

2. *I ask for a fresh anointing of power to heal the sick in Jesus' name.* Nothing can be done in my own strength; it is only by His power.

3. *I remember that the name of Jesus is the most powerful name.* I do not need to fear any other name because it is at the name of Jesus that every knee will have to bow (Philippians 2:10–11). I have someone working in me and with me who is greater than he who is in the world (1 John 4:4). So I do not fear the enemy or any demonic spirits when I am ministering to people in His name. I put on "the armour of God" (Ephesians 6:10–18). The power of God is greater, so I can minister in confidence![1]

4. *I affirm that all healing is to be done in the name of Jesus.* I will not waste words, because Jesus never did. It is

His name that brings healing. Though I pray "Be healed in the name of Jesus" I never tell them, "Now you have been healed", but I usually ask them how they are feeling after the prayer. If they are taking medication for a condition, I encourage them to go back to their doctor to see whether it is still needed.

5.   *I acknowledge that all power and authority belong to Jesus.* He chooses to let me use it in His name.

If you didn't receive before, ask Him now for His power and authority to heal the sick and cast out demons.

Let us pray and ask Him for that now:

Please come, Holy Spirit, and cleanse me. Thank You, Jesus, for what You did for me on the cross. Thank You that all power and authority belong to You. I declare that the name of Jesus is the name above all other names! All power and authority belong to Jesus and I ask You, Lord Jesus, to impart to me the power and authority in Your name to heal the sick, cast out demons, and set the captives free. I lay hold of it now for Your glory and honour. Thank You, Lord. Amen.

6.   *I open my spiritual ears and eyes.* I want to actively listen to the Holy Spirit and see what He is doing in a person. I will ask the Holy Spirit to show me what He sees and help me to hear what He is saying, shutting out any negative or distracting thoughts.

7.   *I ask Jesus to help me every step of the way.* I want to rely on Jesus, leaning into Him, learning from Him. Sometimes He prayed for someone more than once to receive healing, so I will stay open and willing to spend more time with someone I am praying for. People may also receive their healing away from the meeting, which is why I am looking to Jesus to always lead me as I pray. I do not have a set pattern because everyone's needs are different and Jesus knows what those needs are.

Why don't you look at the points above in italics and turn them into a prayer? Remember it's not important to get all the words right; it's an attitude of our heart that we just present ourselves before the Lord for Him to use us. After a while it will become an automatic thing to just surrender yourself to Him and to tune into the Holy Spirit as you start to do prayer ministry.

WHERE IS THE HOLY SPIRIT WORKING?

Sometimes at an event or a conference, a lot of people come forward for prayer ministry. Ask the Holy Spirit whom He wants you to go to. This may be indicated by you having a "knowing" or your gaze may seem to be continually drawn to a particular person. Or, you might look along the group of people and see the Holy Spirit resting on them. This could be a look on their faces of being engaged with the Lord, a sheen, a trembling or shaking or crying in the act of receiving from Him. This suggests that the ministry may progress more quickly and you will be able to pray for a lot more people. Also, some people need to "soak" a little and wait upon the Lord before they are in an attitude of receiving. We don't want people to rely on us praying for them but for them to be expectant of meeting directly with Him themselves.

I don't usually approach someone who is still struggling or striving to meet with Him. I might whisper to that person, "Don't strive; just receive the Holy Spirit, He wants to meet with you. I will come back to you in a minute." This helps the person to realise they are not abandoned and can take their time to receive. Sometimes among those who have come forward for prayer, someone may be used by the Holy Spirit to launch a fresh powerful wave of the Holy Spirit upon the whole congregation. That is why it is important to go to those where the Holy Spirit seems to be working powerfully. We can only do what we see the Father doing (John 5:19). After saying all of this we just want to be following what the Holy Spirit is doing. He might direct you to minister to someone who is standing quietly and hardly engaged at all with the Holy Spirit. He may give you a "word" or "revelation" especially for that person. As always, follow His lead.

IMPORTANT THINGS TO REMEMBER

Here are some things to remember that will help when involved in prayer ministry:

1. Keep your eyes open so that you can see what the Holy Spirit is doing.

2. Stand to the side or in front of the person, not behind them (it makes the person uncomfortable to stand behind them and you cannot see what the Father is doing).

3. Lay a hand gently on the person's head or shoulder.

4. Invite the Holy Spirit to come upon the whole person (mind, body, emotions, will).

5. Make sure that there is at least one other person with you of the same sex as the person you are ministering to. Be aware that the person you are ministering to may be vulnerable and could have been abused. Be sensitive to the fact that having someone of the opposite sex praying over them may be disturbing. Realise that a prayer ministry time involving people of the opposite sex can easily develop into something that ends up being unwise, or even sinful, if safeguards are not taken. If you are in a conference or a public meeting and part of their ministry team, be aware that you always need to be seen to be doing what is right, not just doing what is right. For instance, if the accepted model of ministry is "same gender ministry" (male to male, female to female) and you are ministering to your wife or husband, no one will know that the person you are praying for is the one you are married to. It will seem as if you are going against the guidelines of ministry.

PRAYER MINISTRY STEPS

Here are some of the things I try to do when praying for someone who needs physical and/or emotional healing.

1. Ask the person's name and tell them yours.

2. Ask what they want Jesus to do for them – "I can only do what I see the Father doing" (John 5:19).

3. Invite the Holy Spirit to come upon the person in the name of Jesus.

4. Wait for the Holy Spirit to begin working.

5. Keep your eyes open so that you can see what the Holy Spirit is doing. Also watch the person's body language – for contortions or expressions on their face, etc.

6. Look for signs of the Holy Spirit on the person (see a list of some of these "signs" further on in this chapter).

7. Ask the Holy Spirit to come into the mind, the emotions, and the will – every part of the person.

8. If they join with you in praying (look for their mouth moving) as you minister, then suggest to them that they relax to receive rather than pray.

9. Ask for more power. Encourage the person to receive by saying something like, "Just receive" or "Let Jesus do what He wants" or "Be a receiver".

10. Wait expectantly.

11. Ask the Lord, "What do You want to do now?"

12. Ask the Holy Spirit, "What is the root cause?" (if appropriate).

13. I often ask, "Do you want to say something, Lord?" There may be a word of encouragement, comfort, or strength coming to you via a picture/s or impression or words. Please note that if you have a picture come into your mind ask the Lord what it means. If you have a picture of a tree but nothing else it may be better just to hold on

to this as this could distract the person being prayed for if you just mention that with nothing else. Alternatively this may well be a revelation to the person you are ministering to. If the Lord wants you to give it, then He will no doubt impress this upon you until you give it! It is about being sensitive to the timing of giving the picture or word as well as not distracting the Receiver from any healing they are in the middle of receiving.

14. If it's a physical condition, then speak to the condition in Jesus' name: "I speak healing to this knee in the name of Jesus" or "I speak to this broken bone in the name of Jesus and tell it to be healed."

Follow the prompting of the Holy Spirit. He may indicate to you that you need to pray for the person's hormones, blood supply, or a particular organ. He may further give you a word of knowledge or a prophetic word. When people come for prayer ask how long they have had the condition. Ask if anything else emotionally or physically was happening in their life at that time. In the cases of cancer ask if any particular trauma happened in the person's life a year or six months prior to diagnosis. If so, invite the Lord to come and draw out the trauma or bring emotional or spiritual healing. (This will be addressed in Chapter 3.)

Keep tracking what the Holy Spirit is doing. We only have authority to do what we see the Father doing. Ask throughout the prayer time, "What are You doing, Lord?" Watch for body language, such as the tightening of hands. Remain open to the leading of the Holy Spirit.

Here is an acronym that may help you remember the opening stages of prayer ministry – WELL:

Wait
Engage
Look
Listen

SOME SIGNS OF THE PRESENCE OF THE HOLY SPIRIT

The Receiver may show the presence of the Holy Spirit in the following ways:

- a sheen, like light on the person's face
- a look of being engaged with God – a sense of peacefulness
- shaking
- trembling
- falling to the floor
- eyelids fluttering in an unusual way
- uncontrolled laughter
- tears
- heavy breathing
- rippling of the upper or lower part of the body
- loud crying
- deep groaning
- strange jerking
- one tear from one eye trickling down, then a little later a tear from the other eye.

FALLING TO THE FLOOR

If someone falls to the floor be careful not to take all their weight as you may injure your own back. They are usually falling relaxed, so if you just pull their hand towards you as they fall it causes their knees to bend and you can just then step into position to lower them to the floor. Sometimes it may take you by surprise and you have no time to think! Make sure the Receiver is in a comfortable position, not draped over someone else, and that their dignity is maintained (i.e. nothing is on show that shouldn't be). If possible place a jumper or jacket under their head. Stay with the person and continue ministering to them. If you move away (because there are a lot of people needing prayer ministry) encourage them to keep receiving from Jesus and say that you will be back in a few minutes. Keep your eye on them, as the ministry may change and they may start releasing emotional pain. This can be seen by rapid breathing occurring or the Receiver may start moving their head about. They may also start to clutch their stomach, or their legs may start to do small movements. Or the Receiver may start to look distressed and move their hands to their upper chest. If this starts to happen place your hand where the Holy Spirit indicated and encourage the Receiver to let the inner emotional pain surface. Continue as led by the Holy Spirit.

GIVING A PROPHETIC WORD OR WORD OF KNOWLEDGE

If you get a word, a picture, or a prophecy for the person you are ministering to, remember to offer it sensitively. It is not always appropriate to say it the minute you receive it. If the picture, for instance, is revealing some insecurity, you can always try it out by praying it before actually saying it; for instance, "Jesus, please come and minister to all insecurity, especially anything in the area of..." while watching the reaction of the person to the prayer. You can then ask them if they struggle with insecurity and if they say that they do, you can offer the picture at that point. This can then progress as the Holy Spirit leads you.

Remember, if you feel too nervous to take the plunge you can always ask the Receiver questions. For instance, if you get a word of knowledge that someone had a difficult time during childbirth, you can start off by asking the question, "Have you any children?" and gradually lead in. It is better to go carefully as we learn, being encouraged bit by bit, rather than being stopped at the first post because we make a few mistakes and the person we are praying for has clearly "switched off". If you have a revelation about a sexual problem then this needs to be raised tentatively, indirectly, and certainly not accusingly. We do not want people to be made to feel ashamed and to wish to escape as soon as possible.

SOME PHYSICAL RESPONSES TO PRAYER MINISTRY

Sometimes we can notice that someone is clenching and unclenching their hands. This may indicate frustration or anger. Ask the Receiver if they are thinking/feeling anything in particular. If they admit to anger or frustration ask them where they can feel it. It is usually in their stomach. Ask them to place their own hand there and place your hand gently on top of theirs. Or place your hand in the small of their back – it seems to have the same effect. Ask Jesus to bring the anger to the surface and disperse it. Encourage the Receiver to let the feeling surface. There may be memories attached, so encourage the person to open these also to Jesus. It may be appropriate for the person to release their anger using their body. If this begins to occur in a congregational setting it may be better to respect the Receiver's dignity and the peace and harmony of worship by continuing the ministry out of public view, perhaps in an adjacent room if one is available.

Sometimes you will see someone's eyeballs rolling under their eyelids. This may mean that they are seeing something – reliving a memory or seeing a picture – so you can ask them what it is. If appropriate, ask Jesus to come into their memories and to bring His healing. This can then lead on to deeper ministry, including the releasing of forgiveness.

TAKE CARE

One of the things we never tell people is that they have a demon or an evil spirit in them. This just creates fear in people and it may cause the person to avoid ministry in the future. There is also the danger that we could be wrong. People often make strange noises or cries of agony when they are releasing pain from past hurt, and it is not, in itself, an evidence of demonic activity.

In my third and last section, Pastoral Prayer Ministry, we will look at deliverance from evil spirits. If you are inexperienced in prayer ministry it is better to partner with someone who is in the leadership of your church or a church member with more experience in deliverance. If there is no one else present you can always pray, "I bind anything contrary to the Holy Spirit, in the name of Jesus and with His authority", and pray the peace of Jesus upon the person. At this point you can say to the Receiver, "I feel that may be enough for today. Can we make another time to meet, perhaps with my colleague, who I think can help you?"

A lot of people are frightened of demons but, as we shall see in a further chapter, deliverance is not something that we need to be worried about dealing with; we just have to know how to deal with the situation and help people to be free from further spiritual disturbance.

YOU DON'T HAVE TO DO IT ALONE

It is usually best to minister in twos, as that way you can encourage one another, and because that is the New Testament pattern – Jesus sent His disciples out in pairs. It is good to be able to celebrate with someone when God is on the move. It also offers protection and accountability, saving you from being unnecessarily exposed or vulnerable to attack. Remember to honour the Receiver by not gossiping with others about their lives. Although we cannot promise confidentiality if the Receiver or someone else's life is in danger, we need to realise that it is a privilege for us to hear another's confession of weakness or deep need and we should act appropriately with that information.

As mentioned previously, the enemy will always try to get at you somehow. He will either tell you that you are amazing at ministry (leading to pride), or lead you to believe that you are absolutely useless (leading to "drop out"). Working in a pair or a team allows you to pray for each other if one of you has been affected by the ministry. It also means more gifts of the Holy Spirit will be in operation.

Always minister to others as you would like to be ministered to yourself and remember to encourage each other as you say "Yes!" to being used by the Lord. Let's go for it!

Notes

1. Look up the Scriptures on the "armour of God" so that you are not just informed but equipped.

Chapter 3

MINISTERING PHYSICAL HEALING

Jesus went through all the towns and villages, teaching in their synagogues, proclaiming the good news of the kingdom and healing every disease and sickness.

Matthew 9:35

SOME CAUSES OF PHYSICAL SICKNESS

There are many causes of sickness and disease. It was not part of God's original creation but entered the world through sin (Genesis 3:1–24). It is God's desire to heal.

Also see how many times Jesus healed people in the New Testament. He did it with tenderness, grace, and mercy.

Here are some of my thoughts as to why people are sick:

- It may be that the enemy is afflicting someone.
- It may be as a result of a sinful lifestyle.
- There may be some bodily abuse, including not eating healthy foods or taking exercise.
- There may be issues of self-abuse, including addictions to food, alcohol, or illegal drugs.
- There may be the need to receive forgiveness for sinning against someone else.
- Others may have sinned against them, and the emotional pain that results could be causing sickness.
- Sometimes the body is worn out through overuse and this may be making it more difficult to fight infection.

- It may be just the legacy of man's original sin (Genesis 3:6).
- Sometimes it is the consequences of unconfessed or habitual sin.
- Sometimes it could be an unhealthy lifestyle or an inappropriate diet, or, especially in the case of some developing world countries, a lack of food and fresh water.
- Often we don't know why!

The Lord tells us in the Bible, "I am the Lord, who heals you" (Exodus 15:26). He hasn't changed His mind! We are to expect healing as part of salvation. The Bible tells us that by His stripes (His wounds made by being flogged) we are healed (Isaiah 53:5; 1 Peter 2:24). God heals by the intervention of His mercy.

NOW AND NOT YET

Jesus preached the good news and declared that the Kingdom of God had come near (Mark 1:14–15).

We are living in the "now and not yet" of God's Kingdom. Jesus defeated sickness and death on the cross. He also defeated Satan but has still to destroy him utterly.

That will happen when Jesus comes again in all His glory and His Kingdom comes to earth in all its fullness. Jesus ushered in the coming of His Kingdom by the signs and wonders He did when He walked the earth – mainly nature miracles, exorcisms, and healing. He showed the disciples what to do, then sent them out to minister in His name. While Jesus was on earth the disciples did this with the power and authority of Jesus' name. After He ascended to heaven He sent the Holy Spirit (the power from on high) to empower them to obey His great commission to "do all things that I taught you to do". This included miracles, healing, deliverance, and raising the dead, as well as the good news of eternal life. We still see signs of God's coming Kingdom on earth every time someone becomes a Christian, gets healed, or when there is a miracle. When Jesus comes again there will be no need for healing; when the Kingdom comes fully we shall be made completely whole.

FOLLOWING THE COMMAND OF JESUS

The "now" of God's Kingdom is not a guarantee that every person we pray for will be physically healed but we do it in obedience to the commandment of Jesus when He said, "Heal the sick, raise the dead... and cast out demons" (Matthew 10:8 NLT).

This was Jesus' command to His disciples; since we too are His disciples, we are to follow this same command. I do not have to bear responsibility for people's healing. I can't heal anyone, but I know someone who can! My responsibility is obedience, not success. Of ourselves we have no power, but just like the disciples we can be empowered by the Holy Spirit. Jesus said that we would do even "greater things" than He had demonstrated. I can be expectant of that happening because He said so:

> **Very truly I tell you, whoever believes in me will do the works I have been doing, and they will do even greater things than these, because I am going to the Father.**
>
> John 14:12

After praying for healing I leave the Receiver with Jesus. I don't take them home in my head, debating whether they were partly healed or whether it will be lasting. I know that every time I minister in Jesus' name, inviting the Holy Spirit to come and bring healing and wholeness, He does something good. I know I can simply leave the result with Him.

NATURAL HEALING

Our bodies are made in the most amazing way. Every day different parts of our body are being renewed. Have you ever wondered why there is a lot more dust in your bedroom and bathroom? Did you realise that much of that dust comes from you? Your skin cells! Our skin flakes off as new skin grows. Have you ever wondered about your eyelashes? They only last about six to eight weeks before new ones grow. We all know how fast our fingernails grow. If we cut our bodies the skin will grow over and form a scab, which then drops off to show new skin.

God is renewing and healing us all the time by either putting something in our body to fight and conquer infection or using part of our body that He made to do the job. Unless it is a creative miracle (growing something that isn't already in existence), prayer ministry often speeds something up that would be happening naturally anyway.

WHOLENESS

Healing is a process. If it is instant we may call it a miracle. Sometimes we can get disappointed because our expectation is for a miracle and what is actually taking place is a healing. Healing can happen a few hours later, a few days later, or over a few years.

If the word "healing" is mentioned, often physical healing is what people are referring to. In the Bible more often the word "healing", when translated back to its origin, actually means "wholeness". Jesus is very interested in wholeness. Humans are more often interested in a physical cure because the effects are tangible, but in reality the healing of the whole person is more important. It is a good idea, I believe, to pray for physical healing but also to pray for wholeness – every part of the person. We are not just a physical body. We are "souls".

The Greek word *soteria* in the New Testament literally means "healing and wholeness". It is the word we translate as "salvation". In the Old Testament God called Himself Jehovah Rapha when He said to the Israelites, "I am the Lord, who heals you" (Exodus 15:26). This is the first place in the Bible where healing is mentioned. His name is healing and that is what He does!

Teachers and theologians who study the Scripture in depth explain that in the New Testament the full meaning of some words may be lost in their translation. For instance, five verbs in the Greek New Testament in their English translation come out simply as "heal" or "healing", whereas sometimes they can have a much broader meaning.

- *Laomai*: means wholeness and is translated as "heal" – used twenty-five times and used to describe spiritual healing five times.
- *Soso* (sozo): means "make alive", "make healthy" – used sixteen times by Jesus.
- *Psuchen Sozai*: implies spiritual as well as physical salvation.
- *Therapeuo*: indicates divine healing that is immediate and complete restoration to health.
- *Apokathistemi*: means to restore to former condition of health.

As you can see we miss out a lot by not speaking Greek!

In the Bible we find that many people Jesus healed were not just physically healed but emotionally set free too.

The woman who suffered twelve years of bleeding was healed not just physically but was freed from her suffering of ritual uncleanness that made her an outcast, too. Jesus affirmed her by calling her "daughter". He looked at what she needed as a whole person, not just at the condition that impelled her to seek His help (Mark 5:25–34). Our physical pain cries out for attention, but Jesus is interested in every level of our being and wants to make us whole.

> **May God himself, the God who makes everything holy and whole, make you holy and whole, put you together – spirit, soul, body – and keep you fit for the coming of our Master Jesus Christ. The One who called you is completely dependable. If he said it, he'll do it!**
>
> Thessalonians 5:23–24 The Message

BLIND AND JUDGED

Another person healed in the Bible was the man born blind from birth (John 9). The disciples asked Jesus, "Who sinned, this man or his parents...?" (9:2). The Pharisees said to him, "You were steeped in sin at birth" (9:34). In those days judgments were made on those that were afflicted in this way. This man had lived all his life under that judgment and needed this freedom pronounced as part of his healing so that he could receive his sight. Imagine how awful it must have been to live under such a cloud of others judging him. Jesus replied to His disciples' question, "Neither this man nor his parents sinned" (9:3). And then He healed him! The man not only received healing from blindness, and release from the judgment of others, but the greater blessing was that he ended up believing in Jesus. This man received spiritual, emotional, and physical healing as well as salvation!

There was a further factor in this man's healing. Jesus spat on the ground and mixed His saliva with dirt, forming a paste. He then put this on the man's eyes and told him to go and wash it all off in the Pool of Siloam.

Sometimes in the healing process Jesus asks something of us that may test our faith. This man showed his faith as he fulfilled what Jesus asked of him. An amazing miracle took place for the man blind from birth as he washed in the pool.

I believe it is important to pray for ourselves when we get ill or have physical ailments. Jesus can teach us how to pray for others as we learn to pray for ourselves, and as we follow His model in the Bible. I am not saying that every time I pray for myself I get healed, but so far throughout my life I have received a lot of physical and emotional healing as I remember to bring these problems to Jesus.

AN INSTANT HEALING – A MIRACLE

During the writing of this section of the book I had a visual aid. I was cutting up some salad with a very sharp knife when I suddenly felt the knife slice into the top pad of my ring finger. It felt deep and was very painful and started throbbing immediately. Before my brain could engage too much, I quickly squeezed together the deep cut and started to call out to Jesus: "I know You can heal people, Jesus, and I know You can instantly heal this finger so that it doesn't bleed [I didn't want blood on the salad!]. Please heal this finger now! In the name of Jesus Christ I speak healing to this finger. Be healed in Jesus' name!" I pressed the skin of my finger together for about twenty seconds in all, then I let go and looked. No blood. The pain had ceased as soon as I started calling out to the Lord. In astonishment I put the finger under some water to see if I could make it bleed. Nothing! I looked closely and there was a faint line of a cut. I had some visitors coming so I had to continue preparing the salad. I know the cut went really deep. I felt it slice in. Later on I remembered my finger and looked at it again. A faint line was still there but nothing else. Two weeks later I was telling someone the story, and showed her my finger, still with the faint line on it. Thank You, Jesus, for Your miracle!

PEACE IS A SIGN OF THE HOLY SPIRIT

Sometimes we minister healing and when we ask "What are you experiencing?" the Receiver declares that nothing is happening in their body. In this circumstance I ask, "Are you saying you can sense nothing at all in your body compared to what you were feeling before we prayed?" They may then say, "Oh, I feel peaceful." They might easily have dismissed this as nothing! Peace isn't nothing! Jesus is the Prince of Peace. I will then encourage the person by telling them that this is the Holy Spirit at work, bringing the peace of Jesus. Sometimes this might be the start of healing spreading through the person's life. They may have had prayer for the same condition many times before, but neglected to thank Jesus for His peace. Thanking Him now can lead on to them receiving more.

Receivers with long-term disability may have to bring to Jesus past disappointment at not being instantly healed. There may be a host of negative experiences during past prayer ministry times. Sometimes people with a disability may have had "prophetic words" spoken over them that proved to be false. This can be distressing as the healing does not come to pass. It could also hinder the Receiver from seeking healing for other ailments. The Pray-er needs to be sensitive to the inner emotional pain the Receiver may be suffering that stems from past insensitive prayer ministry.

Not everyone I pray for gets healed physically but that *will not stop me* praying and seeking God for their wholeness.

Often we want to see a supernatural "happening" when we pray for physical healing. But sometimes what is actually taking place is not evident – we don't always see the fruit of the prayer time as it can happen later when we are not present, or God initially may be doing some emotional or spiritual healing. The Holy Spirit is always at work. Sometimes we want to see healing so that it will validate our practice of prayer ministry. We must remember that God will not share His glory with anyone. We should expect healings to validate the presence of God's Kingdom. It is not our ministry but *His* ministry of compassion for His Kingdom.

CLEANSING

If someone has a problem with their skin, or perhaps something wrong with their eyes, I minister cleansing, asking Jesus to come by the power of His Holy Spirit into their bloodstream and wash them. The Holy Spirit may also prompt me to use this same cleansing prayer for other conditions or internal diseases.

If the person confesses sexual sin or perversion, including involvement with making or viewing pornography (after leading them into asking Jesus for forgiveness, receiving that, then repenting and renouncing the sin), I would also ask Jesus to cleanse them with His purity and wash them inside and out. If appropriate I would also look the person directly in their eyes and speak cleansing into their soul. The Bible tells us that our eyes are the light to our soul (Luke 11:34). There may also need to be a prayer of deliverance, in Jesus' name, binding anything contrary to the Holy Spirit, breaking the power of sexual sin or anything unclean and telling it to go to where Jesus directs it (see Chapter 15 for more on deliverance).

Someone who has been sexually abused usually feels dirty inside and out. They may often feel disgusted with themselves, blame themselves, or hate themselves (see Chapter 14 "Hannah's story" for more on this area of healing).

DEDICATING THE BODY

If sexual sin has taken place (this can cause physical sickness, as can any habitual sin), when indicated by the Holy Spirit I would also ask the Receiver to dedicate their body or a particular part of their body to Jesus. This can take place after cleansing (see above).

> ... offer your bodies as a living sacrifice, holy and pleasing to God – this is your true and proper worship.
>
> Romans 12:1

FAMILY SICKNESS

It could be that the person you are praying for has others in their family, past or present, that also suffer from the same condition. If so, that needs to be broken in Jesus' name. Say out loud: "In Jesus' name I take the sword of the Holy Spirit and set you free from..." and/or, "In Jesus' name I break the power of anything unclean or infirm coming down your family bloodline." I would also speak the cleansing of Jesus. At the same time, if appropriate, I would place my hands on their ears and break the power of words from a family member who may have spoken words such as "You will get... because all the females/males in our family have it" (or some similar phrase). Obviously we need to remain open to the Holy Spirit to lead us and show us anything that may be blocking the healing. Also ask the Receiver if anything has occurred to them during the time of prayer. Are they sensing anything – having a memory, seeing a picture, etc.? The Pray-er should remain open to any picture or words of knowledge.

There are books covering almost every type of physical healing recorded in the New Testament, and many helpful books containing a theology and sound doctrine for healing and wholeness, such as:

Come Holy Spirit, by David Pytches

Power Healing, by John Wimber

Healing, by Francis MacNutt

Your Healing is Within You, by Jim Glennon

Deliverance from Evil Spirits, by Francis McNutt

Demolishing Strongholds, by David Devenish.

I have included a number of books on healing and wholeness in the recommended list at the back of this book, including many books by Mary Pytches.

BLESSING OUR BODY

We don't speak positively to our body much, do we? When we get a tickly throat we can speak negatively to our body: "Oh no! I am getting a cold!" instead of "There is no way I am going to receive anything into my body; with the power and authority of Jesus Christ I tell this sore throat to clear up, and pain – stop it! Jesus, You took all my pain and sickness upon Yourself at the cross, so I am not receiving this sore throat." Then, "Jesus, thank You for my throat; I bless it now in Your name." Many times I have used this sort of prayer at night and in the morning the pain has gone.

How many people have you heard saying, "My feet are killing me" or some other negative thing to their body?

I realised many years ago when I first sprained my ankle (I have done it on numerous occasions since that first time) and I had it propped up covered in ice, that I had never appreciated the fact that my ankle usually just got on with its job without any thought from me. Here it was damaged, yet I was feeling very negative towards it – as if it had let me down. I realised that I had never appreciated or blessed parts of my body which were working well, but became annoyed with different parts when they were going wrong. In the Bible it says that my body is a temple of the Holy Spirit (1 Corinthians 6:19). That sounds as if I should honour my body. I realised that I hadn't. I didn't respect it and probably abused it a lot by neglecting it.

This caused me to say sorry to Jesus, and when different parts became sick or damaged I began to thank Jesus for the job they had been doing. This may sound whacky, but the Bible does say, "Love your neighbour as yourself" (Mark 12:31). We are not meant to be *in* love with ourselves but to love what Jesus has made – to respect and look after it.

Physical pain can result from shock or emotional hurt that has been suppressed and never properly processed.

Emotional pain may sometimes develop into a physical condition. Think of how stress can cause a headache or migraine, or even an ulcer.

I have known of cancer starting as a result of trauma from a divorce or a major stressful event (see "An emotionally absent parent" in Chapter 9), though this is not true in every case. For some it may be genetic, because of an environmental issue, an affliction from the enemy, an unhealthy lifestyle or a whole host of other reasons.

SPEAKING TO CONDITIONS AND SICKNESS

Jesus not only spoke the word of God but in John's Gospel we see that He actually is the living Word: "In the beginning was the Word, and the Word was with God, and the Word was God. He was with God in the beginning. Through him all things were made" (John 1:1-3). He spoke the world into being. "Let there be light", and there was light. These were creative words.

Jesus spoke to conditions and diseases. He commanded

bodies to be healed. He didn't try to persuade or plead with His heavenly Father to do it. With just a few words they were healed. Power was released.

- He told ears to "be open", and the man could speak and hear (Mark 7:31–35).
- He *rebuked* the fever in Simon's mother-in-law (Luke 4:38–39).
- He told the leper, "Be clean!", and immediately he was cleansed of leprosy (Matthew 8:3).
- He spoke to the man with the withered hand – "Stretch out your hand" – and it was immediately healed (Matthew 12:13).
- The centurion said to Jesus, "Say the word and my servant shall be healed" (Matthew 8:8). He did, and he was healed!

Some people find it embarrassing to hear their own voice commanding someone's body to be healed. The more you do it, the less you will be embarrassed. Remember you are doing it with the power and authority given to you in Jesus' name. Be prepared to be a fool for Christ. John Wimber used to say, "I am a fool for Christ – whose fool are you?"

MODEL FOR PHYSICAL HEALING

Here is a guide for praying for someone who needs physical healing.

1. First of all, ask, "How long have you had the sickness/ disability? Was anything going on at that time emotionally? Did any major event happen in the family at that time?" If appropriate, minister into the area of trauma or anything that requires emotional healing. See "Releasing trauma", Chapter 4.

2. Ask Receivers experiencing physical pain to tell you on a scale of 1–10 (10 is highest) the level of their pain. If

appropriate, ask them to tell you on the same scale the level of mobility.

3. Invite the Holy Spirit to come upon the person with power (we never command the Holy Spirit; we invite Him to come).

4. After waiting to sense that the power has come, declare out loud, "Jesus, I know that You heal people today. Thank You that You love [name] and want to bring them healing."

5. Place your hand on the place where pain is felt (you might ask the Receiver to put their hand there, then place yours on the top if that seems more appropriate – for example, if a woman is experiencing breast pain).

6. Say out loud, "With the authority given to me by Jesus Christ, I speak to this [limb, organ, or ailment] in the name of Jesus, and command it to be healed."

7. If appropriate, speak out loud to the blood supply, hormones, tendons, muscles, ligaments, or whatever else may be appropriate or as the Spirit leads, in the name of Jesus, commanding it to be healed.

8. If the person has pain, speak out loud to the pain and say, "In Jesus' name I command this pain to *stop it and lift off*." We don't shout but we do firmly tell the pain to "stop" and/or "lift off", with the authority given to us as believers in Jesus' name.

9. Stop and ask the Receiver to reassess their mobility/pain on the scale of 1–10.[1] Repeat all of the above as many times as necessary, as you hear and see healing take place. Don't forget to ask the Receiver each time the number on the scale of improvement.

10. If appropriate – if the pain becomes stronger rather than weaker, or if the pain moves about the body, it is usually something spiritual – break the power of the spirit of affliction or infirmity. Bind anything contrary to the Holy

Spirit in Jesus' name.

11. If things get worse, there is a possibility that the enemy is binding the Receiver with some shame, guilt, or unforgiveness that they are holding on to. This will need to be dealt with. To proceed, see the sections in Chapters 8 and 9 that cover these subjects.

12. In the case of cancer, curse it in the name of Jesus and command tumours to shrivel up and die.

13. Do likewise in the case of other infections and viruses, and speak cleansing of the blood in the name of Jesus.

14. Speak healing to organs and wholeness to the body.

15. During this time the Holy Spirit may give you a word of knowledge or a prophetic word or an insight into how else to proceed. Take a moment to listen.

16. Sometimes the Receiver will feel clicks in their limbs, neck, or spine, as recovery is taking place.

17. It may take one, two, or even a few times of laying on hands in the process of healing. This can be because the enemy is resisting the healing taking place and refusing to lift off, or there may be some spiritual or emotional inner pain that needs to be addressed.

18. Sometimes prompted by the Holy Spirit I might also say, "I bring this [knee, hand, kidney, etc.] under the lordship of Jesus Christ." The Receiver may sense a feeling of heat, warmth or tingling around the affected part. This encouragement will encourage the Pray-er to persevere in ministry. When appropriate, ask the person to move any damaged part of their body to see if things are working any better.

Sometimes the healing will continue throughout the next minutes, hours, or days. Sometimes not much improvement is felt at the time but may occur later.

Obviously internal sickness cannot be tested in this way but often the Receiver will know when something is taking place internally. Never tell anyone that they are healed, as we are not qualified medically to do that but encourage the person to visit their doctor before coming off any medication, and then only at their doctor's direction.

The more people you pray for, the more you will see getting healed and made whole. As we increase our experience, so our faith and wisdom will grow.

It is worth studying how Jesus and His disciples exercised the ministry of healing. Here are some of the key passages:

JESUS: MIRACULOUS HEALING AND DELIVERANCE

Matthew 4:23–25 Healed crowds of every disease and sickness

Matthew 8:2–4 Man with leprosy cleansed and healed

Matthew 8:5–13 Centurion's paralysed servant healed at a distance

Matthew 8:14–17 Peter's mother-in-law healed of fever

Matthew 8:28–33 Two demon-possessed men delivered and the demons cast into the pigs

Matthew 9:1–7 Paralysed man on mat healed

Matthew 9:18–25 A dead girl raised

Matthew 9:20–22 A woman bleeding for twelve years healed

Matthew 9:27–31 Two blind men healed

Matthew 9:32 A deaf and mute man delivered, set free, healed

Matthew 15:21–28 A demon-possessed child delivered

Matthew 17:14–18 A young boy delivered and healed from seizures

Mark 1:23–26 Man in synagogue with evil spirit delivered

Luke 7:12–15 Raised widow's son from the dead

Luke 17:11–19 Ten lepers cleansed and healed

Luke 22:50–51 Jesus heals servant of high priest whose ear was cut off

John 5:1–15 Paralysed man at pool healed

John 9:1–12 Man born blind from birth healed after washing in Pool of Siloam

DISCIPLES: MIRACULOUS HEALING AND DELIVERANCE

Matthew 10:1 Jesus sends them out to deliver and heal
Matthew 10:8 Heal the sick, raise the dead, cast out demons
Mark 6:12–13 Preached repentance, drove out demons, and anointed sick with oil and healed them
Luke 9:6 Preaching gospel, healing people everywhere
Acts 3:7–10 Man crippled from birth healed
Acts 5:16 Crowds healed and delivered
Acts 9:34 A paralytic named Aeneas healed
Acts 14:8–10 A man crippled lame from birth healed
Acts 16:16–18 Slave girl delivered from evil spirit
Acts 19:12 Paul the apostle's handkerchief brought healing and deliverance to many
Acts 28:8 Chief official's father healed of fever and dysentery
Acts 28:9 All the sick on the island of Malta were healed

Notes

1. The idea of asking for a scale of 1–10 regarding pain and mobility was borrowed from Robby Dawkins from Aurora Vineyard and is shared with his permission. Using this idea focuses the Receiver on the progress of healing and releases faith in both Pray-er and Receiver as the level of improvement is identified after each prayer. When receiving prayer for physical healing, we may not communicate clearly the level of improvement, and as the Receiver is still and may be quiet, it is not always clear; so it is very helpful to have this indicator for pain level and mobility.

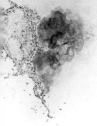

Chapter 4

PRACTICAL APPLICATION

In this chapter I will be exploring practical areas of prayer ministry.

TRAUMA AND SIN

As we have already noted, healing and wellbeing are holistic, and illness can come about for a variety of reasons – spiritual and emotional, as well as physical. When we pray for people with physical problems we remember to remain open to the possibility that it might be the result of others sinning against them, their own sin, or the enemy afflicting them. If there was an accident at the time that they received an injury there might be a need to release trauma attached to that accident before the person can receive healing. There could be a need of forgiveness to be released before they receive their healing as in the following story.

JANEY'S STORY

Janey was involved in a terrible car crash. Someone was killed, so Janey suffered a lot of emotional stress as well as her own injuries. As a result of her terrible experiences, her severe persisting pain required several operations. During our prayer ministry I asked Jesus to draw the trauma out of Janey into Himself. Her whole body started to tremble until she let it go into Jesus. Next, Janey needed to deal with the guilt she assumed at surviving the crash, unlike the other passenger. I explained that Jesus became the guilt offering on the cross so she didn't have to carry this any more. I asked Janey to bring the guilt to Jesus at the cross and let it go. She did this and said she felt relief. It is okay to speak to people while we are ministering; we just need to be sensitive to where and how they are journeying with the Holy Spirit.

I sensed Janey felt very angry with the driver for causing her such pain and suffering through the accident. I asked her to bring her tense feelings towards him to Jesus, and tell Jesus about those big emotions. The next step was for Janey to say sorry to Jesus for her hostile feelings towards her friend, the driver. This she did, and received the forgiveness of the Lord. Then I indicated that Janey needed to extend this forgiveness to her friend. While crying she expressed forgiveness to him as she spelt out the suffering he had caused her. She had made a start on the journey of forgiveness but would need to do it regularly until it wasn't painful any more. We then ministered healing to her body in Jesus' name.

This prayer ministry took place during a conference, so I don't know the final outcome of that story. I left it with the Lord. All I know is that she had done business with God by dealing with her unforgiveness and allowed some trauma to be released. For Janey that was as much as she could allow to take place. Sometimes we may only see part of the healing process, or we may be involved again at a later date with the same person.

Often trauma is linked with fear. This will be covered in the "healing from past hurts" section in Chapters 7 and 8.

RELEASING TRAUMA

If trauma needs releasing because of an accident or incident, ask permission to place your hand on the upper part of the chest below the throat (the area from which emotions are often released) and ask Jesus to draw the trauma out of the Receiver's body into Him. After this you may be prompted by the Holy Spirit to place your hand on the Receiver's stomach and similarly ask Jesus to draw the trauma out into Himself.

You can ask the Receiver to put their own hand on this part of the body and you can place your hand on top and speak release to the trauma. Encourage the Receiver to let it rise up and into Jesus. Ask Jesus to draw the trauma out of the person into Himself. Sometimes, if someone has had an accident resulting in injury, there may be trauma to be released before physical healing can take place. Please realise that in no way do we ever receive anything of that person's pain or trauma into ourselves. We don't receive it and then pass it on to Jesus. It's a direct channel from the Receiver to Jesus.

FORGIVENESS

Time and time again I have seen how the whole area of unforgiveness can keep a person in bondage. I have included below some prayers addressing forgiveness for people who are bound up. We must never force people to forgive before they are really ready; otherwise it will mean they are just going through the motions without a change of heart. When the time is ready we can point out that Jesus commands us to forgive, and this appears to expel residual poison inside.

We must also be sensitive to the Receiver's emotional condition before suggesting they forgive someone during prayer ministry. They may be angry with themselves and bitter about someone else's treatment of them. We can cause damage by insisting they forgive another person before recognition is given to the immense amount of suppressed pain that will need to surface first. I want to reiterate that forgiveness must indeed take place, but acknowledgment and acceptance of the person's pain or anger is of great importance. Pain or anger may be buried so deep that a longer period is required for it to surface, and more than one ministry time might therefore be necessary. Encourage the person in allowing that pain or suppressed anger from the past to come to the surface and be released. Let them take it at their pace.

If the person is ready and willing to release their unforgiveness, you can offer to lead them in a prayer as you minister to them. Encourage them to pray out loud, as it is an affirmation to the Lord (and to the enemy) that they want to be free. You might choose words like this:

> *Dear Jesus, please forgive me for my deep-rooted anger/hatred/bitterness towards [name the person]. I am so sorry. I repent of it and release the one who has hurt me into Your hands. I will not hold on to it any more. I choose to bring this all to the foot of Your cross. Please forgive me and release me now, in Jesus' name. Amen.*

Encourage the person to receive the forgiveness of Jesus and, if appropriate, pronounce His forgiveness over them as follows: "The blood of Jesus Christ, God's Son, cleanse you from all sin. I pronounce His forgiveness over you now. Receive His forgiveness now with thankfulness."

You might also wish to sign the person on the forehead with the sign of the cross saying, "I sign you with the sign of the cross – the sign of His love and peace... everything He did for you was enough."

At this point the person may have already released some pain and may be weeping. Encourage them to continue to release forgiveness to those who have hurt them. It may help them to forgive by extending the forgiveness they have just received for their own sin. It usually helps for them to say out loud, "In Jesus' name I choose to forgive you [name the person] for [they need to speak out what the person did to them]." At this point more tears and pain may be expressed. It is further beneficial if the Receiver also asks Jesus to bless the person who hurt them, and if the Receiver blesses that person with the love of the Lord, in Jesus' name.

If the Receiver finds this difficult to do, explain that forgiveness is a choice we make because it is actually a commandment of Jesus; it may sometimes be hard to make that choice. We may not feel warm and affectionate towards someone we forgive, nor are we obliged to; we are only setting them free, and by so doing we set ourselves free too. Explain that by forgiving someone, it does not mean that what was done to us was right. It simply means that we choose to be free from the poison of unforgiveness spoiling our own lives.

If we are ministering to a number of different people with emotional pain from abuse we may find their suffering affecting us. It can feel overwhelming. After a while I realised that I needed to confess this to Jesus as I had taken responsibility for others and was carrying their pain around with me. I had not passed it over to Him. As soon as I did this I felt relief. If you realise you have a habit of doing this, after a time of prayer ministry bring each person you have ministered to before Jesus and let go of them to Him. I also find it helpful to say to Jesus, "These people belong to You, Jesus, not to me."

USE OF OIL

> **They went out and preached that people should repent. They drove out many demons and anointed many sick people with oil and healed them.**
>
> Mark 6:12–13

I have oil available in prayer ministry, as sometimes the Holy Spirit leads me to anoint a Receiver as part of His work of physical or emotional healing.

It is good to study how oil is used in the Bible, to familiarise yourself with the reasons behind the ministry of anointing. This will give you helpful guidelines and make you alert to situations where it may be beneficial. Listen also to the Holy Spirit – it is not necessary on every occasion.

I mix olive oil with some organic essential oils. My favourite is myrrh and bergamot because it isn't too flowery a smell, so it is suitable for men or women. You might consider having an option of oil free of fragrance, in case allergies pose a problem. I then pray over the oil and dedicate it to Jesus, asking Him to anoint it and use it for His purposes. I may use it to symbolise the work of Jesus on the cross in bringing healing and deliverance, or to symbolise the anointing of the Holy Spirit.

When led by the Holy Spirit to do this, I dip my finger in the oil, and trace the sign of the cross on the Receiver's forehead, with words such as these: "In Jesus' name I sign you with this sign of the cross, as a seal that what Jesus has begun in you today He will continue for your healing and blessing" or "In Jesus' name I sign you with this sign of the cross. Receive all that He has done to bring you healing. Amen."

But there is no set or necessary formula; these words are guidelines to help you find your way as you follow the leading of the Holy Spirit.

DON'T LAY HANDS ON SUDDENLY!

It is best to have their permission before praying for people. If someone comes forward for prayer in church in a wheelchair, they may not want you at that moment to pray for them to be out of their wheelchair. They may just have a bad headache. It would be patronising to pray for something they were not asking for. You may want to ask the Receiver what they would like Jesus to do for them. If the Lord gives you a specific word of knowledge or prophetic word, then be sensitive as to how to deliver it.

If a person asks for prayer for someone else and asks me to go over in church and pray for them I usually ask them, "Do you want me to pray for them or did they send you over to ask me for it?" I will then chat with the person concerned and find out what they are wanting. It is important the Receiver believes healing is possible and wants to be prayed for at that moment in time.

It is also wise not to lay hands suddenly on someone with severe mental illness. See the sections on "mental illness" in Chapter 12.

LAYING ON OF HANDS

In the Old Testament we are shown how people laid hands on their children and blessed them (Genesis 27:1–27; 48:18–20), and

Jesus many times laid hands on people when He healed them. He also laid hands on children and blessed them (Mark 10:16; Matthew 19:13). We see the disciples laying hands on people during healing or anointing. It doesn't tell us in the Bible where on the body Jesus laid His hands but we are told:

- Jesus "spit on the ground, made some mud with the saliva, and put it on the man's eyes" (John 9:6).
- "After he took him aside, away from the crowd, Jesus put his fingers into the man's ears" (Mark 7:33).
- "Then he spit and touched the man's tongue" (Mark 7:33).
- "But he took her by the hand and said, 'My child, get up!'" (she was raised from the dead) (Luke 8:54).
- "So he went to her, took her hand and helped her up. The fever left her" (Mark 1:31).

I am often prompted by the Holy Spirit to lay my hands on different individuals in different ways. I would like to share this with you for guidance and suggestion only, not for you to try prescriptively one after the other. In ministry you must listen for yourself to the Holy Spirit and His direction as to "how and when".

As always we must be sensitive and appropriate as to where we lay our hands.

While standing at the front or to the side of the Receiver:

One hand lightly on the shoulder or forehead

As I do this I invite out loud the power of the Holy Spirit to come upon the Receiver. I ask Him to visit the person's mind, emotions, and will.

One hand on each shoulder

When I have done this I have observed that the person has received in a deeper way. Sometimes the Receiver has said to me that even when I am only resting one hand on them they have experienced two hands placed on the shoulder.

Two hands on either side of temples and head

I sometimes sense a prompting to do this when people feel fearful. Last year I was interested to discover during a training day with Deep Release Ministries that this area deals with the fight or flight part of the brain, and that part of the brain (called the amygdala) stores memories of emotions. It was interesting to see that what I had sensed intuitively had a relationship to the working of our body systems.

One hand tips of fingers just below left shoulder, above person's left breast, taking care to observe propriety

I often place my hand here if there has been a call to people to come to "have the heart of Jesus" or to "see what He sees" with regard to the broken and marginalised. Sometimes if I am being prompted by the Holy Spirit I will do this as an anointing of the heart with the compassion of Jesus. Most times the Receiver will weep with His tears or be moved or even have a sense of some particular ministry He is calling them to take up. Sometimes the Holy Spirit may prompt you to anoint the Receiver with oil.

Hand on top of the Receiver's hand on their stomach

This seems to be the area from which inner pain is released, especially if it has been there for a number of years. Speak release and freedom in Jesus' name and encourage the Receiver to let the pain surface.

Neuroscientists sometimes speak about "the brain in the stomach" as there are so many thousands of neurons in our brain that are also found surrounding our stomach. This may explain why we say, "I have a gut feeling" about something: there is a specific intelligence connected with this area in the body.

Tips of fingers either side of waist while standing partly behind (but not directly behind)

If the Receiver is very overweight this can be less intrusive for them than on their stomach. Speak release and freedom in

Jesus' name. Sometimes I have been prompted to place my hands here even if the person isn't overweight. I have no idea why!

Hand in the small of the Receiver's back

This area seems less intrusive than putting one's hand on someone's stomach. It seems to have a similar effect. As I am doing this I will usually encourage the person to allow their suppressed emotions to surface. Sometimes I speak out "release" or "freedom" in Jesus' name as I minister because Scripture shows us that this is what the mission of Jesus was (Luke 4:18).

Both hands forming a cup over each ear

Hearing is one of our main senses. I have found that for some reason, when I am doing this (prompted by the Holy Spirit) the Receiver seems to experience the love of Jesus in a much deeper way than previously received. Also this may be used when someone has had words spoken over them as a curse, or if they have had negative, cruel, destructive words or lies spoken over them. Break the power of these words in Jesus' name. Speak the truth into the Receiver. Then encourage the Receiver to speak out, rejecting the lie, curse, or negative words. Proceed by asking the Receiver to proclaim the truth out loud.

Be sensitive when speaking directly into someone's ear at close range, as the Receiver may be wearing a hearing aid which may cause discomfort if switched on!

Both hands forming a cup over each eye

This can be done for those with eye disorders or if there is a need for cleansing because of what their eyes have seen.

Tips of fingers in the palms of Receiver's hands

Don't hold the Receiver's hands as they may feel trapped, but gently place your fingertips in the palms of their hands. This can be used when anointing (setting apart for a specific purpose) and also for imparting a gift of the Holy Spirit. Sometimes you may be prompted by the Holy Spirit to anoint the Receiver's hands with oil.

WHEN NOTHING SEEMS TO BE HAPPENING

Many of us have had that sinking feeling when the ministry feels like praying for a block of wood. At such times stop and ask the Receiver, "What do you sense is happening at the moment?" They usually reply, "Nothing". After years of this happening, in desperation one day I asked the Lord, "What shall I do now?" He replied, "Ask them what sort of nothing." Feeling an utter idiot I asked the question. The Receiver looked at me as if I had lost my mind. Then the Lord whispered, "Ask them whether it is a numbness, a barrier, or a brick wall." Without knowing where this was going I asked about that. This is what I discovered.

Numbness: The Receiver may not be connecting to their feelings. They are switched off. This could arise from grief. Ask the Receiver if they have been grieving the loss of something. Or it could be that they have made a "vow" never to feel or show their feelings. See the sections on "vows" in Chapters 8 and 9.

If the numbness is from grief, invite the Holy Spirit to show the person (if not obvious from what they say) what they are grieving. If the Receiver is just "switched off" for some reason, again ask the Holy Spirit to show them when this switching off first happened – the root cause. It may be that the Holy Spirit gives you a word of knowledge at this point to proceed.

A brick wall: A brick wall could be an inner protection that has been put there by the Receiver and built brick by brick. This could be caused by a whole host of things. Ask the Receiver if there is any anger with God, a sense of disappointment or being let down because He didn't answer their prayers, or if they have blamed Him for something bad that happened in their lives. Explain that God always wants the best for us. In the midst of trouble and distress, it can be hard to imagine that, and we cannot always understand what God can possibly be doing: but even so, His ways are perfect (Matthew 5:48; Psalm 18:30). So for our own healing, we need to come to Jesus and say sorry for blaming Him and turning away from Him, then ask His forgiveness. We build barriers between ourselves and God when we are angry and resentful towards Him, and only we can remove them. Explain that Jesus doesn't remove Himself or change His attitude towards us, even if it felt as though He had turned His back. After confession, pronounce forgiveness: "In Jesus' name I pronounce His forgiveness over you – just receive it now." This can help the Receiver take down the brick wall. Proceed by inviting the Holy Spirit upon the Receiver. Also at this point one of the "visual room" exercises may be appropriate (see Chapter 11).

A barrier: Jesus hasn't changed. Nothing can separate us from His love (Romans 8:38–39); the barrier is always of our own making. In my experience, issues of self-worth or self-esteem are sometimes behind this. I ask the Receiver the following sort of questions: "When you receive prayer do you have any expectation of Jesus coming in power upon you?" "Do you believe that God loves you?" "Do you like yourself?" If it seems appropriate, I may ask if the Receiver self-harms in any way. Explaining to the person that there is a reason underlying their inability to receive can be of help. Then I ask the Holy Spirit to bring to the surface and reveal to the Receiver anything in their past that has damaged or diminished their self-worth. I may suggest they read Mary Pytches' book *Who Am I?* (if out of print it is usually available online). Another helpful book is *Mirror Image* by Arianna Walker.

LEADING SOMEONE TO JESUS

Explain to the Receiver that Jesus has been longing for this moment. Try not to be intense or worry that you will do it wrong.

Jesus and the angels are standing by ready and waiting to usher this person into the Kingdom!

The process of receiving Jesus is very simple. The following pattern of words may help you when you find yourself in the wonderful position of leading someone to Jesus:

> Repent
> Renounce
> Receive
> Rely

Make this prayer ministry as simple as possible. Lightly lay your hand on the person's shoulder and suggest that they shut their eyes so that they are not distracted. Quietly invite the Holy Spirit to come upon them. Explain that you are just inviting the Holy Spirit who is the power of God to come and meet with them.

Pray aloud with words like the following:

> *Jesus, I thank You that You love [name] so much that You chose to die on the cross to take their sin and shame. Thank You that You want to come into [name of Receiver's] life and share it.*

Then invite the Receiver to say sorry to Jesus and turn away from anything they may have done in their life that isn't perfect (they can do this quietly and privately).

Ask the Receiver to renounce (or turn away from) evil (this clears up anything they might also have done with regard to the occult). At this point you may wish to ask them if they have been involved in any occult practice, such as a séance, or playing with a Ouija board. Many people have dabbled in these things. If so, they need particularly to repent (turn away from this) to Jesus, naming the things for which they are saying sorry.

When they have done this, ask them to say "Amen" so you know they have finished. Encourage them to receive the forgiveness of Jesus. If it seems appropriate, pronounce the forgiveness and cleansing of Jesus upon them.

Then encourage them to both invite Jesus into their life and surrender their life to Jesus. It is important for the person not just to invite Jesus into their life but also to surrender to Him; otherwise they are asking Jesus to join their life but are not preparing to surrender.

All the time be praying in the Spirit and staying connected with the Holy Spirit. Explain that the Holy Spirit is the power of God and that you are going to ask Him to come and fill them with the power and presence of Jesus, to live this new life with Him.

Watch what is happening, staying open to any prophetic word of encouragement, comfort, or strength.

After saying "Amen", tell the Receiver that they now belong to Jesus. Now they are a Christian it would be good to chat to Jesus every day as their friend. Let them know that all heaven is rejoicing and the angels are having a party! Encourage them to tell others about their decision to follow Jesus.

If possible give them a Bible or a small book for new Christians. Encourage them to rely on Jesus and connect them with one or two Christian friends who can nurture them in their new faith. If possible put them in touch with a church or house group.

SPEAKING IN TONGUES

Sometimes, if prompted by the Holy Spirit during prayer ministry, I may ask the Receiver if they speak in tongues or if they would like to receive the gift. In my experience some people have asked for this gift but do not go on to speak in tongues. This may be through embarrassment, or thinking what they are speaking is gobbledygook, or through fear at hearing their own voice uttering the strange words. The Pray-er's job is mainly to reassure the person to take the step of speaking out. It often helps if the Pray-er starts speaking in tongues first, the Receiver joining in; the Pray-er's voice offers a cloak or cover for the Receiver's experimentation.

The following exercise is one I have used many times; nine times out of ten the person has let rip with a wonderful prayer language:

Encourage the Receiver to ask Jesus for a prayer language or to speak in tongues. Explain that after the count of three you will begin speaking in tongues and they should try to make the same sounds as you do, but they won't be able to as the Holy Spirit will give them their own language. This can help the Receiver get over their embarrassment of hearing their voice speaking out. Many people think they haven't received this gift because they fail to make any sound and articulate it, *when in reality the gift is in place but they are too timid to open it.*

Chapter 5

STORIES OF PHYSICAL HEALING AND WHOLENESS

SPEEDED UP HEALING

In my previous book, *Encounter the Holy Spirit*, I mentioned an accident I'd had which left me with four fractures in my shoulder and another across the top of my arm. I was very thankful to Jesus for the wonderful gas and air that caused me to be shouting out in tongues in the x-ray room, following this up with, "I love all of you nurses. You are so wonderful!" at the top of my voice.

My shoulder and arm couldn't be set in plaster because the breaks were in such an awkward position. For the next ten weeks I relied on a multitude of drugs and the prayers of my friends as I sat propped up trying to recover. After about six weeks I started to re-read a book I had first discovered soon after becoming a Christian, Agnes Sandford's *The Healing Light*. The turn of phrase from 1947 when the book first appeared sounds delightfully quaint now, but I was struck by the simple yet profound message. I started to follow some of the guidance for praying for one's own physical healing. On the first day after reading the book I laid hands on myself – first of all on my head. I always find I receive better when I do this! Then I asked the Holy Spirit to come upon me with the healing power of Jesus. Then I put my hand on the broken parts of my arm and shoulder. The next day I repeated the first part but then didn't ask Jesus to heal me again as I had already asked Him the day before, and I knew Jesus would have a good memory! This time I thanked Him for His healing power. As Agnes suggests in the book, I focused on the healing light of Jesus that lives in me and visualised it in the region of my arm and shoulder, at the same time being aware that Jesus is the light of the world. I found this simple method of praying easy enough to manage in spite of being under the influence of a cocktail of prescribed drugs. While I prayed, I also imagined my arm being fully healed and able to do all the things I wanted it to do. In fact what I was doing was speaking positively to my body.

I continued to thank Jesus for my shoulder and arm (rather than being annoyed at them). At nine weeks I had another x-ray and saw that all the bones had joined together. The radiologist was surprised that the bones had started to heal in such a good position. After ten weeks I attended my first physiotherapy appointment. The physio was amazed at the condition of my arm compared to the first x-rays. In fact I only needed five or six more visits as I made such unusually good progress.

In my mind's eye I had kept the picture of both my arms raised up in worship. When I looked on the internet about my injury I discovered it had been very serious, taking a year to heal in many cases, and commonly requiring the insertion of a pin.

In just under four months I could put my arm up straight to worship. At five months I could swing it completely in a circle and touch behind to my opposite shoulder blade. I enjoyed demonstrating my rapid healing to anyone willing to show an interest! The healing had escalated once I applied the principles set out in *The Healing Light*. My physiotherapist friend expressed astonishment at the arm rotation I could achieve at sixty-three years of age. She pronounced the movement remarkable and said many people would never have reached anything like the recovery I had. In fact my arm and shoulder now work better than they did before the accident. I have a much fuller range of movement.

A HEALING AND A MIRACLE

Speaking at a physical healing seminar, I asked for anyone with a physical problem or sickness to raise their hand. Then I asked the young people to get into same-gender pairs to practise ministering healing by standing next to someone else who needed ministry. As I coached them as to how to pray, I observed that most of the people praying were not used to doing this. At the end of this time I asked for any testimonies of healing. Two young men had been shy about coming forward to me at the front to share their testimonies with everyone present, so they asked my husband Ken to come up instead. One of the boys, Joe, had fallen in the skate park the day before, severely grazing his ankle. After a quick prayer the grazing almost disappeared, and the pain was all gone. His praying partner, Luke, then asked Joe to pray for him, as he was deaf in one ear. Luke's hearing returned. Ken had tested this by asking Luke to cover up his normal hearing ear and whispering in the previously deaf one. When Ken returned to the praying pair, Luke told him that doctors had found a problem with the bone in his ear when he was much younger, which meant he would never be able to hear again!

Praise God for His miracle!

FEAR CAUSING PAIN

Physical pain can be due to fear. I remember praying for a woman who couldn't speak much English. Her name was Douska.

She had suffered many years of intense pain in her side, consulting a number of doctors but never receiving any diagnosis of the cause. As a couple of us ministered to Douska, I asked the Lord to bring wholeness to her. In my mind I invited the Holy Spirit to minister to her mind, emotions, will, and body. Someone received a word of knowledge that her problem was due to fear. We asked Jesus to show Douska the cause and nature of the fear. Then Douska explained in broken English that her husband had been diagnosed with diabetes. I asked how long ago this had happened, and when her own pain had started. Douska's face registered astonishment as she realised the two things had happened at the same time. I asked about the nature of the fear. She said, "That he will die, and I will be left alone."

We ministered into this fear, asking Jesus to stand between Douska and her fear. We broke the power of the fear of death and the fear of being alone, in the name of Jesus. I asked Jesus to stand between Douska and these fears and take them into Himself. I then spoke the abundant life of Jesus into her. She said her pain had lessened but not gone. We felt encouraged; we were on the right track. I then asked Douska to ask Jesus to show her a fear connected to this from an earlier time in her life. She remembered how afraid she had been when her parents divorced, and she started to cry. She had been scared of being left alone. I ministered into that remembered fear, asking Jesus to come and visit that young girl from long ago who needed Him. I said out loud, "Jesus will never leave you; that is His promise to you. You will never be alone. Let Jesus minister to that little girl His love. Let Him in." Jesus did a wonderful healing in Douska as a child. Afterwards she said the pain had completely gone. It was wonderful to watch. I had been worried that the language barrier would prevent healing taking place, as it was difficult to communicate, but of course language isn't a barrier to Jesus! I saw this same person two years later, and she said the pain had not returned since that time.

PHYSICAL SICKNESS AND AN EVIL SPIRIT

Sometimes physical illness is caused by an evil spirit (Luke 13:11). When I discern this, I usually feel sick in the pit of my stomach as I pray. I remember once praying for someone who had intense back pain. When asked, they could not recall when it started. I put my hand on their back (after asking permission to do this). Immediately I sensed a sick, repulsive feeling in my stomach. At once I said, "I bind this pain in the name of Jesus, and break the power of it, and send it into the hands of Jesus!" Instantly the Receiver started retching and coughing, then suddenly they were healed of all pain. It was very swift. I then asked Jesus to heal the whole person, bring healing to the point of entry, and fill the person with the Holy Spirit. Afterwards the person could perform many different movements that back pain previously had made impossible. They had literally, physically, been bound.

HEALING TAKING MANY YEARS

Sometimes the healing process extends over a long period of time.

I had a horse-riding accident in my late twenties. At the time I was told nothing could be done about the damage to my neck and eventually my neck would crumble. Well, it hasn't! Instead, over a period of twenty-five years Jesus brought healing to it in many ways. These days it just causes me some stiffness if I overdo things.

About seven years after the damage to my neck I went to a New Wine conference and received prayer ministry from a group of people. Suddenly my whole body started manifesting the powerful presence of the Holy Spirit. The only way I can describe what my body did at that moment is to compare it to a corkscrew movement of my whole body. Later on, a medical doctor who had been among those praying said those contortions were actually impossible for the body to do! After the prayer I managed to lift both arms in the air, which I had been unable to do for seven years! The healing took twenty-five years from the time of the original injury. I would say that it is now about 90 per cent healed, leaving only an occasional residual stiffness. Praise God!

During these long years of gradual healing, I often had appointments with osteopaths, physiotherapists, and other therapists. Each time the Lord used me to witness to His power to heal and save. Sometimes He even gave me prophecies for those treating me. The ways of the Lord are not our ways, but they are wonderful!

Physical healing can happen in so many different ways: instantly, over a short time, or through an extended time. We never know how or when Jesus will do it. Some people receive emotional, mental, and spiritual healing but seem to experience little physical change. I don't know why this is, and there are probably different reasons in each case, but nothing stops me praying for wholeness. Sometimes Jesus seems to heal someone 80 per cent; sometimes there is only a slight improvement. At other times the person is completely healed physically.

DOUBLE HEALING

My husband had a very debilitating illness diagnosed as cluster headache – a mild term for something absolutely crippling, for which no cure is known. He suffered from these headaches for twelve years, never knowing when each cluster would start. It is said the pain is more intense than the contractions of labour, with each attack lasting thirty to forty-five minutes, occurring every day and increasing to many attacks a day for about three months at a time. It could then recur the following year or miss a year.

We prayed every prayer you could imagine. A few times we confessed ours sins to one another and anointed with oil (James 5:13–18). Eventually I ran out of ideas of prayers to say, and I just put my hand on him and prayed in tongues. When someone you love has a long-term illness and you have tried everything you know, it can feel very frustrating, and I found praying in tongues helped me to refrain from taking responsibility upon myself for my husband's healing. If you don't pray in tongues, I encourage you to ask for it, receive it, and start using it – just speak out in faith and don't worry what it sounds like – or simply use your spirit to connect with the Holy Spirit. Be sensitive to Him as you minister, following His lead (more on this subject and other gifts is covered in *Encounter the Holy Spirit*).

Though we persevered in prayer for his headaches, we saw no healing taking place until my husband was hospitalised for something quite separate – a life-threatening infection in his spine. During his hospital stay, while he was also suffering the intense pain of a cluster headache, people all around the world were praying for his healing from the spinal infection. The infection in the spine was a gradual healing and recovery lasting almost a year, but the healing of the cluster headaches was instant. Eight years have passed since then, during which time he has had no recurrence of his headaches. Sometimes we just don't understand. The Lord's thoughts are higher than our thoughts, the Bible tells us (Isaiah 55:9). We will never fathom God. But He is good and He is able to do much more than we could possibly imagine.

GETTING OUT OF WHEELCHAIRS

At the Soul Survivor Festival in 2012 we saw hurting people getting up out of wheelchairs. A young girl of eleven years old got out of her wheelchair and turned some cartwheels – such a beautiful sight! Later someone told me that she used to do a lot of gymnastics but developed a condition leaving her feet too painful to stand on. A couple of evenings previously Jesus had healed one of her feet, and we were there to witness the moment her other foot was healed.

On the same evening a youth leader in a wheelchair was seen getting out of it and dancing in the aisles having just received his healing.

During those weeks we saw many miracles and healings. Some were more dramatic than others. Some people had self-harming scars disappear; others had legs, arms, or backs healed. One youth leader brought her new baby on stage. The previous year she had been prayed for after being unable to conceive. She had conceived on site after prayer, and here was the proof! Jesus performed these healings and miracles mostly through young people aged fourteen to eighteen as they laid hands on their peer group. We have seen similar healings and miracles for many years as young people minister to one another at the festivals.

HEALING AN UNBELIEVER IN HOSPITAL

At eleven o'clock one night, we heard a loud knocking and a ringing of our front door bell. As we opened the door we saw an untidy-looking young man of about seventeen standing on the doorstep. His eyes looked wild and he had lost one of his muddy trainers. "I'm wanted by the police," he announced. We thought it might be wiser not to invite him in, so my husband chatted to him sitting on the ledge in our porch.

We soon realised he was high on something. He said he had been walking on the common (250 acres of common land) near our house and had been attracted by the light coming from our home. He didn't know where or who he was.

The following day, the police told us this young man had been high on magic mushrooms picked on the common. Once he had come down from the effects of the mushrooms they took him to his home a few miles away.

We thought that this would be the end of seeing Sam, but he called round to see us to apologise for his behaviour a few nights later. But that was not the end of it either. Two weeks later, a young man from our village called Will (not a Christian) visited to tell us Sam had been almost blown up by lighting a cigarette in a bathroom being decorated. The chemical fumes from the decorating materials had ignited when he lit the match! After Will left, I sensed the Lord say He wanted me to visit Sam in hospital.

I fought against this as I was so scared of seeing someone severely burnt. I am a very visual person, and imagined all kinds of gruesome scenes as I thought about it.

But I knew better than to disobey the Lord's prompting, so feeling more than a little anxious I headed off to the hospital. As I entered Sam's room I was shocked to find him wearing nothing more than a pair of boxer shorts. He wasn't in bed, as the touch of any clothes or bedding caused him too much pain. He paced around the room looking agitated.

Sam was a shocking sight. Part of his nose had burned away and half of one ear. One side of his face had escaped burns, but the other side was black and red and oozing. He had massive areas of hair missing. His legs were a blend of different colours and also oozing. Sam's whole body was trembling with shock and trauma. After a while of listening to his story, as I thought of his long journey to recovery, I felt my heart swelling with compassion.

Before I left, I plucked up the courage to ask Sam if I could lay hands on and pray for him, even though there was another young man in the room at the time. I had no idea which part of Sam's body to touch, as it all looked so tender and painful. I asked him about his prognosis of recovery. He gave his permission in a croaky, crackly voice, explaining that his vocal cords had been burned, and the doctors had assessed the damage as permanent. His voice would remain as it was now. He had lost his hearing in the burnt ear. Skin grafts would be started on his face in a few months. Sam lay down, and feeling very daunted I laid a hand lightly on the top of his head. I invited the power of the Holy Spirit to come upon him, asking Jesus' compassion and love for Sam to come in abundance. I spoke healing to Sam's body in Jesus' name, and healing in Jesus' name for his hearing and for his voice. It was a short prayer as Sam couldn't lie down for long as he was so agitated.

I went home with a heavy heart, but a couple of months later Sam came to visit us. His voice had been completely healed and he could hear with his damaged ear! One side of his face was still tender, but healing. When I asked about it, he told me that both his hearing and voice were better from the day after I had prayed, and continued every day to improve.

This healing humbled me. I remembered how I had resisted going to the hospital to visit someone I hardly knew. Though I went in the end, I had been thinking of myself and how it would affect *me*, not of what can happen when God steps in.

I would love to say that out of this Sam became a Christian – but he didn't. He was interested at first and I got him a Bible with pictures instead of words, as he was severely dyslexic. He visited us a couple of times and we watched the speedy healing of his scars with amazement. And then we didn't see him any more. Sometimes we just have to obey that leading of God to do just one or two things and then let it go. That's what we did with Sam.

But though we never saw Sam give his life to Jesus, the Lord has a purpose for his life. Who knows how Sam's story will end?

We never know when or where the Lord will ask us to lay hands on someone. For me it was the first time I had prayed for a near naked young man wearing only boxer shorts! The circumstances may be unusual, but whatever the circumstances I never want to miss something that the Lord is doing. So for me hopefully it will always be – "Yes, Lord!".

WHAT HAPPENED AFTER A WORD OF KNOWLEDGE

"Words of knowledge" are supernaturally revealed pieces of information about people. They may refer to a physical condition or to something from someone's past or something current in their lives at the moment.

The "word" may come into your mind as actual words (or just one word) or a picture, or even as a physical sensation.

On one occasion at a meeting, a "word" given to me, which I gave out, was: "There is someone who is longing to have a baby."

The very first person I went up to pray for had come forward in answer to this word. The Lord will often do this! I encouraged her to invite the Holy Spirit to come into her mind, emotions, and memories. I waited.

The word "hormones" came into my mind. I said out loud, "I speak to these hormones in Jesus' name and tell them to be in the right balance." Next I spoke to her womb in Jesus' name, and told it to be fruitful, still waiting and listening in case the Lord had anything further to say. Into my mind came the words "I will never get pregnant", and I asked the young woman whether she had ever thought this.

She said she remembered thinking many years ago that she probably would never be able to get pregnant, though at the time she had no basis for these thoughts.

I told her to get rid of those sorts of thoughts, as they were not helpful – they were negative. She started to cry. She thought that if she imagined something positive, it wouldn't be trusting

God. We chatted about that and she finally chose to reject those negative words in the name of Jesus. "In Jesus' name I choose to let go of the words 'I will never get pregnant.'" I broke the power of those words in Jesus' name. She then chose to be receptive. I blessed her womb in Jesus' name.

I have not had the opportunity to follow that young woman's story through to the end, but I know how powerful negative thoughts and beliefs can be, blocking natural processes and even causing illness. Speaking positively to our bodies is an essential component of healing.

LONG-TERM ILLNESS

It can be distressing when we contemplate praying for someone who has an incurable illness and must simply learn to "live with it".

Some people embrace their illness to the extent that they come to identify with it, saying, "I am a diabetic" rather than, "I have diabetes." We are more receptive to healing if we distinguish between ourselves and any illness we may have.

When our daughter was twenty-three years old, she was diagnosed with chronic Lyme disease, caused by an infected tick bite. If left untreated the infection spreads, affecting joints, heart, and brain. Our daughter struggled for three years to get a diagnosis. By the time her treatment began, the disease had taken hold and she was in the third stage. It was wreaking havoc on her body. She has been on a very painful journey of recovery. There is no known cure, and the disease can flare up at any time. The incredible thing has been watching her slowly recover not just physically, but emotionally, mentally, and spiritually. She is a completely different person to the one who contracted the disease. Yes, it is something she lives with, but it doesn't define her. During her recovery period she actively separated herself from her illness. She underplayed the effect it had had on her body, and when people asked about it she spoke of what she could do rather than how the illness restricted her.

There is so little known about the long-term effects of this disease. Pregnancy and childbirth can be affected, and there is no clear guidance about the likely health of the unborn child. Remarkably, not only did our daughter become immediately pregnant when she and her husband wanted to start a family, but her pregnancy and birth were normal. Our youngest grandson was born to the laughter of his parents!

It has been a long haul praying through the many different issues in the course of her recovery. Each time her illness plateaued, I would pray specifically about the latest symptoms. At each phase different medications were suggested, and another therapy or direction was taken. Sometimes prayer resulted in emotional release, sometimes mental clarity. This illness causes many symptoms (our daughter at one point had about thirty), so our specific prayers were varied!

Praying for long-term illness, when all the clinicians say there is no known cure, can feel daunting; but we know it makes no difference to Jesus whether someone has a headache or a cancerous tumour.

The hardest thing is to persevere undaunted when there is very little visible improvement or the illness even seems to be getting worse. Even so, "I know whom I have believed, and am convinced that he is able to guard what I have entrusted to him..." (2 Timothy 1:12).

It is also very comforting to know that "nothing can separate us from the love of God that is in Christ Jesus our Lord":

> **For I am convinced that neither death nor life, neither angels nor demons, neither the present nor the future, nor any powers, neither height nor depth, nor anything else in all creation, will be able to separate us from the love of God that is in Christ Jesus our Lord.**
>
> Romans 8:38–39

THREE SHORT PRAYERS

Sometimes I demonstrate physical healing after giving a talk on the subject. Then at a conference I saw Robby Dawkins from

Aurora Vineyard Chicago using a similar model to the one I had been demonstrating for years, but with one difference. Before ministering he asked people to give him a level of pain and mobility on a score of 1–10 (10 being highest) before praying. After each prayer the person is then asked what the score is. This is brilliant as it focuses in on the improvement after each prayer. The model followed is the one described in Chapter 3 on physical healing.

The first time I followed this method, in front of a group of fifty people, the girl I prayed for received progressive healing in her knees after three brief prayers. Then she laid hands on a man with a mobility problem and pain in his shoulder blade. He also received progressive healing which was completed after three brief prayers.

I felt so encouraged I decided two days later to do this again during a seminar. At that conference I was the only speaker offering any talks about the Holy Spirit or healing. This felt very daunting as I don't think there was much expectation among those attending the seminar of seeing miracles of healing at their conference.

During the talk I asked everyone to stand and receive power and authority from Jesus to heal the sick and cast out demons, then towards the end I called six people up on the stage who had mobility problems and pain in their shoulders or arms. Using the same model – Robby Dawkins' method spelled out in Chapter 3 – I prayed for just one person. She was completely healed. I then coached her using the same words to lay hands on the next woman in the line. This second woman received complete healing after the third time of prayer. I then coached the second healed woman to pray for the man who was third in line. He was gradually healed after three short prayers. This continued through all those on the stage. A couple of people were tearful as they tested their range of movement and realised that they were healed and had no pain. One woman started crying as some inner pain was released too. Five out of the six people were completely healed, one woman being led away from the stage for private prayer, as some inner healing was taking place.

I only prayed for one person and coached the rest. To do this required some courage from me and the others who ministered as, to borrow Robby's words, I was "cranking up the risk factor". But what was the worst thing that could have happened? We could have all looked fools! And if we had done, we would have been in good company – "fools for Christ", along with the apostle Paul! (1 Corinthians 4:10).

My desire in telling you these stories is that you will be inspired and encouraged to trust God and have a go yourself, with confidence to practise prayer ministry for healing, taking the authority He gives us in the name of Jesus to make suffering people whole.

I challenge you (as I am challenging myself) to begin doing this ministry, and then continue as often as possible.

Our God is an awesome God!

Chapter 6

NOTES FOR LEADERS: PRAYER MINISTRY

PRAYER MINISTRY: TEAM OR NO TEAM?

A church leader setting out to form a prayer ministry team must weigh up the advantages and disadvantages of different approaches. What format might you follow? I have listed three possible options.

A set prayer ministry team

Pros

1. Some people are gifted in this area of ministry.

2. Knowing your team, it is easier to train, equip, and encourage all who minister, giving better control over methods used, and better accountability.

3. There can be a rota and you will know every week who is going to be on duty.

4. Those unsuitable for this type of ministry can be "weeded out" before causing any pastoral issues.

Cons

1. The team doesn't grow and may even decline unless you are training new people.

2. The congregation may see this as elitist: these are the "special people". This can discourage others from exploring prayer ministry. Those on the team may also be tempted to become possessive about "their" area of ministry.

3. The congregation may start relying on the team, or particular members, instead of on the power of God.

4. Sometimes personality preferences may cause the congregation to avoid certain team members.

No ministry team

Pros

1. Any church member can minister.

2. Everyone feels included, even the new people.

3. We are all the same, all relying on the power of God to minister and heal.

4. It really feels like the body of Christ ministering to one another.

5. There is less likelihood of getting into a rut and limiting our expectations by always doing the same things.

6. A greater number of people ministering means there is never a shortage during holidays or bad weather.

7. Ministry can be directed from the front as it is taking place.

8. Prayer ministry becomes the norm.

9. The empowering of the Holy Spirit is for the entire congregation. As the body of Christ and His followers we may all be involved in this ministry. It is more inclusive to have all the church members available to minister.

Cons

1. It is more "messy" (remember, it is "messy" in the nursery but "quiet" in the graveyard!).

2. Team leaders must look out for those who are not church members and ensure they are appropriately briefed, to maintain accountability and good practice.

3. Team leaders must organise a system for newer members to be paired with more experienced Pray-ers.

4. It is less easy to administrate extra training and equipping with no set team.

5. An increased likelihood of some Pray-ers not ministering appropriately or according to the agreed values may create problems and even put people off.

A combination

To maximise the advantages and minimise the disadvantages, a combination may offer the best way forward. Establishing a team meeting regularly for training, encouraging, and equipping ensures accountability and an agreed good practice. But the team can be open to anyone to join. Team leaders can pair up anyone new (as they come forward to pray) with an experienced Pray-er. After the church service they may then point the new Pray-er to the next training session. This will facilitate their receiving regular sessions for training and fellowship. The team would then be inclusive and always growing and learning, with the extra advantage of encouraging people of all ages to be on the team – not only those who have been members for many years! To encourage participation and increase understanding and accessibility, it is helpful to produce a leaflet setting out how the team works, when and where the ministry is offered, and the core values of the healing ministry in your church.

MEETING BEFORE SERVICES

The team benefits from meeting together before the service to prepare in shared prayer and ask the Lord for words of knowledge to be given at close of worship when the prayer ministry is about to begin. The words of knowledge are then fresh in people's minds, for them to immediately respond, and go forward for prayer. It helps to explain to the congregation that the words of knowledge are the Lord's way of tapping people who need prayer on the shoulder. Without this encouragement, it might not occur to some people to go forward, though the Lord may be waiting and eager to heal and help them.

LEADING EQUIPPING SESSIONS

Introducing prayer ministry into the church should include an initial training and equipping time, along with plenty of opportunity for laying on hands to practise. Thereafter new members' training and equipping should run once or twice a year. This could be a separate meeting, or you might incorporate it into the regular training sessions, to give new members and existing members a chance to make friends, as well as offering a reminder of core values and practice to the regular team, and give them a chance to share their own insights.

Here is a suggested format for a training session of an hour and a half, to be offered on a monthly/bi-monthly basis for regular members:

- time of worship: 15 minutes
- 15 minutes of sharing personal testimony of prayer ministry, or encouragements of seeing the Holy Spirit working during prayer ministry times
- 20-minute teaching time focusing on a specific aspect of the healing ministry; for example, dealing with fear, or healing of memories
- 10 minutes asking the Holy Spirit for words of knowledge for physical or emotional healing
- 30 minutes for people to respond to the words of knowledge and minister to one another by laying on hands.

Doing this regularly will empower the team and bring members closer together.

INTRODUCING MINISTRY IN THE POWER OF THE HOLY SPIRIT

The following suggestions are meant to guide you in introducing prayer ministry in the church service setting:

Start by preparing a series of talks or sermons along the

themes of the Holy Spirit, gifts of the Holy Spirit, the presence of Jesus, and the healing ministry of Jesus.

Explain to the congregation that as well as teaching and reading about the Holy Spirit you would like to give Him space to interact directly and personally during worship. Explain that we are all learning in this, to take the stress out of doing this for the first time. Also explain that we need never be afraid of silence, or of not having every moment in worship structured and planned.

The fear of most leaders is "What if nothing happens?" It is not our responsibility to make "something happen". We are just giving the Lord space to do what He wants. Explain to the congregation that if nothing happens that's okay – we are all learning, practising how to be still and wait. But in the quietness we can be sure the Lord will come and meet with people… because that is what He has been wanting space to do!

An absolute basic essential is that the person leading the service be open to the Holy Spirit leading. An opportune time for "waiting on the Lord" could come at the end of the sung worship or incorporated into the worship time. The leadership team must work closely together, the service leader keeping good liaison with the worship leader. The leader of the service needs to stand in a place with a clear view of all the congregation. If the presence of the Holy Spirit can be strongly felt, direct the congregation to be quiet and welcome Him, encouraging them not to worry about anyone else but simply breathe in the Holy Spirit. Ask Him what He wants to do. You may feel a prompting to call forward some people for a fresh touch of the Holy Spirit, or for healing or encouragement, or you may receive a specific word for a particular people group – perhaps for those who feel anxious or who are at a crossroads in their life. Encourage everyone to be open to the Lord, receptive of the work He is doing in each of them individually and attentive to the promptings of the Spirit. If no specific word is presented clearly to you, this may be an opportunity to invite anyone sensing the presence of God, through a sense of peace or some other manifestation, to come forward. Encourage members of the congregation, or the ministry team, to lay hands on those who come forward, and bless what the Lord is doing.

Be prepared with tissues and dedicated oil. It's also a good idea to have some mints available for your ministry team, to ensure fresh breath. It can be both distracting and unpleasant for the Receiver if the Pray-er has stale breath.

Start simply, and each time wait on the Lord a little longer. This way people will get used to waiting for the stirring of His word and His movement among the congregation. At first this can feel uncomfortable because we are not used to silence, but once it becomes the norm in your church the stress of waiting in the quietness changes to anticipation at the thought of what the Lord may do. A sense of expectation rises. Even on uneventful days, the presence of His peace and love is something to look forward to.

The time of waiting on the Spirit can happen at any point during the service; it doesn't have to be at the beginning or end. Another time can be after the talk or sermon. Always invite the Holy Spirit to come upon the congregation and *wait*. The disciples waited in the upper room for a *long* time at Pentecost. He is worth waiting for!

Those responsible for public worship often worry that there is enough material to fill the time already, and adding in a ministry time will overload the schedule; but prayer ministry need not take long, and it is usually possible to make time for what we really believe to be important. Some leaders may feel concerned that they may upset members of the congregation by changing the familiar flow of worship and introducing something very different. Personally I would be more wary of upsetting the Holy Spirit and not allowing the Lord Jesus to do something in His own church!

You can trust the Lord to direct you in how to develop the times of listening and ministry as you remain open to Him, but here are some pointers:

- Ask, listen, and watch for the Holy Spirit.
- Wait for Him.
- Be willing to be a fool for Christ.
- Push through the fear of looking a fool.
- Get the congregation on your side by explaining that we are all going on a journey with this.
- Be prepared to change what you have planned.
- Rely on the Holy Spirit.
- Watch the Holy Spirit coming upon people.
- Ask, "What are You doing, Lord?"
- Ask, "What do You want to do or say, Lord?"
- Step out of the boat!

Let the adventure begin!

INTRODUCING POWER MINISTRY TO A SMALL GROUP

Power ministry is a shortened term for ministry in the power of the Holy Spirit. This may include prayer ministry and the use of various gifts of the Holy Spirit including words of knowledge, healing, and prophecy.

This ministry could take place at a house group/cell group or any other small and informal gathering. As with ministry in a church service, invite the Holy Spirit to come and then wait for Him, encouraging the group to make Him welcome. Ask the Lord what He wants to do. This may lead into asking anyone who has a physical or emotional need to sit in the "hot seat" in the middle of the group while members lay hands on the person. This time could also lead into asking for "words of knowledge" for those gathered, or prophetic words (see my previous book, *Encounter the Holy Spirit*, for ways of doing this). During this time it may be an opportunity for members of the group or leaders to lay hands on those gathered and bless what they see the Father doing, the activity of the Holy Spirit evident among His people.

Some may feel more relaxed in a small group, where they know people well, than in the more public setting of a church service. It can be a good strategy to begin prayer ministry in house groups, regularly making time for ministry until it feels familiar and the group members have come to look forward to it. This is good preparation; it shapes expectations in readiness for introducing and incorporating ministry into public worship.

PRAYER MINISTRY IN FULL VIEW

It is a good idea to do prayer ministry in full view of the congregation, not in a separate room. Our model for this is Jesus. He modelled and demonstrated healing in full view, in the synagogue, in the Temple, in private homes, or with crowds around Him in the market place and villages. Sometimes Jesus took people outside the village, and I believe this models good practice in pastoral prayer ministry, which will be covered in Part 3. The only time He asked people to leave the room was when He was raising the dead and those grieving had no expectation of life.

The word "occult" means "hidden" or "in secret", and we want nothing occult about our ministry. If we take people off into another room or a separate area it is as if we are trying to hide something. Others watching may have been considering having prayer ministry but may feel nervous or suspicious because they have no opportunity to see what is going on before trying it for themselves. If people from your congregation have previously experienced ministry that frightened or upset them, they need reassurance that this is a natural and safe thing to do.

We must be careful to not only do what is right but to be open and transparent in our practice, particularly when ministering to young or vulnerable people.[1]

PRAYER MINISTRY AT FESTIVALS OR CONFERENCES

At the Soul Survivor festivals for young people we started off having a set prayer ministry team. After a few years we decided instead to form an "Enabling Team". Sometimes the Enabling Team will minister to delegates who come forward in answer to a call given by the leader. These delegates are then invited to join in ministering alongside the team. At other times the delegates minister to other delegates where they are standing, while the Enabling Team walk around the auditorium/big top directing and encouraging the ministry. The Enabling Team only get involved in the ministry if the delegates seem out of their depth. There is also another team available called a "Connect Team" that can be called upon for those needing follow up when they get home or when serious issues arise. There is also a "chat room" for delegates who wish to talk and receive prayer ministry, and some other festivals/conferences also have pastoral prayer ministry or counselling by appointment.

PRACTICE SESSIONS

Bishop David Pytches always says, "The meeting place is the learning place for the market place," and John Wimber used to say, "The meat is on the street!" It is important to practise prayer ministry at church, not only for the health of the body of believers, but also in preparation for taking this ministry out into our everyday life.

Groups of church members can really enjoy and be inspired by getting together to practise ministry in the power of the Holy Spirit, when it is not too intense but done in a relaxed and humorous way. The pressure to succeed and get everything right to the last detail is lifted away when we remember to reassure participants that it is okay to make mistakes – indeed, we learn valuable lessons from our mistakes. I often run "have a go" workshops, encouraging all participants to raise their hand to agree that they don't mind anyone making a mistake during the practice time.

Get everyone into pairs of the same gender, preferably with someone they don't know so well, as this is what often happens in real life. Ask people to practise inviting the Holy Spirit, using some suggestions from Chapter 4, such as the section on where to put your hands. The experimentation and the excitement of seeing the Holy Spirit move among us is great fun as well as instructive. I am convinced that the Lord loves us to practise. We don't have to be slick!

Ask for feedback as to what people were experiencing during that time. Even though they were only practising, the Holy Spirit is eager to minister. Afterwards, ask people to put their hand up if they would like to receive healing for anything. Then get pairs of people to minister the healing of Jesus to them using the model in Chapter 3. Make sure they ask to receive gifts of healing from the Holy Spirit, and ask Him to bring "the power of the Lord that is present to heal". Asking this alone raises the level of expectation in yourself as well as your group.

Another practice exercise is for each person to think of someone they often pray for, or about whom they feel concerned or worried. Let them take turns to bring their person to Jesus. Talk them through visualising or describing themselves taking the person they worry about by the hand and bringing them to Jesus as He stands waiting at the foot of the cross, handing them over to Jesus and leaving them safe with Him. Ask them to then walk away, leaving the person they are worrying about entrusted to Jesus. For some people, this can be a really deep and significant time, hard to do but bringing considerable release and relief.

Another good thing is to practise asking Jesus for words of knowledge or prophetic words.

The more people practise in a safe, unhurried, relaxed environment the more they will use the gifts of the Holy Spirit. We are supposed to be supernaturally natural!

With all of the above we don't have to worry about God's reputation or worry if nothing seems to be happening. God is quite able to look after His own reputation. If we are worried about our own then maybe that is the part we need to surrender before we take our feet off the bottom of the pool and launch out into the deep.

We naturally fear looking inadequate or ineffective as prayer ministers, but in reality our weakness may be our greatest asset, for God's "power is made perfect in weakness" (2 Corinthians 12:9). It means then I can boast about Him, and it is He who will be given the glory.

It can help to explain to the group that we are all going on a journey and sometimes we may get it wrong. Sometimes we may fall off the bike while we are learning to ride it. We remember that it is God's power we are relying on, and can do nothing in our own strength. We cannot guarantee success, but we can still be obedient to God in trying our best. This gives permission for everyone, including you, to get it wrong sometimes.

Sometimes people will confuse "blessed thoughts" (their own thoughts and wishes for the person) with "prophetic words". Our common sense tells us the difference! Gradually, as people get more practised at listening, more prophetic words will come. It is the same with words of knowledge.

For training purposes you may photocopy the "Ministry guidelines" that conclude this chapter. You may also photocopy any other material in the previous or following chapters. These guidelines are also available on my resources website www. ourhandshishealing.co.uk. Feel free to change or adapt them to suit your local circumstances.

MINISTRY GUIDELINES SHEET

You may have been praying for people for many years or may have been taught a model through attending another church. We would all like to be following the same model and so we would really appreciate your adopting the following guidelines and sticking to them.

Ministering to people in the power of the Holy Spirit is very different from praying for people at a distance. We are asking the Holy Spirit to use us as a channel of His power and the love of Jesus to bring healing, comfort, or deliverance. We are asking for the manifest presence of Jesus to come and bring change.

Ministry times usually begin with an invitation from someone leading the service, for people to respond to the Holy Spirit. In praying for people, the most important thing to remember is that this is God's work – not ours. We are there to encourage those seeking God, and to bless what the Holy Spirit is doing in people. It is not our responsibility to ensure any particular outcome of people receiving a cure for any particular condition. For our own accountability and encouragement we request that you minister in pairs.

A basic guide to praying for others...

We don't want to get in God's way when we're praying for others. We don't want our own needs to be met and we want to glorify Jesus not ourselves.

Same gender

It's worth repeating: only pray for someone of the same gender as at least one of the ministering pair. Prayer ministry can bring up all sorts of stuff, so it's a tried and tested principle to always have at least one person of the same sex as the one you are praying for. Some people find it embarrassing, or for some that have been abused it can be disturbing, to have someone of the opposite sex ministering. Always ask whether it is okay if someone of the opposite sex is ministering in your pair. Whisper this request so the person does not feel intimidated. Even if you're married and wish to minister to your partner in public we'd ask you to bear this in mind to avoid any confusion for others around you. This model is not just about doing what is right but also about being seen to be doing what is right.

Stand in front

Stand in front of the person you are ministering to or to the side. Do not stand behind the Receiver (unless you are laying hands on a painful back, in which case still try to stand to the side) as it can make the Receiver feel uncomfortable or vulnerable if they cannot see you.

Eyes open

Keep your eyes open when you pray for someone. In this way you can observe what God is doing and how the person is responding. It also means you can be prepared if they look as though they may fall over in the power of the Spirit. If this begins to happen get your hand behind the person and let their body slide gently to the floor. Make sure they are left in a comfortable position, not draped over anyone else, and that nothing is on show that shouldn't be! Stay with them as long as needed and encourage them to go on receiving from God. If there is an outpouring of the Holy Spirit and there are not enough prayer ministers available, keep an eye on those who may be laid out on the floor, to keep them safe while ministering to others. Be ready to assist them if they are trying to stand and encourage them to stay sitting on the floor if they wish to do so.

Ministry of power

Please do not use wordy prayers. Allow the Holy Spirit to do His work through you. It is a ministry of power, not of words. Invite the Holy Spirit to come upon the whole person and just wait.

Ask

Don't be afraid to ask someone what they would like you to pray for and what God is doing – even if the Holy Spirit is moving powerfully on them (see Luke 18:41: Jesus asks the blind man, "What do you want me to do for you?"). However, avoid turning this into a long conversation; this is a time for the Holy Spirit to offer counselling, not you!

Speak

If appropriate speak into the situation or condition in Jesus' name. Be sensitive and recognise that you may be wrong. If you have a prophetic word or picture, offer it as a prayer or in such a way that the person being prayed for can make their own decision as to how appropriate your insight may be.

Never insist that your prophetic word or picture is from God. Offer it in such a way that the person can make their own decision as to how appropriate it is. They can test this later. Prophetic words are meant to strengthen, comfort, and encourage the person you're praying for (1 Corinthians 14:3).

Confidentiality but no secrets

The person you are praying for may tell you private things that have happened in their life. Don't appear shocked by any disclosures. Confidentiality is of the utmost importance but *do not* promise to keep anything secret (especially with regards to claims of abuse and especially if the person is underage). If any such disclosures are made to you giving cause for alarm or concern, these should be referred to a leader of the prayer ministry team or a dedicated team member. There should be someone available who knows the proper procedures for reporting or pursuing this. The safety and wellbeing of any young person is of the utmost importance.

Share information only on a need-to-know basis. If an adult discloses to you that they have been abused in the past, and there is reason to suspect another vulnerable person's/minor's life is exposed to danger, refer the information on to a designated person such as the Ministry Co-ordinator or a member of the Leadership Team or designated Child Protection Co-ordinator.

Hands on

Encourage the person to receive from God and be still, rather than joining in. If you see someone moving their lips praying, gently suggest that they receive rather than pray. Some people may show this attitude by opening their hands in front of them. Lay a hand gently on the person's shoulder or forehead. Doing this is especially appropriate with regards to healing (in Mark 1:40–45, Jesus heals a man of leprosy) and as a blessing (in Matthew 19:13–15, Jesus blesses the children). If it is appropriate to pray in this way, be sensitive where you place your hands, always with respect for decency and propriety.

If you suspect an evil spirit

Never tell anyone that they have an evil spirit, not least because you may be wrong! Demonisation is not always obvious and people react in many different ways. If the person is unsure about receiving prayer ministry it's good to have an experienced person with you to help discern the situation. If you feel out of your depth and believe there is an evil spirit at work, inform the Ministry Co-ordinator. It may be that the person needs to be ministered to away from the congregational setting to maintain their dignity, though in general ministry is carried out openly in full view of everyone. Remember the evil spirit can always be bound in Jesus' name until you have had time to assess the situation. Never minister alone in these circumstances.

Listening

Listen carefully both to the person you are praying with, and to God. Ask the Holy Spirit for guidance and encouragement; be prepared to wait. This is God's work, not yours.

Release of emotions

Allowing the expression of feelings is very important. This might involve people crying, shaking, or responding in other ways to whatever God is doing. This is totally okay, but be careful to neither suppress nor exacerbate the situation. We want God to do what He needs to do, and not get in the way of that. However, if those to whom you minister seem quiet and composed, don't be disheartened or assume nothing is happening. People don't have to shake for God to heal them!

And finally...

Not everyone is familiar with ministry and prayer times, and some people are fearful when they sense God is working in them through the Holy Spirit. We must help people who are receiving to feel comfortable and safe, and encourage them to reach out to God. Always be sensitive and respectful. Keep in mind how you would like to be prayed for, and constantly ask God's help.

Reassure those being prayed for that God has heard their sincere prayers and the cries of their hearts, and encourage them confidently to expect answers. Speak healing, peace, and release in the name of Jesus and remember the place of repentance; being forgiven and releasing forgiveness is always important. Suppressed pain will often need to be expressed before the Receiver is able to start forgiving others. Be aware of this.

Do not make appointments to pray with people outside of the meeting. If extra prayer or counselling is needed, ask your ministry team leader or another senior Christian for their advice.

If at any time you feel out of your depth then ask for help. We all find ourselves in situations we cannot handle alone. This is not failure. Our model is to pray in pairs to encourage one another and learn from each other.

Prayer ministry is to take place at the front of the church during services. If someone approaches you in another part of the building take them to the front so that everything remains open and transparent; you are working with a ministry partner and in the context of the ministry team. Avoid one-to-one situations independent of the recognised ministry in your church.

Be confident, expect great things, and always look to Jesus!

PART 2
INNER HEALING MINISTRY

Chapter 7

WHOLENESS

The Lord is close to the broken-hearted and saves those who are crushed in spirit.

Psalm 34:18

He brought me out into a spacious place...

Psalm 18:19

MY STORY

I became a Christian, as a very broken person, aged thirty. I had married at nineteen years old and at twenty-three I gave birth to a stillborn baby. Her brain hadn't grown. Three months later I became pregnant again with our second baby, and afterwards I had a complete nervous breakdown as I hadn't grieved the birth and death of our first baby. Three years later we had another daughter. When she was two years old she tragically drowned in a pool in our garden. All three of these events took place within seven years.

Apart from all this pain, I had grown up with a mentally ill mother who was phobic about a lot of things, particularly food and going out of the house. Mostly depressed, she had suffered from many disorders since her teenage years, but never sought help. She would often take to her bed and withdraw. At the time I didn't realise the effect this was having on me. I grew up lacking in self-worth and self-confidence. My inferiority complex was huge. If someone spoke to me I feared they would discover I was stupid; a blotchy rash would appear down my face and neck.

When I became a Christian, I had no idea I was a sinner. The Bible tells us the Lord doesn't break a bruised reed and a smouldering wick He will not quench (Matthew 12:20; Isaiah 42:3). If the Holy Spirit had shown me my sin and my need for forgiveness and repentance immediately, I think it would have destroyed me completely. Instead, Jesus started drawing me close to Him and healing me. It was about a year after I became a Christian that He showed me what He had done for me on the cross. Before this time I had asked Jesus into my life. After knowing what He did for me on the cross, I surrendered my life to Him and I knew Him as my Lord and King.

This has been a lesson to me in the healing of the broken-hearted. Yes, definitely, people need to seek forgiveness for sin and extend it to others who have sinned against them, but some people are so broken that they need to receive the mercy and healing of Jesus into that deep brokenness first, before they can look outside of that. This is particularly true of those who have been severely abused, and those suffering serious trauma and grief.

Of course this is not prescriptive. For some, the revelation of their sin can occur simultaneously with receiving healing into their brokenness.

We must remain open to the Holy Spirit and His leading and not try to lead people where they are not ready to go.

IT'S ABOUT WASHING FEET!

Our attitude when ministering to people with hurts from the past should be like that of Jesus, who demonstrated the "full extent of his love":

> Having loved his own who were in the world, he now showed them the full extent of his love... [Jesus] got up from the meal, took off his outer clothing, and wrapped a towel around his waist. After that he poured water into a basin and began to wash his disciples' feet, drying them with the towel that was wrapped around him.

... Now that I, your Lord and Teacher, have washed your feet, you should also wash one another's feet. I have set you an example, that you should do as I have done for you.

John 13:1–15

We are to let Him, almighty God, kneel before us and wash our feet. This is such a precious thing, very humbling. After His example we are to then wash others' dirty feet.

WHAT IS "INNER HEALING" OR "HEALING FROM PAST HURTS"?

This is a process in which the Holy Spirit brings the love and healing of Jesus to people who have suffered damage to their spirit and soul (this includes their mind, emotions, and will). This can, of course, in turn cause damage to the body in producing symptoms, whether disease or disability. Some people have suffered over and over in their adult life; others have lived through a troubled or abusive childhood. Maybe as a child they survived somehow, but their coping mechanisms stopped working as they grew up; the past may suddenly burst into their present circumstances, causing distress. Because we are body, soul, and spirit, when bad things happen to us the whole of our being is affected. Though the Lord can heal and release us wonderfully, we will not be completely whole until we go to heaven; but we all have potential for wholeness, and can increasingly receive this while here on earth.

We can feel like midwives when we are ministering inner healing, facilitating what the Holy Spirit is doing, bringing to birth a healed soul.

BODY, SOUL, AND SPIRIT

May God himself, the God who makes everything holy and whole, make you holy and whole, put you together

– spirit, soul, and body – and keep you fit for the coming of our Master, Jesus Christ. The One who called you is completely dependable. If he said it, he'll do it!

1 Thessalonians 5:23–24 The Message

A human being is made up of body, soul, and spirit – but what is the difference between them? Let me offer you my personal understanding of what these terms mean.

The body enables us to enjoy physical awareness of the world around us via our senses – hearing, seeing, smelling, tasting, and touching – and to interact with others.

The soul is made up of our mind, emotions, and will. Because "soul" can be a holistic term meaning "person", it can also include the body as well.

The spirit includes our conscious mind, enabling us to be aware of God and interact with Him.

All three can be abused and damaged.

Luke's Gospel tells of Jesus, fresh from His long fasting in the desert where He was tempted by Satan. Filled with the Holy Spirit, He began His ministry by applying to Himself, as He taught in the synagogue, this quotation from Isaiah:

The Spirit of the Sovereign Lord is on me because the Lord has anointed me to proclaim good news to the poor. He has sent me to bind up the broken-hearted, to proclaim freedom for the captives and release from darkness for the prisoners...

Isaiah 61:1

In preparing for being involved in inner healing prayer ministry we can ask the Lord to speak to us as we set time aside to read quietly and prayerfully through the whole of Isaiah 61. Jesus is the Anointed One but we can also be anointed (set apart for a purpose) by Him. If you haven't already done so, ask for His anointing for prayer ministry and also for "gifts of healing" as mentioned in 1 Corinthians 12:7–11.

PRISONERS AND CAPTIVES

One day while re-reading the passage from Isaiah, it suddenly registered with me that it refers to both freedom for the captives and release from darkness for prisoners. I thought, "Why both? What is the difference?"

Prisoners are detained against their will and are suffering the consequences of their actions. Their freedom has been taken away. In the ordinary sense of the word we think of locked doors and stone walls with small, high, barred windows. In spiritual terms, we might think of people imprisoned within an addiction or trapped inside such sins as hatred, bitterness, self-harm, revenge, unforgiveness, rebellion, self-hatred, adultery, or sexual immorality. Because this sin is unconfessed, the enemy can keep the person locked into their sin. That is why they need release from their darkness.

Captives are bound, enslaved, not free to go. In spiritual terms this may result from some sinful response to being sinned against, robbed of their freedom in any one of a number of ways, and maybe smeared with false accusations or lies.

They may be bound through emotional, mental, spiritual, or sexual abuse. Or they may have never known true love, or been neglected in their childhood. Their inner self may not have been free to develop, and may be held captive by distorted perspectives and oppressive memories.

AREAS THAT NEED ADDRESSING

To receive healing, freedom, and release can involve (in no particular order):
- renewing of the mind
- releasing from a fantasy world
- breaking the power of lies
- releasing, driving out, and dispersing fears
- addressing irrational beliefs
- deliverance from bondage to evil spirits

- breaking binding from sinful or misguided vows
- exposing false choices
- healing of traumatic memories
- redirecting false expectations
- freedom from rejection
- releasing guilt
- releasing shame
- repentance for sin
- breaking the power of self-harm
- healing grief and loss
- healing from neglect
- healing from abuse
- receiving love
- addressing and releasing suppressed misused anger
- breaking strong unhealthy/soul-ties (see Chapter 15 on deliverance)
- healing the inner child
- releasing oppression
- breaking bondages
- healing the spirit
- healing the mind.

In the next chapter I explain how you can use some spiritual tools for setting the captives free and releasing prisoners from darkness. As you gain in confidence you will experience the Lord equipping you with your own spiritual tools to use at different times. Keep in mind that everything is at the lead of the Holy Spirit, and remain open and sensitive to His direction. Follow His leading and keep interacting with Him throughout.

Being set free and healed from any of the afflictions referred to above is life-changing; getting free from the restraints of emotional trauma from the past means they do not control us in the present. Released people can make better choices and be free from harmful patterns of behaviour.

This transformation may not happen all at once. It may stretch over a period of time in an unfolding process. But it can sometimes be instantaneous and then we call it a miracle. I have seen some miraculous emotional healings.

Reading the list above can feel daunting. We may feel inadequate when we listen to the distressing tale of someone's life, or what they are suffering. But by the end of the session we can often be in awe of what we have seen take place. It is good to feel our weakness, as it means we have to let the Holy Spirit work through us, and recognise that the power to change people is entirely His. The Lord's work through the most inexperienced person means He rightfully receives all the glory.

Not every negative experience from the past needs healing. But for some an unresolved root cause becomes a starting point for fear or suffering. Everything else then piles on top. Receivers may not need to relive their past in order to be healed, but we ask the Lord to reveal the root of their problems, asking, "What is the root cause?" and "Please show the Receiver when it started."

During prayer ministry for healing from past hurts, encourage Receivers to give Jesus permission to come into their memories, emotions, and will. Healing will take place only as much as the Receiver will allow. We may see what needs to take place, but we can only go at the pace of the Receiver. This is crucial when someone experiences flashbacks of past abuse, when a fragment of a memory of abuse assails the person's mind. It is very frightening, and can surprise the person anywhere at any time. If the Pray-er interferes by trying to get the Receiver to recall these memories, the mental effect can be severely detrimental. The brain has been protecting the Receiver from remembering. It is as if the memories have been frozen and we must wait patiently as they slowly thaw out. In such a situation the Receiver would benefit from professional therapy, and should see their doctor or get help from a fully trained therapist.

Prayer ministry can help everyone, and God the Holy Spirit is always at work when we lay on hands; but we should recognise our limitations and be willing to refer someone on when we uncover a history of serious abuse or psychiatric illness. This is not failure on our part; it is one more way we have been able to help the person on their healing journey.

KEEPING OPEN TO GOD

Though the depth and extent of need may daunt us, and we may often fear that we will not know how to proceed in prayer ministry, we bear in mind that the Holy Spirit is our Counsellor and Comforter. He is our Teacher, and we can learn from Him as we go. He knows us intimately, and will speak, teach, and counsel according to our personality and understanding. He may lead you into a different way from some of the approaches I am sharing. But He can always be trusted. He prompts us, or gives us a word of wisdom on how to proceed when we feel entirely out of our depth.

It is important to keep open to receiving wholeness and healing for ourselves. Sometimes you may minister to someone only to realise with a shock that you too have the same issues, or need the same type of healing. This is why ministering in pairs is helpful. You can then share this with the person with whom you are ministering. They can then either minister there and then with you or say a quick prayer with you so that you feel accountable and you can then work through this with the Holy Spirit at home. It's good to have a ministry partner to pray for you, but you don't need someone else to minister to you for you to receive healing. Jesus is more than able to do it on His own! Also you don't need everything healed up before ministering to others. If we waited until we were completely whole to begin, we would never minister to anyone!

THE ENEMY'S TACTICS

When we are engaged in prayer ministry, the enemy will try to tell us things like: "You are terrible at this" or "You are good at this – better than the rest of the team" or "I am going to make you/your family suffer if you continue doing this."

We must learn to recognise his voice and reject his accusations and schemes, as the Bible tells us, "Resist the devil, and he will flee from you" (James 4:7).

Whatever our weaknesses or fears are, this is the area that the enemy will highlight. For instance, I hated masks, and was afraid of the dark. When I began doing prayer ministry regularly, the enemy reminded me of my fears. On Sunday nights as I closed my eyes in bed, I would see the most awful frightening masks. As this was an unusual occurrence, I recognised a connection with what I was doing in the daytime on Sundays and what I was seeing at night. Out loud I said to the enemy, "You are not going to stop me doing prayer ministry; whatever you do I am still going to do it." After saying this I got out of bed in the dark (praying silently in tongues). I focused on Jesus, the light of the world, and on His light in me shining out. I stepped out onto the dark landing and forced myself to cling to the banister and go into the darkness downstairs. I felt stronger and more powerful as I continued praying and by the time I reached the bottom of the stairs I had conquered my fear. I felt triumphant as I realised this was an area the enemy could no longer hold me to. I had stood firm, and he did flee – though of course he changed his tactics and was soon trying something else!

The Lord has provided us with all that we need to protect us from the enemy, as we put on the whole armour of God – belt, breastplate, shoes, shield, helmet, and sword (Ephesians 6:10–18).

JESUS SUFFERED TOO

Consider some of the pain and emotions Jesus suffered during His three years of ministry on earth:

He...

- had no permanent place to lay His head;
- was always on the move because "His time had not yet come";
- was misunderstood even by His family and disciples;

- was undermined by those who thought Him just "a carpenter's son";
- was accused of lying;
- often went without sleep;
- went without food;
- was in constant demand;
- was rejected;
- was tormented;
- was accused and attacked by the devil;
- was tortured;
- was ridiculed;
- was humiliated;
- suffered physical abuse;
- was betrayed;
- was separated from His Father;
- suffered seeing others' grief – especially His mother's;
- took the sins of the whole world upon Himself.

These are just a few of the things that happened to Jesus, who was fully man and fully God.

When we hear stories of people's pain, grief, and abuse we keep in mind that Jesus knows all these things; He suffered all of that and more, taking it upon Himself on the cross. Everything necessary for someone to be healed from their suffering and pain was accomplished on the cross.

Sometimes when prompted by the Holy Spirit during prayer ministry I may say, "He is bigger than this! Whatever has happened to you, He is bigger than this! What He did on the cross was enough. He can take it." A Receiver may need gentle encouragement to release their pain to Jesus. Because they are scared at the immensity of it, should it surface, you may want to reassure them that it is not too big for Jesus. He doesn't turn away from our confession of sin, or judge us in our display of anger and rage at what was done to us. Nothing is too big for Him to hear; He knows it already. Sometimes just saying to someone, "Rest in Jesus' arms. They are open wide to you", can be the encouragement they need to let go and entrust themselves to Him.

We must be careful not to show shock or distaste or judgment when something is disclosed to us. It may be something that causes the person shame and distress. It is a privilege to be trusted in this way. If the Receiver tells you something that shocks you, make sure the person you are paired with in ministry prays for you before you go home. Bring it to Jesus and surrender it to Him and let go of it. It is not yours to have.

KEEP ASKING QUESTIONS

During times of prayer ministry for inner healing keep asking the Holy Spirit, "What now?" as shorthand for, "What do You want me to do now?" Ask, "What is it?" as shorthand for, "What are *You* doing?" Ask, "What's the root?" as shorthand for, "What is the root cause?" These arrow prayers to Him are sent up like flares signalling for His assistance. We rely on Him continually, always remembering that He wants this person healed up and set free even more than we do.

Sometimes He does a little healing in just one or two areas, or He might do a huge block of healing. Sometimes it is like peeling away layers. On another occasion He will be exposing a root and cutting it off.

At times during ministry in inner healing it will feel as if you are on edge as you wait for the next direction. Try to relax and lean into Jesus. Just trust Him and don't forget to keep asking the Holy Spirit, "What now?"

Remember *He* is leading; we are just meant to follow!

Chapter 8

TIPS AND SPIRITUAL TOOLS

In this chapter I will be working through, under separate headings, specific discoveries made along the way during thirty years of prayer ministry. I hope my experiences will be helpful for you to learn from and refer to, but as always – remember that the Holy Spirit is your teacher. He will lead you. He will guide you. He will show you bit by bit all you need on each individual occasion.

FIRST STEPS

As you invite the Holy Spirit upon the whole person ask them to invite Jesus into both their conscious and unconscious mind (that is, both the part of our mind we are using in the here and now *and* the part that may be locking away past traumas). Also ask the Receiver to invite Jesus into their current conscious memories. **Wait.**

1. Sometimes at this point you may see the Receiver moving their eyeballs under their eyelids, as if they are watching a scene. Ask them what they are seeing. If it is a memory, ask them to invite Jesus to come and visit them in their past. The Bible says Jesus is the same yesterday, today, and forever, so He can visit their past. At this point *do not* suggest to the person that they are seeing Jesus, or that Jesus is doing such-and-such. It is not up to us to make anything happen. Unless the Lord does it, nothing of value will take place. Let them invite Jesus into whatever scene they are reliving, without trying to influence the nature of their encounter with Jesus in their past. Then proceed by asking the Receiver whatever the Holy Spirit leads you in.

2. *Or*, if prompted by the Holy Spirit, ask the Receiver whether they are sensing or feeling anything. If they are, ask the Holy Spirit to show them what that is connected to.

3. *Or*, ask Jesus to unearth anything He wants to bring up for healing. Ask the Receiver not to try too hard but to relax and let the Holy Spirit do it. You may notice some emotions start to be displayed at this point as you observe the Receiver's body language.

4. *Or*, ask the Receiver if anything is happening in their mind. Sometimes they have been thinking of an incident from childhood, but are struggling because they think it is too trivial a thing to consider. But what may seem minor things to the adult they now are may have been of major importance to a child.

5. The Receiver may recall several incidents or memories. Ask what they are and whether they are feeling any emotions as they recall them. Ask if (and where) they feel them in their body.

6. Proceed as the Holy Spirit leads, gently encouraging the Receiver to allow feelings to surface without being afraid – they are in a safe place. Be guided by the Holy Spirit where to place your hands. If He is not indicating that you move them, don't!

Everyone is different – each with a unique mix of issues, and the way Jesus brings each healing is also unique. However, there are some areas or issues that come up over and over again. I will share some tips and spiritual tools that you might like to try. As always don't follow these as a formulaic prescription but keep interacting with the Holy Spirit; He will show new things, often surprising you in how He brings the healing of Jesus.

GUILT

Psychologists say that the people who carry the most guilt with them are Christians! I have ministered to many people who have not received forgiveness for their sin and continue to feel guilty. Jesus became the "guilt offering" on the cross. Because of our sin something had to die. In the Old Testament it was a lamb, goat, or pigeon that was slain. Blood needed to be shed. We have no need to feel guilty because Jesus has made a supreme offering for our sin, shedding His own blood for us. When people carry guilt, it is as if they are saying that what Jesus did wasn't enough. But He did *everything* necessary to forgive our sin. Any sin needs to be confessed, repented, and fully absolved. Some people may find it helpful to think of approaching the foot of the cross and surrendering their guilt to Jesus. It may help just to think of the word "guilt", and handing it to Jesus. For some it helps to visualise in the mind a symbol of what they are bringing, as it can help focus on surrendering it.

FALSE GUILT

Guilt belongs to things we really have done wrong, but some people are made to feel guilty for things that have been done to them rather than done by them, by the accusations of the perpetrator. This is false guilt. They may have carried it around for years. Children made to feel guilty by predatory and corrupt adults may grow up still bearing that secret burden. Even though they know it is not rational, false guilt is very powerful and some people have profound difficulty surrendering it. They can be set free by naming and bringing false guilt to the foot of the cross, surrendering it to Jesus. Then the Pray-er needs to break the power of false guilt over the Receiver, declaring out loud that what happened wasn't their fault. Speak freedom in Jesus' name.

SHAME

> Then he showed me Joshua the high priest standing
> before the angel of the Lord, and Satan standing at his
> right side to accuse him. The Lord said to Satan, "The
> Lord rebuke you, Satan! The Lord, who has chosen
> Jerusalem, rebuke you! Is not this man a burning stick
> snatched from the fire?"
>
> Now Joshua was dressed in filthy clothes as he
> stood before the angel. The angel said to those who
> stood before him, "Take off his filthy clothes."
>
> Then he said to Joshua, "See, I have taken away
> your sin, and I will put fine garments on you."
>
> Then I said, "Put a clean turban on his head." So
> they put a clean turban on his head and clothed him,
> while the angel of the Lord stood by.
>
> Zechariah 3:1–5

Shame can affect a person deeply. A guilty person can wear shame like clothes of filthy rags, and some feel dirty on the inside too. We can understand why some are even too ashamed to look at Jesus. Those who suffer like this often feel self-hatred or self-rejection. Be open to this, and be directed by the Holy Spirit. Look at the sections on self-rejection in Chapter 14 and self-hatred in Chapter 15.

We can take shame upon ourselves by committing deeds that we are ashamed of, or we can be made ashamed by others as they fill us with shame through sexual or physical abuse, or ridicule and humiliation.

This is how I minister to those dealing with feelings of shame:

1. Explain now there is no condemnation for those who belong to Christ Jesus (Romans 8:1).

2. Where there is real foundation for shame, suggest that the Receiver confess, repent, and receive forgiveness out loud. Some may prefer to do this in a less public area.

> **If we confess our sins, he is faithful and just and will forgive us our sins and purify us from all unrighteousness.**
>
> 1 John 1:9

3. If being shamed by others occurred in childhood, speak to the child: "In Jesus' name I speak to that little girl/boy who was made to feel shame, and say, 'It wasn't your fault. Jesus wants you to know... it wasn't your fault.'"

4. Explain simply that Jesus took over all shame when He was stripped naked on the cross for all to see, and was abused and ridiculed. He has taken our filth and shame. He understands. He does not turn away. We can be naked before Him. He accepts us.

5. Explain that it is as if they wear dirty clothes. Ask them to come and stand before Jesus on the cross and visualise taking off the filthy clothes, handing them to Jesus or dropping them at His feet. Ask them to indicate when they have done it, to say "Amen" when ready to proceed. Keep praying in the Spirit quietly. Ask them to receive anything Jesus may hand back to them. Usually the Receiver will take their time – there may be a lot of anguish and crying. Be patient and ask what is happening, being careful not to intervene too soon. Watch their body language and ask the Holy Spirit what to do next.

According to how the ministry goes you could also do one of the "visual rooms" exercises – see Chapter 11.

During this time the Receiver may start to experience memories coming to the surface. Ask what is happening from time to time. If it seems appropriate, ask Jesus to show the Receiver any area or event where He wants to bring healing.

STORY: BELIEVING A LIE

Prayer ministry can feel like a journey into the unknown with the Holy Spirit leading us.

One young woman looked very fearful as I ministered to her. She had her head in her hands and was visibly shaking. As I put my hand gently upon her shoulder, the shaking only increased. I spoke freedom and release to her in the name of Jesus and broke the power of fear upon her. I spoke into her the perfect love of Jesus, saying a few times quietly, "You are perfectly loved by Jesus." I was conscious of speaking into her soul (her mind, emotions, and will). The shaking slowed, ceased, and she stopped clutching her head in her hands. Then, as I spoke the peace of Jesus into her mind, she suddenly went very limp, apparently released from something that had been holding her.

When she opened her eyes she confided that she didn't know who Jesus was. I suggested to her that she could open the door to Jesus. When negative words, experiences, or connections have invaded a person, not only do they need to send these things packing and bolt the door behind them, but also welcome Jesus in with His light and love.

> **Here I am! I stand at the door and knock. If anyone**
> **hears my voice and opens the door, I will come in...**
>
> Revelation 3:20

The girl replied that when she asked to receive Jesus she had seen horrible eyes. I suggested to her that we ask Jesus where that image came from. I felt prompted to enquire, "Are you scared of Jesus? Do you think He is shaking His finger at you, or has He got His arms open wide to you?" She replied, "In between those two things." Quickly, I replied, "No; He is goodness itself." Then suddenly I received a word of knowledge: "If you have something good, something bad will happen."

It was as if she had been told this more than once, and I was listening in to what had been said to her. I repeated what I had heard, asking her whether that was something she had heard from someone – where did that phrase come from?

She said, "My dad – he always says it to me." I sensed this was at the root of the problem.

I declared, "That is a lie. That lie has become your belief, and that is why whenever Jesus tries to bring you something good, even coming Himself to visit and bless you, that lie kicks in and you can't receive it."

With her permission I broke the power of the lie (naming it, speaking out the phrase) and set her free in Jesus' name.

She renounced the lie in Jesus' name.

I spoke over her the truth that God is good, and brings blessing and truth. I spoke out loud the truth of her salvation, the fact that she belonged to Jesus, and that she could expect blessing from Him with no negative consequences.

I continued speaking freedom over her, and spoke more truths as the Holy Spirit led me.

She accepted the truth and looked radiant.

LIES

The story of that young woman illustrates how easily someone can be bound with lies, and how this constantly affects them spiritually, mentally, and emotionally. Lies are destructive, and can impact people physically if they continue to be acted out.

Satan is a liar and the father of lies (John 8:44). Children believe what adults tell them, so they are very susceptible to accepting lies as truth. As they grow up they can live out of these lies, which then become established as beliefs. Lies can also be accusations from the enemy:

- You are ugly.
- You will never amount to anything.
- You are useless and you always will be.
- You are stupid.
- You will always be...

> **Your eyes are windows into your body. If you open your eyes wide in wonder and belief, your body fills up with light. If you live squinty-eyed in greed and distrust, your body is a dank cellar. If you pull the blinds on your windows, what a dark life you will have!**
>
> Matthew 6:22 The Message

Our major senses are like gateways to our inner being. What we hear, see, and experience affects the quality of our interior life.

Lies usually enter our mind through the gateway of our hearing – negative words spoken to us, affecting our minds and emotions right down into our body.

When the enemy speaks to us directly, or through someone else, he accuses us, speaking into our thought life, "You are...", followed by some negative, destructive words or accusations. Our own thoughts, by contrast, are usually in the first person: "I am..." Jesus said, "My sheep know my voice." The Lord doesn't accuse, condemn, deceive, or lie to us. He may challenge, encourage, affirm, or question us. Even when the Lord convicts us of serious sin, His word to us brings joy in forgiveness and release, not the crippling condemnation of guilt. Encourage the Receiver to pay attention and discern whose voice they are listening to and complying with in their thought life.

Here is a way to minister freedom from spoken negative words, lies, or negative beliefs:

1. Invite the Holy Spirit onto the whole person, including mind, emotions, and will.

2. Wait.

3. Get the Receiver to renounce the lie/s out loud, saying, "In Jesus' name I renounce the lie/belief that..."

4. Place your hands over the Receiver's ears, breaking the power of the lie/belief in Jesus' name.

5. Ask the Receiver to declare that they are no longer going to live by that lie/belief (naming it).

6. Ask the Receiver to declare the truth in Jesus' name; for instance, if the lie is that they cannot do something, they should affirm in Jesus' name that they can.

IRRATIONAL BELIEFS

This could cover a whole range of beliefs. Our carers or parents teach us things intended to protect us as we are growing up, which may settle into our thought life as embedded caution:

Look both ways before crossing the road.

Don't play with matches; you might start a fire.

These are helpful things that keep us safe. But we can also pick up irrational beliefs from superstitions and old wives' tales:

Eating greens makes your hair curly!

Sitting on a cold step will give you piles!

Treading on cracks in the pavement makes you blind!
(I was twenty-five years old and still avoiding cracks in the pavement until I realised what I was doing!)

Some irrational beliefs are laughable and easy to spot; others are more subtle and obtain a hold on our thinking, whether we caught them from our parents or formed generalisations from bad experiences of our own. Sometimes they take root at vulnerable moments when we must make a decision that will determine our development or shape a course of events. Here are a few irrational beliefs I have seen people holding on to:

*   Never trust men; they are unreliable.
*   If something good happens then something bad will follow.
*   Don't let anyone see you cry; it will make it worse.
*   I must do everything perfectly.
*   This is how it is and this is how it will always be.

These beliefs and others like them can profoundly influence and seriously restrict a person's life. Here is the way I would minister in such cases:

1. Invite the Holy Spirit to come upon the whole person.

2. Wait.

3. If directed by the Holy Spirit, encourage the Receiver to invite Jesus to come into their memories and show where any false belief has originated through a memory or experience.

4. If it is a memory, ask Jesus to come and visit that time and place.

5. Encourage the Receiver to "let Jesus do it", to allow Jesus access and freedom rather than them striving to make anything happen.

6. Explain briefly to the Receiver why their belief is irrational.

7. The Receiver can proceed by renouncing the belief, saying, "In Jesus' name I *choose* to let go of this belief that…"

8. Break the power of any false belief in Jesus' name.

9. Encourage the Receiver to proclaim the truth out loud.

During the prayer ministry time in a seminar, it was amazing to hear people declare for all to hear: "It wasn't my fault. It wasn't my fault" – over and over, until the truth of that sank in, bringing them amazing freedom.

I have seen incredible release when space is made for Jesus to come, bringing His healing love and truth instead of lies and irrational beliefs. It can make such a very big difference in someone's life once they tackle this.

Once you get started the Receiver may get into the swing of things and recall more and more lies or irrational beliefs. Just carry on doing the same thing as above with each belief.

Encourage the Receiver to keep on proclaiming the truth

whenever any negative thoughts are surfacing. This is all part of the renewing of the mind (Romans 12:2). Corrective truths setting the record straight can be spoken with regard to the Receiver's personal situation, and proclaiming the truths of the faith from the Bible is also powerful and effective.

FANTASY WORLDS

Children who find their circumstances overwhelming, whether because they are abused or simply because they are unusually sensitive, may take refuge in an imaginary world. Here they can escape – it becomes a survival kit whereby everything is under their control. Some children do this in a mild way when their life is boring. Usually children give up this fantasy world as they get older, but some take their survival kit with them into adult life.

The Pray-er may receive a word of knowledge that the Receiver is living in a fantasy world. This may become clear in other ways. Sometimes the Receiver may seem like a child in their responses. In the process of ministering, the Receiver disassociates. (There can be other reasons for this. Possibly the Receiver is not ready to enter into this area of ministry.) Asking direct questions along the following lines can be helpful:

- Do you/did you daydream a lot?
- As a child did you have a fantasy world?
- Did you go into that fantasy world often?
- Have you ever actively given it up – renounced it?

It can be a struggle for someone to give up their refuge, the sense of something that felt empowering, a safe place.

But Jesus is our true hiding place – we can hide in Him instead of our fantasy world. Jesus is a strong tower for our protection.

> **The name of the Lord is a fortified tower; the righteous run to it and they are safe.**
>
> Proverbs 18:10

> **You are my hiding-place; you will protect me from**
> **trouble and surround me with songs of deliverance.**
>
> Psalm 32:7

Here is the way I would minister to people who retreat into fantasy:

1. Invite the Holy Spirit to come on the whole person – encourage the Receiver to welcome Him into their mind, imagination, and emotions.

2. Ask the Receiver to invite Him into their conscious and unconscious mind, and also their fantasy and imagination.

3. Ask the Receiver as an *adult* to surrender their fantasy world to Jesus.

4. In Jesus' name break the power of the fantasy world of imagination and daydreams. Ask Jesus to bring cleansing, truth, and clarity.

5. Ask the Receiver to invite Jesus to visit the *little girl/boy* who imagined they needed that world to survive.

6. Ask Jesus to bring His healing and comfort, and proceed at the leading of the Holy Spirit. The Receiver may start having memories. Ask Jesus to show the root one which may reveal the origin of the fantasy world.

7. When appropriate, affirm that Jesus is their hiding place, a strong tower they can run into.

8. Don't rush this time; keep asking the Holy Spirit what He wants you to do.

9. After this, break the power of the fantasy world in the child.

10. When appropriate ask the *little girl/boy* to surrender their fantasy world to Jesus.

11. Keep communication going to ascertain what is happening to the Receiver, being sensitive, not

interrupting if they are receiving healing.

12. Remain open to any prophetic words. Finish by blessing the Receiver in Jesus' name. Pray for the Receiver to be filled with the Holy Spirit.

FEARS

In my experience the following are root fears:

- fear of death
- fear of being alone
- fear of being powerless or out of control.

Although someone could have any number of fears, when they are all unpacked, it usually comes down to one of these three root fears.

This is a good thing to bear in mind when ministering. Sometimes because the Receiver has been fearful for many years they will have accumulated all three root fears. Fear increases in power like the ripples from a pebble thrown into a pool of water. The ripples get bigger and bigger. If fear is fully confronted and addressed, it will lose its crippling power; though if severe abuse and trauma has taken place, deliverance may also be needed. I have always chosen to minister inner healing unless a demon clearly manifests. Once the healing is effected there is no place left for demons (see also Chapter 15 on deliverance).

The Bible says that "perfect love casts out fear" (1 John 4:18 NRSV). God is perfect love. He doesn't just love; He actually *is* love. We cannot take perfect love into our hands and also hold on to fear. We have to let one of them go. The Receiver needs to let go of fear and grasp hold of love with both hands. God is love (1 John 4:8)!

This is how I minister to those struggling with fear:

1. Invite the Holy Spirit to come on the whole person, encouraging the Receiver to welcome Him into their mind, emotions, and memories.

2.   Depending on where the Holy Spirit is leading, you may choose to proceed in one of the following ways:

• Ask Jesus to show the Receiver the root cause of the fear – when it first started.

• Encourage the Receiver to invite Jesus into the memory and take the fear.

or

• Ask Jesus to stand bodily between the Receiver and their fear (name it). You could say out loud: "In Jesus' name I place His cross and everything He did on it between you and your fear of…"

and/or

• Speak out the following, with one hand on the person:

Fear of death: "Jesus, in Your word, it says, 'Oh death, where is your sting?' (1 Corinthians 15:55 NRSV). On the cross You said, 'It is finished' (John 19:30). In Jesus' name I break the power of the fear of death now. Receive the abundant life of Jesus. Have life in Jesus' name."

Fear of being alone: "Jesus, You promised that You would always be with us (Matthew 28:20). In Jesus' name I speak to this fear of… and command it to go. I break the power of this fear of being alone, in Jesus' name. May Jesus be always with you until the end of the age."

Fear of being powerless, not in control: "Just bring that desire to be in control to Jesus now and surrender it to Him. Let Him be in control. Everything was made by Him; in Him all things hold together. He has all power and authority. In Jesus' name, I rebuke the fear of not being in control/being out of control and command it to go."

I would vary the ministry above depending upon the circumstances.

Usually there is a memory/root of the fear when it first started. Try to get to this and take it out, as it stunts spiritual and emotional growth.

VOWS AND OATHS

Nuns take binding, lifelong vows of chastity, poverty, and obedience. Lawyers and doctors take oaths: solemn promises, sworn declarations binding by law. During times of trauma or extreme stress, both adults and children may make very strong vows.

> Again, you have heard that it was said to the people long ago, "Do not break your oath, but fulfil to the Lord the oaths you have made." But I tell you, do not swear an oath at all: either by heaven... or earth... All you need to say is simply "Yes," or "No"; anything beyond this comes from the evil one.

Matthew 5:33–37

People can often make vows rashly, declaring what they will always or never do. They do not realise that they may find themselves bound by this choice they have made in the heat of the moment. At a future date when they try to take a different course of action, they may be unable to break free from the power of words they spoke long ago.

The enemy loves this type of choice. An evil spirit can attach itself to such a vow, keeping the person from living any other way until they repent, renounce, and make a positive alternative choice in Jesus' name.

Children may make vows when they are suffering deep pain. Experiencing something they never want to feel again, they may vow, "I will never..." If the child is beaten, and is punished again for crying, they may vow, "I will never let anyone see me cry." Sometimes we hear adults saying, "I will never forgive them for..." This is often the case in family feuds. Family members become bound by their vows. The enemy can keep us chained in this way. It is only when the vow is undone and the seal broken by the power of the Spirit in the name of Jesus that the person can be free.

When someone is freed from a vow that has controlled their life, the transformation can be dramatic as they experience release in many unexpected areas of life.

In prayer ministry, be open to the Holy Spirit showing you when a vow is at the root of someone's inability to live in freedom.

Sometimes the power of a vow is revealed when someone tells you their romantic relationships never last because they always back off. An inability to show emotion or cry could also be an indication of vows that have been made. You may suspect an inner vow if the Receiver wants to do something in ministry but seems unable to do it. If the person struggles to renounce a vow then possibly an evil spirit has attached itself. In this instance, encourage the person to put their will behind their renunciation, and bind anything contrary to the Holy Spirit. As they renounce their vow, break its power in Jesus' name. If they are still unable to do it, ask the Lord what is preventing them and deal with it appropriately.

The Receiver should also ask the Lord to reveal any vow still binding them. Or the Holy Spirit may disclose it to you through a word of knowledge. Offer this sensitively. Ask the Lord to show when the vow was made by revealing some memory or incident.

Pain might be released at this point or later. Encourage the Receiver to work through the memory by inviting Jesus to heal them.

Once any vows are identified, the Receiver should repent, saying aloud to Jesus, "I am sorry for vowing..." and then out loud, "In Jesus' name I choose to break my vow to... I surrender it to You, Lord Jesus." Each vow needs to be dealt with separately. The Pray-er breaks the vow in Jesus' name, by naming it. The Pray-er may then announce the freedom and release of Jesus. If appropriate, bind anything contrary to the Holy Spirit.

Then ask the Receiver to choose the opposite of the vow just broken. For instance, they might say out loud, "In Jesus' name I choose to cry when I want to..." or "I choose to let people close when appropriate."

If you have not already done so, now ask the Lord to come

and bring healing to those memories that caused the Receiver to make the vow in the first place.

Pray for the Receiver to be filled with the Holy Spirit and the love of Jesus.

As always, be led by the Holy Spirit; consult Him at every stage and follow the leading He gives.

As this description of ministry releasing people from vows has been lengthy, here is a re-cap you may find helpful as a checklist:

1. Identify the vow/oath.
2. Admit it aloud.
3. Repent.
4. Receive forgiveness.
5. Tell the Receiver to renounce the vow.
6. Pray-er breaks the power of the vow (if appropriate, binding anything contrary to the Holy Spirit, telling it to let go).
7. Receiver next chooses the opposite of the vow.
8. At some point find the cause of the vow.
9. Allow any pain to surface, and invite Jesus into the past to bring healing.
10. Receiver to be filled with Holy Spirit and love of Jesus.

IMPORTANT ACTIONS

During prayer ministry, some courses of action will seem to crop up time after time. After a while as you pray in the Spirit, words of knowledge may just pop into your head and you will sense what to do. Always be open to how and when the Holy Spirit wants you to use them. Here are some courses of action that will become very familiar as you minister:

- confession... sins, unbelief
- repentance... turning away from habitual sin and established patterns

- receiving forgiveness... as an adult, as a child
- extending forgiveness... to those who have hurt them
- choosing... another way, the right way, to surrender
- declaring... the truth
- proclaiming... who God is, who they are in Him, renouncing evil, lies, destructive patterns
- receiving... forgiveness, healing, love, affirmation, truth
- allowing... pain to surface; to feel; change; Jesus access
- surrendering... body, spirit, soul, attitudes, patterns, irrational beliefs
- releasing... opinions of self-guilt, shame
- enabling... inner child to have a voice
- loving... the inner child, others, the Lord
- asking Jesus... to show the root cause, to bring healing and mercy
- listening to Jesus... His words of love; His words of release
- listening to the Holy Spirit... His leading, His comfort, teaching, counsel
- using gifts... asking for and stepping out using them
- binding... anything contrary to the Holy Spirit
- breaking... power of the enemy, soul-ties
- loosing... into Jesus' hands
- cleansing... eyes, ears, bodies, thoughts, soul
- asking Jesus... to show the root cause, to bring healing and mercy
- asking Jesus... to show a root memory and surface it.

It is always good to keep referring back to the New Testament to see how Jesus ministered. Look at the words He used when ministering healing, freedom, and release to people: "Be free", "Be clean", "Be free from your suffering", "Go and sin no more!" To evil spirits He said, "Come out!", "Stop it", "Be quiet."

We too can use these words. Jesus didn't pray long prayers publicly. Prayers in the healing ministry are best kept short. We are supposed to be letting the Holy Spirit do it. Our part is to be a channel of the Holy Spirit and not get in His way.

Chapter 9

STORIES OF INNER HEALING

The following stories focus attention on ministry in specific areas of the lives of different individuals. Sometimes healing takes several sessions, peeling off one layer, then a few weeks or months later another part is ready to be healed. Sometimes it seems as if knots are being untied until the weight to which they are attached tumbles free. At other times something is cut off at the root so all the knots no longer matter. As you can see I am a very visual person! This has been an advantage during prayer ministry. But my husband is not visual *at all* and this in no way stops him being used by the Lord for inner healing. Jesus knows how to lead and prompt each of us individually.

LABELLED WITH A LIE

In a seminar once, I mentioned that some people are called names that go on to become part of their identity. They are trapped in the false identity self-imposed with the name.

At the end of the seminar a young woman came up to me, her face blotchy from crying. Repeatedly, emphatically, she said to me, "I am NOT a disease!" She then explained that at school the other children came up to her and said, "You are a disease." They taunted her by wiping their hands with antibacterial tissues, as if to rid themselves of contamination. The young woman told me, "I have just been prayed for and said out loud, 'I am not a disease.' I feel completely released from this horrible identity."

AN EMOTIONALLY ABSENT PARENT

On a ministry trip overseas, visiting a church for the weekend, I joined someone from our team who was already praying.

Carolyn stood with her arms crossed tightly across her chest, at the same time clutching the hand of her husband who stood behind her.

First of all I asked her if she could let go of his hand, as it would be good to deny herself his comfort so as to be free to receive totally from the Lord. This she agreed to. Looking at her body language, my question to the Lord was, "Why is she protecting herself?"

After a little while of praying in the Spirit without knowing the way forward, I suddenly said to her, "Your heavenly Father will not break His promise to you." I sensed I had heard this from the Lord in my head – I knew I had to speak it out.

She burst into tears. I continued to pray for her to be restored. I thought that her earthly father may have abandoned her.

After a while, I asked her what was happening. She said that she had breast cancer and that God had promised she would have full healing but her cancer had returned three times. I asked her when she first got it and she said twelve years ago.

I asked Carolyn if her earthly father had left her, but she replied, "No." She said her father always hugged and kissed her and told her that he loved her. For some reason (it must have been the Holy Spirit), I didn't feel satisfied with this answer, so I asked for more details. Then Carolyn said, "I always wanted a daddy, but what I got was a father." I asked her what she meant. Carolyn told me that her father had gone away on business often. When he returned, he approached her but she never felt able to approach him. He always seemed busy with the TV, the phone, or the newspaper. She felt as if she was secondary to all these other preoccupations in her dad's life.

I noticed Carolyn had a frozen look about her – expressionless.

I asked her to see herself in a room as a child. She did so, saying that she was seven years old. She went to the door and invited Jesus to come in and meet with her, as I encouraged her to do.

It looked as if some healing was taking place. Then I asked Carolyn to also enter the room at the age she was now. I told her the little girl in the room needed her love. She started to cry. Later, she said she had always kept that little girl locked away – separate. We decided to meet up again after the evening service to continue prayer ministry.

That evening we met up and I invited Carolyn to see herself once more in a room as a child. This she did. Once more I asked her to invite Jesus to be there too, and then later to walk into the room as an adult. Continuing in the same vein I asked her to go closer to the little girl and say sorry to her for shutting her away and not letting her be seen and heard. Lots of emotion showed on her face. She told the little girl (her inner child) that she loved her. At this point I also asked her what the little girl wanted to say to Carolyn the adult. Carolyn entered into this and started to ask to be accepted and loved. I then asked Jesus to integrate the inner child with the adult. Carolyn nodded – this was what she wanted. Later on she described an amazing moment when this part of herself that had been separate suddenly became part of her. She said the feeling was almost indescribable and thought that if she tried to explain it to anyone else it would make her sound as if she were mentally ill!

I asked Carolyn if as a little girl she had ever made a vow about showing her emotions. She immediately agreed. She verbalised the vows she had made of not connecting to her emotions or displaying them. Out loud Carolyn renounced the vows. I broke them in the name of Jesus and then she chose out loud to connect and show her emotions. I pronounced the freedom of Jesus upon her. At that moment she started laughing. Her whole face lit up in a way I had not seen previously. Muscles started moving in her face that previously had seemed frozen.

I didn't think this was the end of the healing process for

Carolyn, but I was blessed in appreciating some big progress had been made in finding freedom from the pain she had been carrying all these years.

As we chatted, I found myself explaining to her that often when we pray for healing our expectation is for a miracle. A miracle is instantaneous; healing is a process, which is why it is called heal-ing. Hearing this Carolyn became excited, saying, "That explains a lot to me – that's why I have been so disappointed about my cancer. I *was* expecting a miracle." Then I explained about wholeness and that the ministry of the last two sessions formed an important step towards receiving wholeness – that Jesus came and brought not just healing of the body but also spiritual and emotional healing. I described the story of the paralysed man let down through the roof to be healed by Jesus (Mark 2:1–12).

First of all Jesus called him "son", bringing him affirmation of sonship and of belonging. Maybe he had never been affirmed by his earthly father. Then Jesus told him his sins were forgiven – this was healing to his spirit. After that Jesus healed his body, telling him to take up his mat and walk. Carolyn's eyes got bigger as she realised that Jesus wanted to do more than heal her body.

I would have loved to see what else Jesus was going to do in Carolyn's life, but we were leaving to go to another church. I left encouraging Carolyn to pursue wholeness daily and to continue to get to know her "inner child". I encouraged her to celebrate, play, and let the spontaneity of that child spill out into her life. She looked excited as she thought of that happening. Thank You, Jesus – You do all things well!

The following year we returned to the same church. We attended all four services. About eleven o'clock at night, after a long time of prayer ministry, we were just leaving the church when a woman walked past me and stopped. She called my name, and with great delight I realised it was Carolyn. She looked amazing! She looked so alive and healthy. She had put on weight (she had been painfully thin the previous year) and looked so joyful. I asked her what had been happening since I had seen her last. She said no trace of cancer had been found and she had steadily improved. The Lord had continued to bring inner healing to her since the time we prayed. She said that she felt like a different person.

As you can imagine this was a wonderful thing to hear. Isn't God good!

Sometimes, if we are ministering away from our own church, we never know what unfolds in the lives of people to whom we minister. We just leave it in the Lord's hands, because we cannot be responsible for others' healing. We are just told to minister healing. We have to leave the results to Him. The healing belongs to the Lord. Sometimes He lets us see what happens as a result of our prayer, but if we knew what happened each time I am sure it wouldn't be good for us. This way He gets the glory!

HEALING FROM FEAR AND COMPULSIVE DISORDER

My husband and I ministered to a young man with severe Obsessive Compulsive Disorder. I will call him Paul. As we chatted with Paul his body couldn't keep still; he was constantly on the move. This was part of his disorder.

I asked Paul when it had started. He said it had begun a couple of years previously during his exams. He then confessed to a sin, saying that if he told us what it was, we would never want to speak to him again. I held his hand and looked into his eyes and told him that during many years of ministry I had probably heard almost every type of scenario and it had never altered my opinion of anyone – we are all sinners.

He confessed his sin and we encouraged him to take it to Jesus at the cross, repent, and ask for forgiveness. He did. We pronounced forgiveness over him in Jesus' name and asked him to really receive it. He was to bring to Jesus at the cross any other guilt getting in the way of him receiving. He became really calm as he received forgiveness; before that his body couldn't keep still. After a while I asked him what else had happened to him before this incident – did anything really frighten him? He affirmed that on holiday a few years before, he had gone on a roller coaster that was supposed to be the most terrifying in the world. At one point he suddenly realised he could hardly breathe. Usually on those sorts of rides people scream or shout or explode with their feelings. He didn't – he imploded. His sister questioned him afterwards as to his silence. I asked him, "What did you think would happen?" He said, "I thought I was going to die." I asked him, "Did you think, 'I never want to ever be in that situation again'?" "Yes!" he said.

He had been traumatised by fear. Afterwards he had decided to ensure he was always in control, taking measures to protect himself by obsessive rituals. We asked Jesus to come and visit him on that roller coaster – to come and sit beside him and bring healing through His perfect love, instead of leaving him in that fear (perfect love casts out fear). Afterwards Paul said it was like being on the ride with someone better than your best mate. Jesus transformed the whole thing into fun. He told us the fear had gone. During the time Paul had been experiencing fun with Jesus I had been quietly praying against the fear of death!

But I had a knowing that there was still more. I asked him what else had happened. Paul said a burglar had come into his home one night while he was asleep. He was awoken by his dad telling him an intruder had been in the house, who had now left. "How did this make you feel?" I asked. Paul replied, "Invaded." I explained that a fear of not being in control had traumatised him, and the invasion had left him feeling powerless. I asked Paul to see himself in the bed, then going to the door to let Jesus into his bedroom. I encouraged Paul to ask Jesus to come with the light of His love – His power into Paul's powerlessness. He did this. While this was happening I prayed against the fear of not being in control, feeling powerless. We let him receive healing from Jesus while we continued silently interceding. After a while he opened his eyes and said he had never experienced such a stillness and peace. He felt ecstatic. We asked what he had experienced. He said Jesus sat on his bed and held him. He was amazed at how he felt. He then said he loved how he was feeling now, but wondered how it would be in the future as he still had more exams. I asked him to envisage himself in the examination hall – which he did. Then once more I said, "Jesus is standing at the door; go and let Him into the examination hall." This he did. We asked after a while what was happening. He said Jesus led him by the hand around the room, sat with him at the examiner's table and then sat with him at his own desk. At the end of the ministry time I suggested that when he thought about his exams, he needed to do this and let Jesus speak to him. Also every day he needed to give control over to Jesus. He looked a different guy at the end of the ministry time.

Paul said he had experienced peace in the past, but now he felt an utter stillness – it felt incredible. From this we see that Paul experienced all three root fears:

- on the roller coaster ride: fear of death
- in bed feeling invaded: fear of powerlessness, not being in control
- in the exam hall: fear of being alone.

Perfect love casts out fear – Paul now knew he was perfectly loved by Jesus.

We do not know what happened after this time, but we saw Paul transformed before our eyes. Hopefully he has gone from strength to strength. If ever he is afraid again, he knows what to do now.

TWO COURAGEOUS YOUNG MEN

At the end of a seminar on loss, a young man of about nineteen came up to me and said that his father was in prison and his mother was an alcoholic. His brother was on drugs. He said, "All my life I have been abused in as many ways as you could possibly think of. Last year I became a Christian and joined a church, but they let me down badly. I haven't been able to cry since I was a very young child. Today during the seminar my eyes felt wet, but I couldn't cry. Can you tell me, how can I start to get healed up from all that is inside me? There is so much pain, but I don't know where to start."

My heart went out to this brave young man who was willing to tackle all that needed to be done but was confused as to where to begin. I explained that usually God does it gradually, bit by bit, so that we can bear it. First of all I suggested that he might like to choose with his mind to undo the vow he may have made about crying, when he was a little boy. Next I suggested he ask the Holy Spirit to surface something He wanted to heal. When he knew what that "something" was, he needed to lift it to Jesus in prayer every day, and to keep seeking healing until it came. I encouraged him to be specific so that he would see specific answers. When the first thing he identified was healed up, he could move on to the next thing and the next thing, repeating the process until he had worked through all the areas that needed healing. I suggested it would take a while! I called over another guy to join me in ministering a quick prayer for the young man, as we had to clear the venue for the start of another seminar.

The next evening, in the big meeting gathered for worship and teaching, I suddenly heard a voice I recognised coming from the stage. Speaking into the microphone was the young man I had met the day before, saying, "I have lived a very abused life, but I could never cry about all the pain I had suffered. Tonight I cried like a baby and I feel such freedom. Not only that, but I stood up and made a decision that when the time comes I am going to be the best dad I can possibly be!" I ran towards the stage to meet this brave young man as he descended the stairs. I gave him a big hug with tears streaming down my face. Afterwards I was draped over a barrier as I felt overcome with emotion, sobbing at the immensity of the words he had just said. He had come from such an abusive family. It is very common for people growing up with continued abuse to either go on to abuse others or turn the abuse inwards on themselves. I felt uplifted and encouraged to believe this abuse had been halted from travelling through generations. Almighty God had stopped it, by enabling this young man to cry and then make a positive declaration of freedom.

As I was still weeping I felt a hand on my shoulder. I looked up and saw another young man, wearing a chequered hat with earflaps. He introduced himself as Rob. I explained why I was crying – rejoicing in the goodness of the Lord at bringing healing. On hearing this, Rob explained that his own father had left his mother when Rob was still a young boy. Rob had chosen never to see his dad again, because he felt so angry at being rejected. "This evening," Rob said, "I left the meeting and contacted my dad on Facebook. I told him I have forgiven him and want to meet up." At this news I burst out with a fresh lot of sobbing. What an amazing God.

When I eventually regained control of my emotions I reflected on the kindness of Jesus. Usually when at a festival with thousands of people I hear their stories and see people's pain being released, but I don't often hear what happened. During the next hour as Jesus continued His healing, I moved from person to person laying on hands, seeing God's power being released. I saw person after person with a tear-streaked face, released from suppressed anger or inner pain, then receiving healing and peace but never knowing how their story would end. So it was extra special and very humbling to have a glimpse of the wonderful ways our God brings about His inner healing, long after we have stopped doing the bit He has asked us to do.

> Praise God from whom all blessings flow
> Praise Him you creatures here below
> Praise Him above ye heavenly host
> Praise Father, Son, and Holy Ghost!
>
> Part of a hymn written by Bishop Ken Thomas
> in 1674 while walking in the gardens of the Bishop's Palace in Wells

DAISY MADE A VOW

Daisy went down on the floor under the power of the Holy Spirit. She did a little crying, but somehow it didn't sound as if she was releasing her emotions. I asked her what she was feeling. She said, "What I always feel – dead inside." When I asked her what made her feel like that, she replied, "It's complicated." I asked if she had ever decided not to feel because it was too painful, and she said, "Yes." I asked her to break the vow she had made. She said she had vowed to never feel any emotions. I explained that this could be reversed. She could choose to feel again.

You will see from what happened next that sometimes the Lord can heal people very simply; not everyone has to go through a process of reliving, remembering, or bringing pain to the surface.

Daisy said, "I choose to feel. Amen." I interrupted, "No, first of all you need to break that vow before you choose to feel."

Again she said, "In Jesus' name, I choose to feel." Once more I interrupted: "No, I am sorry but first of all you need to break the vow."

This happened three times, but at last she did it!

I then broke the power of that vow in Jesus' name and spoke out the freedom of Jesus.

Suddenly Daisy was gasping repeatedly, as if gulping in air.

I prayed, "Fill her with life, hope, and laughter, Lord!" And He did! Wonderful!

She received life into all that deadness inside her. She laughed and cried at the same time. It was amazing to watch. She came alive before our very eyes.

BOUND BY AN OATH

After I had spoken on "loss" at a seminar, I prayed for a woman in her early forties. I will call her Kate. She explained that since giving birth to her daughter, she had suffered in so many ways: physically, emotionally, and mentally.

I asked Jesus to show her if there was any reason why she had suffered in this way, and if there was a link.

During the time of prayer she realised that after she had had two boys, she tried to bargain with God by saying, "If you let me have a little girl next time I will suffer anything."

This rang alarm bells in me. It seemed as if she had taken an oath and was now living in the consequences. By doing this she was suffering the consequences of her actions; she had opened a door through which the enemy could attack her.

She chose to say sorry to Jesus and receive His forgiveness. Then aloud she renounced the oath that she had made. In Jesus' name I broke the power of those words, and she was free. Then Kate chose the opposite of her original vow. Out loud, Kate chose to declare, "In Jesus' name I choose to now receive every blessing in my body and in my life that you want to give me, Lord." After a little while she went through some more healing and then she cried out, "Oh, I have let go of the control! I have always controlled everything about myself and suddenly my shoulders have dropped to the right place after forty years of holding them up!"

RELEASING FORGIVENESS

A woman came for prayer knowing she wanted to forgive someone. She didn't want to say what her story was. I asked Jesus to come into her pain and bring it to the surface.

She cried a lot. I asked her if she still felt bad feelings towards the person and she said, "Yes."

I asked her to tell Jesus what those feelings were, and encouraged her to come to Him at the cross. She needed to ask forgiveness from Jesus for her bad feelings. She did this, and I pronounced forgiveness over her in Jesus' name. After a little while I asked her if she had received it – she said she had. I then asked her to take the unforgiven person to Jesus at the cross and extend what she had just received to that person. I indicated that she needed to say the person's name out loud and say, "I forgive you for..." I told her to list all the things that had been done to her, and spell out how they made her feel.

She cried deeply, and then as she quietened down I asked her to say "Amen" when she had finished, so that I would know. She did, and I continued ministering the love of Jesus to her. Afterwards she told me that the person she forgave had nearly raped her and had locked her in a room for some time. She thought she was going to die. This had happened many years ago, but had severely affected her everyday life. I saw her the next day, when she said she felt so different. The fear had all gone.

A VOW AND WORRIES

A young woman I will call Molly came for prayer ministry, saying that every time the Holy Spirit came upon her she felt dizzy in her head. I asked if it was like a not well sort of dizzy, like fainting, or a more relaxed dizzy like falling in Jesus' arms. She said she wasn't sure.

I used one of the "rooms" exercises (see Chapter 11), suggesting she envisage herself at home. She invited Jesus into the room and I encouraged her to speak to Him. Molly said as soon as she began to speak to Jesus, all sorts of people and their worries started to fill her mind. She said she desperately wanted to laugh with Jesus, but she couldn't. I sensed she had a "vow" issue. I asked Molly, "Did you ever decide after something happened in your life that you would never laugh again?" She looked startled and said, "Yes!" Tears started to flow down her face. She broke that vow. I then out loud broke the vow of those words, "I will never laugh again." I asked her to let any other vows surface. Then she had to choose the opposite of those vows. Out loud Molly chose to laugh, to have freedom, to have fun, and to be spontaneous. I broke the power of all these negative things in her life, releasing her in Jesus' name. Molly then named to Jesus all those she worried about, bringing them to Him at the cross one by one, and surrendering them. Her dizziness completely went, and she seemed transformed as she was filled with the Holy Spirit. All this took about twenty minutes. Thank You, Jesus.

FREE TO BE SUCCESSFUL

Bill asked my husband Ken and me to pray with him at a conference. He told us he was very fearful and this was holding him back in his job working for the church; he also said he felt a lack of self-worth. Bill explained that when he woke in the mornings, a dread came over him and he didn't want to face the day or do anything.

We laid hands on Bill and he asked the Holy Spirit to come into his memories. We asked Him to show Bill what He wanted to heal today.

I immediately had the thought that boys at school had called him "gay boy", but didn't sense that I should share this at that time. (This is a common occurrence and for some can cause a painful doubting at a very young age.)

Bill suddenly said, "I have a memory, but it is not really a painful memory for me so I am wondering why I thought of it." I explained to Bill that as an adult he probably wasn't aware of what that memory had done to him as a child, but obviously God knew. I asked about the memory, and he explained that he was young and playing football for the school team, but a group of girls sitting on a wall were mocking him, calling out cruel names and laughing at him.

I asked Jesus to come into that time in Bill's memory, where the girls were mocking. Then I asked Bill to look for Jesus in that place. After that I asked Jesus to put the cross between Bill and those mocking girls.

Bill started to sob. Afterwards he said he couldn't see the girls any more, as the cross was blocking the view. Suddenly Bill had another memory. This time he was in the changing rooms with boys after the football match. In this memory he was a teenager. Bill said he was very successful at playing football and the boys in the changing rooms didn't like it! I asked if they were jealous. He said, "Yes." Bill cried again. I realised that as Bill was in a changing room, he would be unclothed – more vulnerable, no covering. The words of these boys – their lies –

had gone deep into Bill; into his soul. The Holy Spirit showed me that Bill had a fear of being successful, as if he succeeded painful consequences would follow: he would be rejected and punished, becoming the object of abusive words. I realised he had been crushed and rejected. He had discarded that part of himself. He wasn't free to succeed. People often feel afraid to fail but he had the opposite problem!

I asked Bill to see himself in that changing room again. This time he said he was no longer a teenager but a child of six. This surprised me, but then I realised this was not the first time such things had happened. Bill must have decided it was a problem for him to be successful from the age of six. Continuing with the prayer ministry I asked Bill the six-year-old child to go to the door of the changing room, open it, and let Jesus in. I asked Jesus to affirm Bill and set him free to be successful. I placed the cross of Jesus between Bill and the fear of speaking of his success. He cried deep sobs. I realised the fear had gone very deep. It all started with that little six-year-old child. Later on, he told us that as a young boy he had come home with his success stories but he couldn't tell his dad because his sister wasn't as clever as her other siblings. Bill felt he always had to play everything down and deny his success so his sister could shine!

As that little six-year-old boy he opened the door to Jesus.

I asked Jesus to do whatever he wanted to free that little boy and his wounds from lies. Suddenly Bill called out, "They used to call me a gay boy!" I remembered that the Holy Spirit had shown me that at the beginning of the prayer time. Bill sobbed again. I placed my hands over his ears and broke the power of the lies that had gone down into his soul. I asked Bill the adult to come and meet that little boy – to walk in the room where he was.

He did, and spoke words of comfort and affirmation to that little boy. Then I asked him to go to that same room as a teenager to meet himself as a little boy. He did. He cried again as he was reconciled with those parts of himself that had not been integrated.

Then I said to him, "Your problem was not a fear of failure but a fear of success, because you feared the consequences and the actions of others. You fear standing out above others." Bill renounced this fear in Jesus' name.

He then chose to be successful – to be who God made him to be. I broke the power of his vow of failure and his fear of success in the name of Jesus.

Immediately Bill started to cough loudly, retching as the Lord delivered him.

Sometimes in ministry words seem to bypass the brain as the Holy Spirit simply uses us as a channel. It's a bit like the times when prophecy is released from the mouth when only the first two words have come into the mind. I spoke release in Jesus' name; and then simply acting in the power of the Spirit with no premeditation at all, I put the cross of Jesus between Bill and his father. I broke depression in Jesus' name in him and in the family line.

Bill coughed again, and he was freed. We prayed the infilling of the Holy Spirit and anointing. After the ministry Bill was exhausted but felt free.

Sometimes when a person receives healing from something like this, for a while the old habit may persist until the realisation sinks in that they really are free.

So I explained to Bill that Jesus had freed and healed him, but the enemy would continue to whisper negative things to him. Each time this happened, Bill would need to say, "No."

It's rather like having a door that sticks and can only open half way. We trim the bottom of the door so it can open fully, but for a while through force of habit we continue only opening the door half way and not fully. Then we get used to the new freedom and open it fully every time.

At the start of the ministry time with Bill I did not have a clue what was wrong or what needed healing. Prayer ministry often takes us on this kind of journey. As you get used to trusting the Holy Spirit to lead you, instead of feeling nervous you discover a sense of excitement as you watch how the Lord guides you through.

ALWAYS TRYING TO PLEASE

A man came forward for prayer – I will call him Nick. He said that he had been conceived on his parents' honeymoon, and they often thoughtlessly referred to this as having been a great mistake. Nick explained that he had come to think of himself as a mistake, and was always trying to make up for the fact that he was an unplanned child. He felt loved by his parents, but could never shake this off. He also felt very angry with God since he had prayed for healing for a friend, but the sick man had died.

I asked Nick to see himself as a child – any age – in a room. Then I asked him to invite Jesus into the room ("I stand at the door and knock", Revelation 3:20).

I asked Nick what he had seen. He said it was great – he was having a really good time, with Jesus carrying him about on his shoulders and playing games with him.

Then I asked Nick to go into the room as an adult to meet this little boy that was his inner child. He did that, and said he didn't feel anything. I asked Nick if it was a numbness or a distance. He said he felt distant. I asked him if he could choose to get closer to this little boy.

He said he could, and started to walk closer. Nick looked very emotional and told me afterwards that he went up to the little boy and held him close for a long time. He said afterwards that it felt better inside his chest whereas before it had felt really tight inside.

This simple healing brought release to a man who had come from an essentially loving family. The unintentional effect of his parents' thoughtless words remind us to bear in mind what power there is in the things we say – to bind or to bless, to hurt or to heal. It did not take much to set right this one small thing that had blighted his life – all Nick needed to do was invite the Lord Jesus in. The very simplicity of it makes it easy to remember and learn from: to be careful what we say to others, and to invite Jesus in to heal every hurt inside ourselves.

Chapter 10

MINISTERING TO THE INNER CHILD

Jesus said, "Let the little children come to me and do not hinder them, for the kingdom of heaven belongs to such as these."

Matthew 19:14

We are meant to be child-like, though not childish, as children of the living God. God demonstrated His love by coming to earth as a vulnerable, holy child to lead and reconcile us to our heavenly Father.

Children growing up affirmed, knowing they are loved by their parents, mature into confident adults able to be spontaneous and face challenges. For many of us that hasn't happened, and the inner child becomes restrained, frightened, or feels unloved.

WHAT IS THE INNER CHILD?

This is the aspect of the self linking back to the early formative years – the internal record of all the emotional experiences, memories, feelings, and unhealed attitudes stored up in the soul during childhood.

Unhealed negative experiences in childhood can result in an adult living out of the hurt inner child. Instead of becoming the spontaneous, loving, creative, free, and responsive person God intended, they can be stuck in childishness. This can show itself in the following ways:

- running away from problems and situations
- thinking that everything revolves around them
- stamping their feet when annoyed
- resisting change of any sort
- crying as a means of getting their own way
- speaking in a timid, childish voice
- always blaming others for their problems.

Just as Jesus spoke to parents encouraging them to bring their little children for Him to bless, so He wants us to bring our "little child" – our inner child – to Him, to get healed up and set free.

Some people whose inner child is very hurt may experience the inner conflict and suffering of their adult self judging their child self, a form of self-hatred expressed by wanting to punish or reject themselves. This can usually be traced back to something frightening, humiliating, sad, or painful happening in childhood, remaining unresolved and in need of attention. As part of the healing process, the adult self will need to speak to the inner child and release them from this blame and punishment. Often the healing process is very moving to witness, as the adult self embraces the childhood self, giving permission for the inner child to grow and be made whole.

I have ministered in this area on many occasions, and seen Jesus bringing reconciliation between the adult self and the inner child. It can have a huge effect on someone's life.

HEALING STORY: INNER CHILD

My husband and I met a man called Adrian at a conference, when he came to us for ministry. He said we had prayed for him on a previous occasion a couple of years before, when he was grieving. After that ministry he had been released from his pain of loss.

Since then, over the course of about a year, Adrian had been suffering severe anxiety manifesting as fearfulness about his health. He had physical symptoms with no known medical basis that had affected his career and options at work. When I asked about his family, he told me that his mother and grandmother had been anxious too. I explained that our parents' attitudes very easily communicate to us through their words and behaviour, and become our own character traits in turn. This is all the more likely when reinforced by parents saying to their child, "You are so like me..." Adrian went on to tell us he had been a very anxious child, and that when he was born he had required care in an incubator for two weeks.

We invited the Holy Spirit to come upon Adrian, and as we waited I asked him to visualise himself coming towards Jesus (if Adrian had not been a visual person I would have asked him to just think about doing this). Adrian looked peaceful. When I asked him what was happening, he said he could sense Jesus with him.

Prompted by the Holy Spirit, I said to Adrian, "This may sound strange, but why don't you take the hand of yourself as a child, and in the other arm carry that little newborn 'incubator' baby, and so bring both these parts of yourself with you to Jesus?"

As Adrian did this I could see deep emotion welling up inside him. His chest heaved and tears streamed down his face. I sensed he was still unprepared to hand himself, as a baby or as a child, over to Jesus.

So in Jesus' name I cut him off from everything to do with anxiety and fear passed down to him in his family line from his mother and grandmother.

I put my hands over his ears and came against any negative words, and set him free in Jesus' name. At this point Adrian began to manifest release by making big movements of his body. I asked Jesus to release him from his thought-life prison.

Next I asked Adrian to see himself as that little baby in the incubator. Immediately his face crumpled and he looked full of anguish. He started crying like a little baby. I knew that control and fear of letting go were major issues for him.

I asked Adrian as an adult to go back to the baby in the hospital incubator. He suddenly changed, and instead of crying like a tiny baby his chest started heaving with strong emotions. Afterwards he said he couldn't bear seeing himself as a baby all alone. He knew the baby needed his mummy. He said he picked the baby up, and it felt so good because the baby was frightened. I asked him if he could invite Jesus to come into the ward with him. He nodded. He looked really content.

I came against the fear of death in Jesus' name, and told it to lift off. I asked Jesus to bring him into abundant life. My husband and I spoke blessing and truth over him.

Afterwards Adrian said he felt completely different. He said it was a wonderful experience being together with himself as a baby with Jesus in the hospital. He told us he had always been very afraid of hospitals, and now understood why that was.

In total this life-changing prayer ministry took about fifteen minutes in the coffee break!

ATTACHMENT

Babies receive a lot of reassurance, security, and comfort in their early months of life, through attachment to their mothers. If for some reason a baby is separated by distance, perhaps for a hospital stay or because the mother is an alcoholic or mentally ill and may need inpatient care herself, the baby may suffer trauma. Mothers who have never received love themselves, or were numbed by trauma as a child, may be too emotionally distant and detached to give love easily or effectively as adults.

I discovered that a friend of mine had suffered deeply from lack of attachment. She explained it to me.

Evie had grown up in a very dysfunctional family where she had not experienced love; but at the age of five she knew Jesus, and He would speak to her. This was a lifeline to Evie because attachment was a huge issue for her. As an adult, she used to observe a particular close, loving family in her church. She couldn't stand watching their affection and demonstrations of love for each other. It made her really angry, reminding her of the reality that she had never known anything like this. But this family consistently loved Evie, including her and making her feel welcome and wanted. Evie learned to love as she had the chance to see and be included in their love for each other.

The Circle of Security parenting course, an international relationship-based early intervention programme designed to enhance attachment security between parents and children, considers how parent/child relationships can be strengthened. It offers a unique approach to teaching parents and carers ways to understand and respond to children's needs and behaviour. Parents who may never have attached to their own parents when children form a circle of commitment to each other at the beginning of the course. A series of exercises helps them to explore their children's inability to attach, and discover how this has affected the children. Further exercises enable those on the course to discover and understand the process of attachment for themselves. If the parents in a "Circle" have to go away for some reason, others in the Circle are there for their children, as adults in an extended family would be. In modern life, attachment within families is a growing issue. The Circle of Security parenting course gives those who struggle with attachment the tools they need to develop and express their capacity for love.

The Bible tells us that love is the greatest thing. Jesus calls us to work with Him in extending His love to people through His body, the church. He asks us to commit to loving individuals who have suffered severe abuse, incest, and severe rejection, resulting in attachment issues – to be committed and love the person whatever their response. They may struggle to either give or receive love. If we are willing to work with Jesus in bringing love to life, we can see some amazing results. Jesus can heal the numb and frozen world of the lonely, the neglected, and the abused.

ABANDONED CHILD HEALED BY LOVE

During a time of powerful prayer ministry in South Africa, I prayed for Ella, whom I judged to be about ten years old, though

I later discovered she was thirteen. She had covered her shoes and socks with words of self-hatred written in ink, and inscribed destructive words onto her hands and arms. Her face contorted often into an ugly grimace. As I ministered to her, she started to manifest; she was clearly demonised. Her face contorted with hatred as she growled in a deep voice and her limbs started to thrash about violently. I felt a caution in my spirit not to cast these demons out. I bound anything contrary to the Holy Spirit and asked her if she would like to go to the prayer room later in the day, where I thought we could offer her more privacy, as the manifestations were attracting a lot of attention. In the meantime I discovered that Ella lived in an orphanage. She had been abandoned by her mother and wider family after she had told her mother that her father had repeatedly abused her sexually. This we discovered was a common occurrence in her cultural environment, where a belief prevails that a man can rid himself of AIDS by having sex with a virgin. Sometimes fathers rape their own children in the hope of curing the disease.

I was very disturbed to discover from others in our team that local women had already tried many times to cast demons out of Ella, without success. I was introduced to a young married couple from a nearby church who visited the orphanage regularly to befriend and pray for the children. They told me Ella would often manifest demons at the orphanage, and all the other children were frightened of her. They told me that Ella seemed to enjoy having this power over people, and I realised that the demons made her feel powerful. Later that day, two of us met up with Ella. We ministered in the area of inner healing. She cried a lot and released pain, and Jesus came and met with her. During the evening, a group of children from her orphanage were filled with the Holy Spirit, and spoke in tongues for the first time. Ella was among this group. Speaking in a beautiful love language to Jesus delighted her. She especially loved the sense of being included, as the other children gathered around her instead of rejecting her. The married couple we met earlier said that they wanted to take their young daughter to the orphanage, and start taking

Ella out for treats to give her a taste of what family life could be. They loved Ella and wanted to show her the love of Jesus. I believed that this was God's merciful love for Ella – such a broken, damaged little girl.

The following year we returned to South Africa. During a time of worship I was filming all the young people worshipping to show our church back home. A lot of them were sitting on the floor. Suddenly through the lens I saw a remarkable sight. Ella was standing up worshipping with all her heart and soul, her arms lifted high. She looked beautiful. She now looked her age – fourteen. I met with the young couple who had committed to loving her through the past year. They said they had frequently ministered the love of Jesus to Ella in prayer and regularly took her out with their daughter. It was such a wonderful healing that even now I feel deeply moved by what Jesus did in loving Ella through people who loved Him enough to love a little child back to life.

To receive healing, a person with attachment issues needs to be in a close, loving community. I have seen such healing take place in a close community church with enough members on hand that the person never felt abandoned. These abandonment issues go back really deep, to being a tiny baby. Some may suffer rejection from their very earliest days, while still in the womb.

A BABY AND A BLANKET

In the course of the more than three decades I have been a Christian, I have received very deep healing of emotions and memories. It came as a surprise to me even after all that time to receive further deep healing relating to affirmation in my babyhood.

My mother's history of mental illness began when she was a teenager. Not only did this create long-standing struggle and suffering in her life, it also had a huge effect on me as her child – more than I realised until my experiences on a Deep Release Ministries training day. During these days, instead of just hearing how to help others, we are often directed to look at our own inner child and need of wholeness.

On this particular occasion, we went through an exercise using a folded up small blanket. What I am about to tell you may sound bizarre – believe me, when I saw the exercise demonstrated before embarking on it myself, I too thought it strange! Even so, I felt intrigued and very moved by what I saw unfolding before me. I have since undertaken this exercise with both individual men and women and with groups. I have seen some remarkable healing take place.

To begin with, we were all partnered off with another person. Then the teacher and a woman from the group sat cross-legged on the floor, looking into each other's eyes. The teacher held a small folded blanket out to the woman, saying, "This is the part of you that no one ever sees. It is a hidden part." When the teacher handed over the blanket, the woman grabbed hold of it and threw it across the room. After a while she collected it and started to examine what she had been given. A lot of personal experiences unfolded from that time, the teacher all the while encouraging her to inspect and discover areas of the folds of the blanket, asking her to articulate her feelings. Eventually the teacher asked if she could touch the blanket, and the woman placed part of the blanket on the teacher's lap, in a gesture of acceptance and trust.

Soon it was my turn to go through the exercise with my partner, who happened to be a rape crisis counsellor. I had never met this woman before, and received only the briefest introduction before we began the exercise.

As she handed me the small blanket, I quickly hid it inside my cardigan. I started to stroke where it was hidden. My partner asked, "What is happening?" Tears started to flow down my face and I said, "It's a baby... it's me as a baby." I felt as if I was nurturing myself as a tiny baby, protecting myself. At the same time, part of my mind was screaming, "What? You must be out of your mind! What are you doing?" I ignored it (it was probably the enemy). My partner asked, "May I see?" I carefully brought the blanket baby out from under my cardigan, holding it tenderly. She asked what I wanted her to do. I offered her the blanket baby, saying, "Hold her; hold her close." She took the blanket baby tenderly in her arms just like a real live baby. My sobs were by now increasing to the point where it hurt really badly in my stomach. My partner then said, "Is there anything else you want me to do?" Sobbing louder from deep within, I gasped, "Look her in the eyes, look her in the eyes! She has never had someone to look her in the eyes." This she did. It felt so good watching her. It brought such deep healing to me. I never realised before this time that my mum had not looked me in the eyes as a baby; but my inner child knew. A baby needs their mum to look them in the eyes when they are feeding and when they talk to them. It feeds something inside a baby, a sense of belonging and of being affirmed. It was an incredible healing for me that day.

Afterwards I wondered what difference it would make in my life. What would be the fruit and growth of wholeness from that time?

Two weeks later I preached the sermon at our morning church service. Afterwards, I would usually think of all the things I should have said, or would go over and over making sure I had done it right, or judging myself as to whether it was good enough. I was almost home when I realised I hadn't done that! Suddenly I realised that the healing I had received was affirmation. I no longer needed to be affirmed by any other person than Father God. Although I had received affirmation from Him in the past, the experience of the folded blanket exercise had found my area of need for attachment and belonging as a tiny baby, and restored to me the affirmation I needed.

God knows our needs, and will work gently with us, healing deeper and deeper through all the layers of past experience, restoring us.

Isn't God amazing that He can bring healing through using a folded blanket?

PRE-BIRTH HEALING

It is a wonderful thing that not only can Jesus reach us as a child to bring healing, but He can also visit us as a tiny baby, even in the womb before our birth! After all, the Bible says God saw our unformed body when we were hidden in the secret place (Psalm 139:15).

Jesus brings His light and healing touch to the baby in the womb. Sometimes the Receiver may want to lie on the floor and assume a foetal position. I follow the leading of the Holy Spirit in determining how to proceed. The Receiver may experience fear, or have trouble breathing as they are experiencing distress prior to birth. The person may even re-enact the birth experience under the power of the Holy Spirit.

Being born is often referred to as our most dangerous journey. Some did not want to be born; others felt frightened before or during birth. It is remarkable to watch Jesus bring healing into these primal stages of life. The sensitivity of the neo-natal infant is not imagined. Research programmes offer evidence of suffering in the child if the mother is abused, as chemicals released by the mother find their way along the umbilical cord. To find out more about this subject read the fascinating book *The Secret Life of the Unborn Child*, by Thomas R. Verny.

Though we are not obsessively searching for a damaged inner child in every individual who presents for healing, in ministry we come across much to confirm that life in the womb and the journey of birth affect our personalities and attitude to life, right the way through into adulthood. The Holy Spirit reveals the need for ministry to the child in the womb, through a word of knowledge. Perhaps the Receiver may mention that they often feel something tight around the neck, or have a distressing feeling of being squeezed and unable to get out. At other times the Receiver may assume the foetal position during prayer ministry, making sounds like a tiny baby. Healing of the baby in the womb can have a profound effect on the Receiver's life.

VOICE OF THE PARENT AND INNER CHILD

There can be other factors at work affecting the Receiver that cause them difficulties in making choices or decisions to change. Some people have the inner voice of their parent still echoing with the "should do, ought to". Or they may have the childish voice of the inner child that is self-centred. Their inner adult voice needs to come to an informed decision.

- *The parent's voice* is picked up as we grow up. It is full of the "must and the must nots", the "shoulds and the oughts" from our parents or carers.
- *The child's voice* is usually self-centred and expresses its needs.
- *The adult's voice* listens to the other two voices and makes an informed choice.

> **When I was a child, I talked like a child, I thought like a child, I reasoned like a child. When I became a man, I put the ways of childhood behind me.**
>
> 1 Corinthians 13:11

To understand this there are two very good books on the subject: *Yesterday's Child*, by Mary Pytches, and *Making Peace with Your Inner Child*, by Rita Bennet. If out of print both are available online.

The "twelve steps recovery programme" indicates that the healing of the inner child is one of the essential areas in the stages of recovery from addiction, abuse, and trauma, including post-traumatic stress disorder.

There are some really helpful booklets available from Deep Release Ministries on the subject of the inner child. They also run training days and church training days on a variety of subjects. See www.deeprelease.org.uk for more information.

DISASSOCIATION DURING PRAYER MINISTRY

Sometimes people are so traumatised by thoughtless or abusive treatment in childhood, often suffered over an extensive period, that when we invite the Holy Spirit to come upon them, they choose to retreat into an unreachable state. They become disconnected, or disassociated, from their memories. If the person's mind goes blank, and memories of childhood are unavailable, this may be the brain's way of protecting the individual from facing trauma they are not ready or emotionally able to recall. To force this in any way could be dangerous for the Receiver.

On one occasion, a young woman receiving ministry began to jerk her head around as if she were seeing something terrifying above her head. Her eyes appeared glassy and I could no longer connect with her. She looked like a rabbit caught in headlights. The Holy Spirit prompted me that I must be very cautious. The ministry must stop to make it possible for her to return to reality. I started to chat about everyday things, to reassure her and divert her from whatever had so transfixed her attention. I got some water and dabbed some on the back of her neck, to bring her back to normality in a gentle way. After a while she regained full use of her faculties. I spoke to someone from the group she was with, stressing that prayer ministry was not in the young woman's best interest for now. She needed a different way – inclusion in a loving community where she felt safe enough to build up confidence and security, so that whatever was troubling her could safely surface without doing any further damage. Unfortunately, I couldn't let everyone know at the conference that this young woman was not to be ministered to – it was in the early days of prayer ministry and everyone was keen to get involved!

Several times I returned to find this young woman in the same predicament and had to bring her back to reality with reassurances that she was safe. I sensed her to be re-enacting something from very early childhood. The whole thing felt very unsatisfactory as she appeared to make no progress at all. However, her church group seemed very caring and loving, and I felt sure they could be trusted to nurture and protect her until she grew in confidence as time went on.

The following year I met up with her again. I couldn't believe the transformation. The group had shown her a lot of love during the year, until she felt safe enough to reveal what had happened to her. She told me her heart-breaking story. She was a victim of incest, sexually abused by her father for most of her childhood. During the year since I had last seen her she had plucked up courage to go to the police and tell them her story; her father was now awaiting trial, and she had agreed to testify. During the next few days Jesus met with her many times, gently bringing healing into her horrific memories. The following year I met her again, and this time I saw even more transformation in her life.

Sometimes I have ministered to people experiencing similar reactions, and had to ask them to use their will to choose to come back. I help them to ease back into present reality by friendly questions about their day, what they have been doing, what they will be having for lunch, and where they are staying. On other occasions I have told the person directly that it is safe to come back. I repeat this until, by the second or third time of reassurance, they begin to respond. Ministry in the power of the Holy Spirit is wonderful and brings great healing, but timing is important too. People who have experienced profound trauma should not be rushed. They may not be ready to look at their pain.

> There is a time for everything, and a season for every activity under the heavens...
>
> Ecclesiastes 3:1

Usually when someone is resting under the power of the Holy Spirit, you can speak to them and they will try to respond even if it is difficult. When the Receiver is disassociating, they will feel unable to come back to reality because it is too painful. They want to switch off. They may appear trance-like, or experience lack of control over their body or some part of it. We obviously need to discern whether it is the Holy Spirit, man's spirit, or an evil spirit at work. Sometimes people have an evil spirit that is troubling them, but even so I believe this is not the time and place to cast it out of them. If the spirit is cast out and they are not healed up, more spirits may return with the original spirit, leaving the person in a worse state than when we first prayed for them (see Luke 11:25–26). In this instance I would bind anything contrary to the Holy Spirit but not cast it out.

We also need to bear in mind that when people have experienced terrible powerlessness in the past, they seek the comfort of feeling powerful, and evil spirits can give a sense of power. Sometimes the demon may become the victim's identity, and the Receiver may feel threatened at the prospect of giving this up. We need to be sensitive in ministry, finding out what to do and when. Above all we have to keep in tune with the Holy Spirit, taking our direction from Him.

Sometimes when I am unsure how to proceed, an idea pops into my head as I pray. Only when I follow it through, and it turns out to be just the right thing, does it dawn on me that this was the prompting of the Holy Spirit!

If someone is disassociating in a time of prayer ministry or pastoral prayer ministry, I suggest they seek professional therapy. They can always come back for prayer ministry at a later date.

NOT READY TO LET IT GO

At a church where I had been invited to speak, a woman came forward for ministry in answer to a word of knowledge I had given out, for someone who felt very lonely, which manifested itself as a physical pain.

This woman suffered from agoraphobia (a disabling fear and anxiety of large open spaces or crowds of people) and bouts of depression. She talked incessantly. Two of us prayed for her, asking Jesus to meet her in her loneliness. After a minute or two it looked as if inner pain was surfacing, as her breathing became laboured. She looked as if she might cry. Suddenly she swallowed it all down, opened her eyes and started into a whole stream of stories about other people's problems. I cut through, saying,

"Shall we let Jesus come and release you from your loneliness?" She agreed, but the same thing happened – she swallowed it all down, opened her eyes, and launched into stories of others' problems. Not to be put off, I tried again, reassuring her that she had no need to be afraid of Jesus.

After the third attempt failed, I put a hand on each of her shoulders, saying, "Every time your pain starts to rise up, you immediately shut it down. Are you afraid of what it might feel like?" "Yes," she replied. "It's like the size of a volcano and I am afraid of it erupting, it's so big." I sensed this to be neither the time nor the place for further ministry. She wasn't ready to let it erupt. I gave her a copy of my book, encouraging her to work through the exercises. Discovering that this woman had not been a Christian very long, I encouraged someone in the church to call in and help her do the exercises, so she would feel less alone. I could easily have felt disappointed that we saw no resolution, but I took comfort from the fact that this woman had made some positive steps:

- She had responded to a word of knowledge, walking out to the front of the church with everyone watching.
- She had admitted she needed Jesus to help her.
- She had acknowledged the size of her inner pain, and her inability at that moment to let it erupt.
- She had accepted a book, and promised to read it and follow the exercises.

Sometimes we have to leave it with Jesus knowing that He will not let that person go. They belong to Him, not us!

> **I am confident of this, that the one who began a good work among you will bring it to completion...**
>
> Philippians 1:6 NRSV

Chapter 11

USING VISUAL ROOMS

*Jesus Christ is the same yesterday and today
and forever.*

Hebrews 13:8

INTRODUCING THE CONCEPT

I hesitated to include this section in this book because it can so
easily be misconstrued or mishandled. It is easier to learn this
by observation of real ministry than from principles described
in writing.

However, I have used the following exercises and seen
Jesus powerfully bring healing from the hurts of the past to
many people, using variations of the theme outlined. Once again,
let me stress there is no formula, because prayer ministry is
not a technique; but there are a few tools that we can use while
listening to the leading of the Holy Spirit. Sometimes the Spirit
will prompt us to pick up and use one of these tools. Even then
each time in prayer ministry is unique, because it is essentially
about the intimate relationship between God and a human being
– and that can never be prescriptive or formulaic; it is personal.

So, though these exercises have been developed over years
of prayer ministry and I believe they all evolved at the prompting
of the Holy Spirit, they are only pointers and suggestions.
Central to all prayer ministry is the leading of the Spirit. It is
most important never to suggest a diagnosis, or in any way to
intrude with our own preconceptions upon the Lord's work in
someone's life. Our task is to watch and listen, to follow His lead
and obey His prompting; neither less nor more than that.

Because every person is unique something different may

happen every time. We stay open to that, not restricting or restraining the Holy Spirit in His work. I would never plan in advance to use these exercises – it's just that various things pop into my mind while I am prayerfully ministering. As they are still evolving, the Holy Spirit continues to surprise me when He whispers what to do next. I never want to get to the point where I think, "Oh yes, I'll start with a room visualisation and then we can bring the inner child to Jesus…" Jesus said that "he can only do what he sees his Father doing" (John 5:19); "Whatever I say is just what the Father has told me to say" (John 12:50).

A couple of simple exercises can help the Receiver let go of matters that are troubling them. The exercises may also bring to the surface some suppressed emotions.

During prayer ministry, if the Receiver is anxious about someone they love, ask them to visualise the person (or think of them) and take them by the hand to Jesus at the cross. Give them time to do this, enquiring if they are able to do it. Then proceed by asking the Receiver to put the person's hand into Jesus' hand. Some may struggle to do this, but encourage them to hand the person over to Jesus. When they have done this, ask the Receiver to walk away and leave the person with Jesus. At this point there may be a release of suppressed emotion.

This exercise can also be used if someone is grieving the loss of a loved one. For some to relinquish a child in this way can be very healing. This exercise can also be used for those who have had a break-up of a romantic relationship or broken engagement.

When the Receiver is anxious about any particular situation, ask them to visualise this as a parcel labelled with the words describing the difficulty. Encourage them to come towards Jesus at the cross with their parcel (or they may just wish to put their hands out, bringing something that is symbolic to them that sums up the situation or problem). Encourage them to hand over their parcel or symbolic object to Jesus, and walk away leaving it with Him. Again there may be a release of suppressed emotion at this time.

The Receiver may go on their own creative journey after the initial first stage of either of these exercises. It is okay to interject and ask what is happening during the exercise. Sometimes the exercise may also lead into deeper ministry.

We need to keep interacting with the Holy Spirit, and if the Receiver is visualising we must be careful to refrain from suggesting scenes for them to see; they are on their own journey with Him; it is not ours. We facilitate the ministry taking place but we must not hinder it by using the power of suggestion. We offer our hands, but it is His healing.

THE NON-VISUAL RECEIVER

First of all I want to introduce to you the idea of using "rooms" or "safe places" in someone's memory. If I am a bit stuck in ministry or it seems as if the person is not really receiving, I ask them, "Are you a visual person?" If they are unsure, I test it by asking them to shut their eyes and visualise an object such as a rose. If they can do this, and a picture presents to their mind's eye, then I go forward with the following exercise. If the person is not visual and struggles to picture an imagined object, I ask them to think back and recall childhood photographs they have seen of themselves, to help facilitate visualisation. For a non-visual type of person, using the word "think" instead of "see" is helpful.

Not everyone is comfortable with visualisation. A small number of people find this a difficult concept (especially cerebral types – highly intellectual, or with very analytical minds). Sometimes it will help this type of person to surrender their intellect to Jesus and then give Him access to their imagination. Some people are not used to working with that side of their brain.

VISUAL MINISTRY

I invite the Holy Spirit to come upon them and encourage the person to welcome Jesus into their conscious and unconscious minds and their memories. After waiting a while for the presence of Jesus, I ask the person to do *one* of the following things:

- See yourself as an adult/at the age you are now at home – in a room you like.
- Imagine a room that you would love to be in at the age you are now. You can have anything you want in this room. Decorate it how you would like it to be, in any colour, and put in it anything you would love to have, anything that reflects your personality, skills or hobbies – anything you think you could never have.
- See yourself in a room when you were a child – a room where you felt safe, or where you liked to be, your special place.
- See yourself in a place that you used to go to.
- Make for yourself a room as a child – a room that you would have loved to have had. You can have anything in this room: the colour you would you like, and anything necessary to make it feel lovely and safe.
- See yourself as a child in a room, or outside – at any age. It can be in someone else's house if you prefer.

With this in place, I ask them to describe what they can see. How you proceed has to be a prompting and reliance on the Holy Spirit – He is the Counsellor and Comforter. I can't tell you what He will do next as this is different for every person, depending on what happened to them there in the past. The description of the imagined room can reveal vividly how someone is feeling as a child. Sometimes people say, "There was nowhere safe – no room in the house ever felt safe." This can be very helpful and revealing. It tells you that something bad may have happened in the house – in every room. If this happens, I would encourage the person to either make up their own room or go to a place outside, or to someone else's house – any location, so long as they feel safe.

When describing the room they are in, the person may tell you they are in bed under the covers, or hiding in a wardrobe or under the bed. This lets you know what a scary place their bedroom was. If this is the case, sometimes I will ask them to make up their own "safe room". Later on in the ministry I might ask them if they would like to take Jesus to the room that was scary, or they can ask Jesus to go in there ahead of them and shine His light and love into that place. Another possibility is to ask the Receiver, "Do you want to take Jesus to another room in the house or to somewhere else?" This can allow the ministry to develop at the pace of the Receiver.

During this time the Lord might prompt you to pray something like, "Bring Your healing there, Jesus" or "Shine Your light there, Jesus."

To help the person open up to Jesus, I ask them to look around the room to find the door or, if they are outside, look for a gate. I explain, "The Bible tells us Jesus says, 'I stand at the door and knock; if you open the door I want to come in and eat with you.'" Then I make it clear that Jesus comes in only by invitation – the handle is on their side. He wants to come in and meet with that little boy/girl who needs Him. At this point just wait and watch, observing the expression on the person's face. After a while, ask, "Have you managed to open the door?" If they say no, just ask, "What is stopping you?" Sometimes people need encouraging, but no more than that – not suggestion! Maybe say something like, "Jesus loves that little girl/boy: He wants to come into that room/place. Could you allow that little girl/boy to let Him in?" At times the reply has been, "I can't reach the handle. I am too little." In such a case I ask if there is something in the room they can stand on.

Then I wait and quietly pray, "You do it, Lord. Do it Your way." This encourages the person, because you are declaring your faith; you believe that He will come and meet with the little child who is hurting. At some point I also explain that the person does not have to see Jesus, conjure Him up – He doesn't have to appear in a white gown to be there! Some people see an impression or a figure or bright light that they can respond to. Anything they see as their expression is okay.

It is important to make the distinction between encouraging

the Receiver to allow Jesus in to meet with the little child in the room they have imagined, and planting suggestions in their mind. It might seem that saying, "Jesus loves that little girl/boy: He wants to come into that room/place" *is* suggestion.

But prayer ministry is never pushed on a person, only offered at their request. If they have come to you asking for ministry, you already know they want to meet with Jesus – you have nothing else to offer. There is not, and must never be, any hint of coercion. The encouragement to allow Jesus in is not to push them into a meeting they don't want, but to help them believe in a meeting they long for.

Suggestion would be planning the details of their safe place for them, or insisting they open the door right now, or getting impatient with their slow visualisation and having Jesus gatecrash their safe room (which He would never do).

Keep praying in the Spirit while this is taking place. Connect with the Holy Spirit and keep your spiritual ears and eyes engaged with Him. Be an open channel to whatever He may be prompting you to say. This is a precious time; many things can happen as people invite Jesus into their yesterdays. Some feel very peaceful; others experience Jesus holding them or speaking to them. Out loud I usually say, "Tell Jesus anything you want to – this is your time; you can do anything you want." I am very conscious of the fact that I can't do anything. Only He can. I don't want to get in the way of what He is doing, and how.

Sometimes the Receiver can find that when they open the door there is no one there. This can then lead on to deeper ministry. I ask them what they were expecting when they opened the door, and this can lead on into a different direction. Sometimes the Receiver had no expectation of anything good ever happening – only bad. Then the Pray-er can ask Jesus to show the Receiver what the root cause of that expectation was.

Before trying this as a one-to-one with someone in need of healing, experiment with someone else willing to learn new ways in prayer ministry. First, try it with them seeing themselves in a room as an adult, or at the age they are now. I have done this with a group of ten, twenty-five, and even 200 people. One fifteen-year-old told me a few weeks afterwards that she had tried this group exercise with some of her youth group. They had all entered into it fully, and had some lovely times with Jesus.

This "see yourself as an adult" room exercise can be a useful tool for the Receiver to use when they go home and are alone. They can revisit this safe room where they have experienced the touch of Jesus, and continue to use it as a place of prayer and healing where they meet with Him. It can become their prayer refuge. For some people life is lonely, and they find it difficult to connect with Jesus in solitude. This exercise helps emphasise that Jesus wants to come and bring healing to us when it is just us and Him. We don't have to wait for ministry from someone else before Jesus can come in and bring healing to us. It is easy to make the mistake of thinking we can only seek healing at church or in a small group situation. Of course some of the other visual exercises may also be used by the Receiver at home but they may prefer to do them with the Pray-er as they may fear that it could be overwhelming when alone. For others this may be more liberating, meaning they can "let rip" with their emotions.

> **There's no need to go to this place or that place in search of the kingdom of God; it is within you.**
>
> Paraphrase of Luke 17:21

It is important to note that, for some people, remembering isn't an option. Their way of surviving has been to disassociate from feelings or memories of bad stuff that has happened. During prayer ministry at conferences, at times of power encounter, I have occasionally seen people go through what appears to be very traumatic remembering. When I have asked what is happening, they may have had no idea the manifestation could arise from past trauma, because the memory is so painful they have blocked it. The good news is we can minister the power, love, and light of Jesus into these hurts without the person having to remember anything when events are too painful to recall. We must be careful to respect the pace of the person we are praying for, as the mind does all it can to protect itself from going over the edge.

A way of gently moving forward when everything seems stuck is to ask the Receiver to see themselves as a child and to go into the hallway of their home, or to the front door. Then proceed to say: "Jesus stands at the door and knocks. He wants to come in but only you can open the door – He is outside." After a little while, ask if Jesus has come in. Then you might continue, "Would you like to take Jesus to any particular rooms?"

Sometimes the Receiver has no-go areas of the house. This again can offer an opportunity for opening up the ministry to explore why that is. Sometimes the Receiver may take Jesus to another place altogether – perhaps their school. This again deepens the ministry and leads it on.

MAKING A ROOM – REBECCA

I remember using the "make yourself a room as an adult" exercise with Rebecca. She had a wonderful time and described to me in great detail what her room looked like. It was yellow with a lovely big sofa and chair. The sun shone in through the large, clear windows; everything was clean and co-ordinated. She didn't have to do anything in the room; it had all been done. This instantly took a lot of pressure off her. With unusual confidence, she rushed to open the door to let Jesus into this special place that was hers, a safe place that made no demands on her. Her face was beaming as she opened herself up to Jesus in her made-up room. Rebecca told me afterwards that she had never experienced anything so wonderful; she loved the time she spent with Jesus in her room. Because of a deprived childhood, Rebecca had never had much to call her own; memories of her childhood had been colourless and empty. The room exercise had filled her with hope for the future. She also knew that she could return to this room whenever she felt stressed and tired or far from God. It was as if He had given her a present and a blessing.

ADULT AND CHILD – ANNA

Twenty-year-old Anna had never experienced the love of Jesus. She looked sad and empty. I asked her to see herself in a safe place as a child. When I asked her where she was, she told me she was under the bedcovers. I asked her whether she could get to the door and open it to Jesus, but she said, "No, it's too scary." I said to her that under the covers probably wasn't a safe place for her; was there anywhere else? She replied, "No." Then I said, "Make up your own room; anything you wanted as a child, you can have in that room." Anna described the room to me: "It is yellow – nothing else in it, just yellow – I like the space!" She saw herself in the room but when I explained that Jesus was at the door wanting to come in, she said she couldn't open the door. She said she wasn't scared, she just didn't know how to. I realised that the adult Anna was probably protecting her inner child, so I asked her at the age she was now to walk into the room where Anna the little girl was. Anna started to cry, saying, "I want to hold her." I encouraged her to do this. After a while she invited Jesus to come into the room and felt His love embracing both Anna the little girl and Anna the adult.

IN A FIELD – LAURA

During a time of ministry, after Laura had received some deliverance, I asked her to see herself as a child somewhere she could feel completely safe. She told me she saw herself in a field with a big tree; she was sitting at the base of the tree. I told Laura to look for a gate, go to the gate, and open it to Jesus. "He wants to come into your field and spend time with you." After waiting a while and watching her expressions change, I asked her what had happened. She said, "It was wonderful; for the first time in my life I felt loved." Laura had suffered an emotionally abusive childhood, and had been thrown out of her home aged only sixteen. I encouraged her to go into the field and meet that little girl and Jesus together. Laura cried as she met them both in the field. Afterwards she said she experienced Jesus loving her as an eighteen-year-old in the same way as He had earlier loved her as a little girl. I found it intriguing that she couldn't access that concept intellectually; she had to experience it to know that it was true! Jesus always knows the right way for each one of us.

FORGIVING HIS INNER CHILD – PETE

I saw a young man standing as if he wanted prayer ministry but felt too shy to ask. I went over with another man and asked if he wanted prayer, and he said, "Yes." I asked him if he was sensing anything and he said that his chest ached a bit. After a while I received a word of knowledge in the form of a picture, which I relayed to him. He acknowledged that the picture was significant to him and helped him know that he was safe with Jesus. I asked him to imagine himself as a little boy in a room, and asked him to invite Jesus into that room with him.

When I asked what was happening, he said it was good. Jesus was close to him and he felt safe. I then asked him to visit the same room as an adult. He said he was standing at the open door, but not going into the room. I asked what was stopping him. He said he didn't know. I asked what he was feeling; he said, "Nothing." I asked him if it felt numb or distant when he looked at the little boy. He answered, "Yes! That's it! I feel distant." I asked him if he judged that little boy for what he (the little boy) was like. He said yes, he didn't want him to be like he was – not standing up for himself. I suggested it would be good if he forgave that little boy for not being what he wanted him to be. He did that. Then he was able to go closer and embrace the little boy. Afterwards he said he felt a lot better.

SPLIT INTO THREE – MICHELLE

She saw herself in a room, not as a little girl but as a tiny baby. The baby ended up in Jesus' pocket, where she felt really safe! Then I asked her to go into the room as an adult. She found that difficult until I suggested she go in as a little girl first. I realised that she had been somehow separated into three parts, no part integrated with another. The little girl then entered the room and received from Jesus – now she was relating to the baby. Then she entered as an adult and all three, with Jesus, made their peace. She said she felt different afterwards.

There are too many stories of using "rooms" to recount, but each one is a surprise to me. I have experienced people meet Jesus in their safe place on the top of a mountain, in the woods, hiding under a shrub, hiding behind a chair, at their gran's house, up a tree, behind a wall, in the playground...

If you try this, keep it simple. Start off with: "See yourself as an adult in a room, a safe place." It may help to ask, "Did you have a safe place when you were a child?" If not, ask if they had a place they liked to go to on their own, or if they preferred being in someone else's house. If none of that applies, ask if they preferred being outdoors. It works just the same inside or out. The important thing is to establish a safe place in the imagination.

After using this a few times you will gain in confidence to let the Holy Spirit guide you.

USING ROOMS TO RELEASE ANGER AND PAIN

The "rooms" exercise is also useful in helping a person vocalise pain or anger towards someone, using a "safe place" to let it out. This is also helpful for the Receiver who needs to feel strong, to say something to someone of whom they are frightened.

If your Receivers have been used to working with "rooms" to receive from Jesus, they are usually open to using a similar scenario for relieving pain.

First of all I encourage the person to see themselves in their safe place, one they have remembered or one they have made up. When they have invited Jesus into the room with them, ask what might make them feel more powerful in the room. Receivers offer all sorts of responses, ranging from hiding behind Jesus or behind a big chair, or suddenly becoming like a giant! I encourage them by saying, "This is your room – no one can do or say anything in this room unless you say so. Everyone who comes into this room, from now on, has to obey you. They can only speak if you say so." Then I ask, "How does this make you feel?" This alone can have an empowering effect on some people. At this point you must proceed carefully, taking your lead from the Holy Spirit, always checking with Him what you should do next.

I have been prompted to follow a wide variety of different courses of action. As always, my own experiences do not provide a formula or technique, just an indication of various ways healing can take place as we allow the Holy Spirit space to work.

You might ask:

- Is there someone you would like to say something to? Something that you would never dare say to their face? Something that needs to be said?
- Is there someone you are angry with?
- Is there anyone you are frightened of, that you wouldn't like to have in this, your special room? This can lead on to talking with Jesus about the situation.
- Are there some people who need to know what you think or feel about something you have kept hidden?
- Is there anyone standing outside the door whom you wouldn't like to enter your room? Who is it? Or ask, "How do you feel towards them?" You can take the ministry forward from here as directed by the Holy Spirit. If the person standing outside their door terrifies the Receiver (look at their body language for clues), do not insist they invite them in; just use this as a springboard

for the Receiver to talk to Jesus about their feelings. They may never have acknowledged their fear.

- Is there a group of people outside the door with whom you are angry or unhappy? Who are they? If it seems appropriate, ask, "If you ranked the people outside the door in order of whom you are most angry or unhappy with, what would the order be?" You can use this to facilitate the ministry as the Holy Spirit leads.
- If the little boy/girl could say something to these people, what would it be?
- If you had a line of people outside the door who made you feel powerless, who would they be?

The ministry develops into the Receiver inviting someone into their special room where they feel in charge, or choosing somewhere else to face them. Some people love their safe room so much they don't want to let in these threatening individuals in case they spoil it! Even in this instance the exercise is useful, because it helps the Receiver identify those with whom they have issues, and why.

Options could be:

1. If the person outside the door entered the room, what would you do to make yourself still feel safe in the room?
2. Where would you make the person outside sit or stand if they came in, so it still felt safe?
3. What animal/vegetable would you like the person from outside the room to be, so they could be acceptable inside your room?

I have had various answers to the questions above. Some of them are:

Replies to questions 1 and 2:
- I would be in Jesus' arms.
- I would be behind Jesus or another person.

- I would make them sit down and I would stand up.
- I would make them lie down on the floor.
- I would put a big plaster over their mouth.

Replies to question 3:
- A spider so that I can squash it.
- A seal so I can make her do what I want her to do.
- A very tiny person.

There have been so many amazing encounters using these exercises. Some have entered in and been able to give vent to anger, disappointment, and frustration, speaking out words they had never felt able to say to those who had hurt them. Others have had the time to speak words of love they never realised they still felt. Other scenarios have enabled people to take Jesus into rooms in their home, or classrooms at school, bringing His love and power into that place. Often this has dispelled fear associated with these places.

At other times it has been heart-rending to hear the person cry out with a hateful accusation, or their inner child cry out their need to be shown love. When someone lets rip from the depth of their pain, it is an awesome moment. I usually feel a mixture of respect and privilege at being allowed to witness such a thing, aware that Jesus is about to do an amazing healing. I never know how it will happen so I usually say, "Let Jesus do it" or "Do what you want to do right now – Jesus is still there." Even as I write this, my eyes fill up remembering some truly exquisite times of sensing His healing taking place. I wait until the time is right before asking, "What is happening now?" or "What happened?" I never cease to be amazed at the variety of ways Jesus heals people.

FEAR IN THE DENTIST'S CHAIR

This is a story of my own, concerning how helpful I found the "rooms" exercise at the dentist.

I was in the dentist's chair feeling very worried, as I had been suffering agony from a tooth that, unknown to me, had a fracture in it. After a week on painkillers the pain had subsided, so I visited the dentist. My dentist filled the tooth and I had no more pain. But a couple of years later the same tooth fractured further, and this time I needed a crown fitted. Remembering the past agony of the fractured tooth I felt nervous about having anything done to it. I had an injection but I could still feel pain when the dentist started drilling. After a further two injections, neither of which worked, the dentist applied yet another. By now I had sweaty palms, and felt very hot and fearful at the impending drilling of a tooth where the gum was not numb enough. At this moment I suddenly remembered the rooms exercise. I practised this in my head, going to the door and opening it to let Jesus in. The Holy Spirit came upon me powerfully; I felt quite drunk, and my body felt heavy – so much so, that when the dentist finished drilling most of my tooth ready for the crown, I could hardly sit up to wash my mouth out. I slurred my words like the worst drunk, as the dentist asked me what had happened to me earlier. Puzzled, I asked what she meant. She continued, "Something happened to you earlier, after I injected you. Usually the patient's tongue is fighting to relax and let me do my job, but suddenly yours completely relaxed and your whole body changed. It made it so easy for me." I struggled to speak, still slurring as she insisted on knowing what had happened. I explained that I was a Christian and described the exercise to her. She and the nurse were so impressed they quizzed me about Jesus and healing for the next twenty minutes! Thank You, Lord!

GOING WITH JESUS TO A SPECIAL PLACE

Some people who have lived through an abusive childhood would not like to be "in a room". At times I have asked people, "If you could go anywhere now with Jesus where would it be?" Lots of people say, "In the sun on a beach." I invite them to see themselves there with Jesus, or think of themselves there. After a while I ask them if they can sense Jesus there. Then I just say, "Jesus, do what You want to do. Bring [name] Your healing now; do it Your way." I have heard wonderful stories of how Jesus brought them freedom through this. One young woman I remember started to put her arms out, with a smile on her face. Later on I asked what was happening. She said Jesus lifted her up in His arms and started to take her up from the beach into the air. As she went up with Him all the horrible voices of her childhood – her parents shouting and arguing – started to fade. He lifted her high up, and she could see beautiful colours she had never seen before. He washed her mind of all the abusive shouting from her past that so often filled her head. Afterwards she looked radiant.

This is just one of so many stories of Jesus visiting His people.

A NON-VISUAL PERSON

It is not necessary for someone to relive or even visualise a memory for Jesus to heal it.

During a talk on inner healing I explained that we were going to do a visualising exercise. I encouraged those who were not visual to invite Jesus to come in anyway, just thinking it rather than visualising it. During the first exercise, John said he hadn't been able to enter in very much. However, when we asked Jesus to show us ourselves as children, he had a very clear memory of himself and saw Jesus visit him. Following on from that, Jesus ministered some deep healing to him and ended up sitting with him inside a locked cupboard. This was where he had often been sent as a punishment by his father. John received a deep healing through this visualisation, following an exercise he didn't think he could do. The exercise became accessible and effective for him, a non-visual person, because in fact John was not imagining anything, but recalling memories. Praise God for His healing.

PART 3
PASTORAL PRAYER MINISTRY

Chapter 12

INTRODUCING PASTORAL PRAYER MINISTRY

HE WASHES OUR FEET!

Pastoral prayer ministry (PPM) is a term used for extended prayer ministry, usually neutral ground on church premises away from any interruption. It offers time and space for longer, deeper inner healing prayer ministry, typically three to six sessions of between sixty and ninety minutes. Membership of the PPM team is usually at the discretion of church leaders.

> Having loved his own... he now showed them the full extent of his love... he got up from the meal, took off his outer clothing, and wrapped a towel around his waist... and began to wash his disciples' feet, drying them with the towel that was wrapped around him...
> "Now that I, your Lord and Teacher, have washed your feet, you also should wash one another's feet. I have set you an example that you should do as I have done for you."
>
> John 13:1–17

This Scripture says Jesus showed the disciples *the full extent of His love*! I find it amazing that He washed Judas' feet – the one who would betray Him – showing him, too, how much He loved him. Can you imagine the state of the disciples' feet? They were probably sweaty from living in such a hot country, toes oozing dirt and dung from camels and donkeys. Washing twelve lots of feet would have involved time and effort but He did it with love.

You cannot wash feet unless you get down to their level. Feet are not the most pleasant part of the body. Jesus chose to do this because it was usually the job of the lowest servant present: He came to serve. Pastoral prayer ministry is serving people – spending time, joining Jesus in washing feet. It says in the passage above that, as His followers, we are to do the same as Jesus. We cannot wash other people's feet unless we are willing to have our own washed by Him.

Pastoral prayer ministry is to be done with the attitude of a servant. We acknowledge that we are all the same, all needing our feet to be washed. We are all sinners. None of us is completely whole. I was healed, I am being healed, and I will be healed. I am still one of the walking wounded. I like to keep that in mind when I am ministering.

QUALITIES OF A POSSIBLE PASTORAL PRAYER MINISTRY TEAM MEMBER

Here are the main qualities to look for in a PPM team member:

- committed member of the church for at least a year
- regular attender at church home group/cell group
- accountable
- teachable
- anointed by the Holy Spirit for the work
- regularly involved in church ministry team
- open and pursuing own wholeness and healing
- has common sense
- able to hear God
- willing to be used as a channel of the Holy Spirit
- likes people
- will give God the glory
- has received some healing from past hurts in their own life.

The following traits are undesirable in a PPM team member:
- needs to be needed
- judgmental
- gossip
- rescuer (overly co-dependent)
- has control issues
- status seeker.

COMPASSION AND MERCY

What a privilege it is to be allowed to join Jesus in His healing ministry. Being alongside someone opening up to the Lord, seeing the depth of their inner pain, can be very humbling.

Who am I to be given this opportunity to see Jesus my Healer healing someone else's wounds? But didn't He say that with the comfort I have received, I should comfort others? That I should set the captives free with His love and power? Yes, He did! Thank You, Jesus, that You can use a sinner like me!

Sometimes I feel a sense of the compassion of Jesus for hurting people, almost physical at times. Whenever I sense this during the prayer ministry I know Jesus is about to do something special; it is often followed by deep inner healing. If it happens at other times when I am with a group of people I know some significant healing is about to take place. Before Jesus did something out of the ordinary – a miracle or a healing – the Scripture often says He was moved by compassion or looked upon the person or people with compassion. This word "compassion" in Scripture implies "a wrenching of the guts", a far stronger term than we are used to understanding "compassion" to mean. In the story of raising Lazarus from the dead (John 11:38–44), Jesus saw the grief of all the people: in the original Greek, His reaction is described as snorting like a horse or snorting in the Spirit. In the Greek the word carries connotations of anger or deep emotion. Some commentators interpret this as Jesus being angry with death. Jesus was, and is, moved by the plight of an individual, by their pain or distress. An example is the widow about to have her only son buried – he is being carried out by the coffin bearers (Luke 7:11–15). Jesus, moved by compassion, brought her son back to life miraculously with a word. He knew the boy's mother had already suffered the death of her husband – with both male members of her immediate family gone she could now be desperately vulnerable as well as heartbroken.

The compassion of Jesus feels different from experiencing the love of Jesus for someone. It compels us to act.

When we feel the compassion of Jesus it may be twinned with His mercy. The mercy of Jesus is so beautiful. This is another gift we can ask Him for. During ministry when using the gift of mercy we can suddenly be almost in the other person's shoes, experiencing what they are feeling without it depleting our own resources. It leads to a deeper outpouring of the love of Jesus that brings healing. At times as I have used this gift I have had a deep assurance that the person is receiving a profound healing.

Ministering with compassion and mercy has a great impact on ministry. It brings a spiritual dynamic. I spent a long while asking Jesus to show me what He sees, continuing for about a year to ask Him to show me how to love people. After a while, I found myself starting to cry at the most unlikely things.

If an advert on TV displayed any form of injustice, I would weep. At times I would walk into my lounge as my husband was watching a movie, and would suddenly find myself weeping if it included scenes portraying injustice. Injustice seemed to shout at me from magazines and newspapers. I was often moved to tears by the beauty of nature or photographs of children. I seemed to spend a lot of the time in tears! If I watched a whole programme where people were being sinned against in some way – whether drama or documentary – I would spend quite a long time sobbing. In some ways this felt disconcerting, but I realised Jesus was softening my heart and answering my prayers. He was sharing His compassion as He showed me His hurting world.

> He has shown you, O mortal, what is good. And what
> does the Lord require of you? To act justly and to love
> mercy and to walk humbly with your God.
>
> Micah 6:8

Mercy is exquisitely tender – it is sparing us from something we really deserve. It is letting someone off the hook. It is very powerful. It is blessing someone when they deserved to be cursed. Mercy is a gift of the Holy Spirit and we can ask for it. Why not do that now?

The sacrament of Holy Communion is a good place to receive forgiveness for sin, forgive others, and receive healing. Encourage the Receiver to bring their inner pain to Jesus as they go forward in church to receive the bread and the wine.

THE PERSONAL COST

A pastoral prayer ministry team gives an opportunity for church leaders to refer on any member of the congregation struggling with a deep-rooted or long-standing issue. House group or small group leaders can also refer on members whose needs are of a magnitude that would unbalance the pastoral care possible in a small group meeting.

Because pastoral prayer ministry requires an extended time, timing is important. People cannot concentrate on receiving ministry if they are worried about collecting a child from children's ministry, anxious to get home to cook dinner, or are rushing off for a lunch date. Ministering into deep issues cannot be rushed, so it may be better to schedule a separate time for PPM.

LIVING OUT OF HEALING RECEIVED

Habits are hard to break, and a person can receive healing without properly appropriating the freedom now won for them. If the Receiver has for many years been accused by the enemy, and believed the lies, even after receiving freedom and healing they still need to break the habit when they hear such accusations in the future. Not only does Jesus heal and forgive us, He gives us the power to break old habits – we just have to remember to step into that freedom and really live from our healing.

It might happen like this:

First step: Thought and accusation – some time after hearing an accusation, the Receiver wakes up to what is going on, and counters the accusation with truth.

Second step: Thought and accusation – half-way through receiving the accusation, the Receiver realises, and counters with the truth.

Third step: Thought and accusation – as soon as the same old accusation starts up, the Receiver stops it right there in its tracks with the truth.

This then becomes the new habit.

Even after the new habit is in place the enemy may try again to see if there is any access.

This is what I mean by living in the healing. It can help to arm the Receiver with verses from the Bible, to be affirmed out loud. Scripture then becomes not just words but a two-edged sword, a living word, and a lamp to the feet (see Chapter 18).

Memorising Scripture in this way is very helpful in countering the attacks of the enemy and laying down new habits of freedom. Proclaiming the promises of God assists us in appropriating for ourselves in daily life the freedom Christ has won for us.

God's word to us in the Bible can seem dry and dusty until we see it applied as living truth that sets us free – then it becomes exciting. The movement of the Spirit in power ministry is always exciting, but needs to be firmly rooted in Scripture so that we do not mistake our own emotions and enthusiasms for the leading of the Spirit. As the old saying goes:

> Too much Word and we dry up;
> Too much Spirit and we blow up;
> With the Word and the Spirit we grow up!

SOME REASONS PEOPLE COME FOR PPM

There are many different reasons why people may need an extended time of prayer ministry.

Those who suffer trauma, neglect, or abuse in childhood usually develop coping strategies for survival. When they grow up, they establish a pattern of behaviour to protect themselves against further hurt – seeking to either avoid or control situations where they feel vulnerable and overwhelmed. This fearfulness and defensiveness stunts personal growth and affects all personal relationships – including the relationship with God. These coping strategies can be so ingrained that they feel normal. The Receiver may not realise there is any other way to approach relationships, and cannot work out why their life seems so stuck.

Living out of irrational beliefs and lies also inhibits growth to full adult maturity. If for instance we believe that "This is how you are and this is how you will always be", we will have no expectation for growth and change and will not be open to God's healing and transformation.

No one has perfect parents, carers, teachers, siblings, or friends. All of us at some point experience pain inflicted by those we trusted and relied on for love and support. Children who were not allowed to communicate when they felt injustice had been done, or when they were punished for something they didn't do, can bury their pain for fear that if they express it they will be further punished. Some children have suffered parental abandonment or lived with emotionally absent parents. Some may not connect emotionally with one or both parents. Some parents have never experienced love themselves and are incapable of expressing spontaneous and natural affection.

Others needing pastoral prayer ministry may have suffered a broken engagement or divorce, or they may be children of divorced parents. The Receiver may have been adopted and never known who their birth parents were.

Some may be bereaved, whether because a loved one has

died or through other sorts of loss, such as redundancy or children leaving home. Younger people may have left home, and be struggling to find their feet in the world – perhaps they are in debt or finding it hard to get started in a career. Maybe it is not easy to find the money to pay for accommodation, or perhaps they are going through a broken relationship.

A current loss may crack open a past emotional wound still unhealed. The pain that surfaces feels huge. This can be a big shock, as the current loss does not seem to warrant such extreme feelings.

Each person is unique and we should not make judgments on anything anyone tells us. Neither should we look shocked at people's confessions. For some, just the disclosure or confession may release huge burdens.

RECOGNISING WHEN SOMETHING ELSE IS NEEDED

We recognise that we can only do what we can do, and leave the rest to Jesus. We are not counsellors or therapists. There are professionals who do that. It is helpful to read some books on inner healing and see how the mind works. Some useful books are listed at the back of this book. Some counselling and listening skills are useful, but we remain clear that we are not offering counselling as part of pastoral prayer ministry. Personally I don't seem to remember much that I read, but that doesn't seem to hinder the Lord using me, so please do not be put off if you find reading and remembering difficult. He will find some way to teach and show you as you are faithful in doing only what you see the Father do, and allowing the Holy Spirit to lead and guide you.

Some people need to talk a lot and get things out of their system before attending prayer ministry. From the first or second session it should be obvious whether the Receiver needs prayer ministry or should be referred for professional help.

It is a good idea to have ready a leaflet giving details of local counsellors and therapists, as well as contact details of any Christian counselling services offering sliding-scale charges depending on earnings. If you don't know anyone you could recommend, the Receiver could search the internet for accredited help. If they are seeking counselling they will need to find someone who is fully trained.

In every town there is usually a free counselling service for those under twenty-five years old. Counselling offered from the doctor is usually only up to six sessions.

Do not begin pastoral prayer ministry sessions with someone who is having counselling or therapy unless their counsellor or therapist is in agreement. Even then, only minister into the area the counsellor or therapist is currently working with. It could be necessary for some to see a psychotherapist. As well as unravelling past pain, a therapist will be able to equip their client with tools to help them in between sessions. Some may benefit from the support of bereavement counselling. In all cases of mental illness, refer the Receiver to their doctor for treatment.

Do not ever suggest that someone stop taking medication, even if they appear to be healed. This is the doctor's job, not ours! If they are healed their doctor will let them know.

If the Receiver appears to suffer from depression, you will need to suggest that they see their doctor. They may be depressed if they are suffering from some of the following symptoms:

- loss of appetite
- crying all the time
- no desire to get out of bed in the morning
- difficulty sleeping
- sleeping most of the day
- mostly negative thoughts
- suicidal thoughts
- panic attacks.

It is imperative not to take responsibility for someone else's illness. They are not our responsibility. They should be under the care of their doctor. Sometimes a Receiver may refuse, saying, "Oh no, I don't want to take tablets! I want God to heal me." In such circumstances I usually reply, "God can work in many different ways – through doctors, nurses, therapists, and counsellors. I am sorry, but if you won't visit your doctor I cannot see you for prayer ministry." I explain that prayer ministry usually takes us down into our painful feelings before it lifts us up, and this can be emotionally tough. I would hesitate to offer ministry to someone who is clearly unstable.

HAVING BOUNDARIES

Anyone engaged in pastoral prayer ministry must maintain clear boundaries. Differentiating between what prayer ministry can offer and what needs a doctor's care is an essential boundary to have in place. Another is that when I go to church I am there to receive through fellowship and worshipping the Lord in a community of believers. I need space to do this and to meet up with friends afterwards for coffee. I will minister to people after the service in the time allotted for prayer ministry, but if I see someone who is "in session" with me in pastoral prayer ministry, I will not usually go up to them and ask how they have been feeling this week. I will explain this in advance at the first session. This gives the ministry team space and avoids embarrassing situations while they are trying to chat with friends, maintaining the proper boundary between their personal life and their work as a prayer minister. Even in the prayer ministry time I will not automatically go up to them if they come forward for prayer – they do not become "mine". They may be coming up for something totally unrelated to the sessions we are having. The only time I will go to them is if I am called over or the Holy Spirit directs me to go – perhaps because their pain has fully surfaced and they need to be with someone they know is familiar with their situation, so they can let rip with their inner pain.

I do give out my mobile number, but I explain that I am not available to text backwards and forwards (some people have a habit of this); it is only to be used in emergencies or if they need to cancel a session.

This may sound harsh but such boundaries must be in place. The pastoral prayer ministry team also have other responsibilities and can get worn out. The church could soon have no members left on the team if the work becomes all-consuming.

We need to be aware that some Receivers may seek to form a long-term attachment. Pray-ers can find this an extra burden to carry, and may feel the only way to escape is to withdraw from the ministry altogether.

Others may want Jesus to wave a magic wand and take away all of their inner pain, but this doesn't usually happen. I have seen miracles of instant inner healing, but the following verse explains the usual way the process works:

> Continue to work out your salvation [or "wholeness",
> from the Greek word *sozo*] with fear and trembling,
> for it is God who works in you to will and to act
> according to his good purpose.
>
> Philippians 2:12–13

He works it in us but we have to work it out. For some, healing can be a slow process, and maintaining boundaries enables us to stay in the ministry for the long haul.

We need to keep a balance between ministering to others and giving time to our family and friends. It is also important that we enjoy refreshment spiritually, emotionally, mentally, and physically. Having fun is important!

Keeping proper boundaries in place helps us observe this balance of life.

MENTAL ILLNESS

I have not covered the question of ministering in the area of serious mental illness in this book, not because I believe that Jesus cannot heal a serious mental illness, but because

I have less personal experience in this area. Mental health is certainly affected by spiritual and emotional inner pain and forgiveness. Healing in these areas enables a person to receive some healing of their mind. Several of the stories I have shared include evidence of mental healing, but each case is unique and I feel a real concern about drawing generalised conclusions or giving any direction into the area of mental illness. Deep prayer ministry for inner healing can cause someone to feel more vulnerable and exposed, resulting in those with serious mental health issues becoming unstable. There is a right time for prayer ministry, and a time to exercise restraint. We must be led by the Holy Spirit in discerning when to offer ministry and when to refer someone on. I believe full-on prayer ministry alongside any therapy already taking place should proceed only with the backing approval of professionals. This avoids the Receiver being pulled into different and potentially conflicting approaches to healing at the same time. Inexperienced Pray-ers could do more harm than good if they proceeded without due caution into working with an exceptionally fragile and vulnerable individual.

We must be aware that some mental health issues may result in creating emotional and psychological dependency unhelpful to both the Pray-er and the Receiver.

This does not mean we turn people away or refuse any kind of help. We can always pray generally for the blessing and healing of Jesus upon someone, without getting into deep ministry. My belief is that the person still receives from Jesus and can progress in the area of healing. He always hears our prayers, and blessing cannot be anything other than beneficial.

I have ministered to people with severe mental health issues by praying a short prayer of peace, and the healing love of Jesus. I have also prayed His security and safety upon the person. This has taken place at the front of church after the service in the ministry time. On some occasions I have asked others of the team if they will go and pray a short prayer, so no dependency issues arise and the Receiver feels the benefit of being in a loving community. This in itself can confer the beneficial effect of feeling accepted within the congregation.

SOME PRACTICAL POINTS

If their problem derives from a bad relationship with either their father or mother, some women can receive in a deeper way if the prayer ministry is from a married couple. For others the nearness of a male – even the smell of his aftershave – can be very disturbing, especially if they have been sexually abused by a man. Sensitivity must always be used.

Of course a man may also have been sexually abused, whether by a man or woman, or have been physically abused by their father. Be sensitive to the needs of the Receiver at every stage, ensuring they have the opportunity to express any discomfort they may feel from either gender.

Always respect the Receiver's personal space, watching for body language that may show discomfort over any aspect of the prayer ministry.

Look at Chapter 18 for sheets you can photocopy, so Receivers have something to take home between sessions. This may feel reassuring and supportive, and may also assist the healing to progress, helping the Receiver to seek healing directly from the Lord between prayer ministry sessions.

Chapter 13
MODEL AND PRACTICE

In this chapter I will take you through a summary of pastoral prayer ministry, to give you an idea of how to begin in the first session, and ways you might proceed in subsequent sessions. As always, you are following the lead of the Holy Spirit and always listening to Him; but having some structure and the benefit of what others have found useful may give you confidence and support.

I recommend the booklet *Pastoral Prayer Ministry Training* by Mary Pytches and Prue Bedwell, first published by New Wine and now available in a revised version, also from New Wine.

SESSION 1

Ministering in a same-gender pair, or as a married couple:

1. Book a room at church or a place neutral to the Receiver: somewhere no phone calls or person will interrupt or disturb you.

2. Turn off your mobile phone and ensure others do the same.

3. Have tissues and glasses of water available for everyone.

4. Make sure that the Receiver is not facing the door if it has a glass panel, so that they can be hidden from view.

5. Explain to the Receiver in advance that each session will be about one to one and a half hours long.

6. Explain that four to six sessions are on offer, depending on how things go. If more sessions seem necessary, they can recommence after a break of a few weeks or months. Some people may only want one or two sessions.

7. Make it clear that pastoral prayer ministry isn't counselling. Talk to the Receiver regarding their responsibility during and in between sessions. Their commitment to actively seeking Jesus for their healing outside of the sessions is vital. The Receiver must commit to praying a simple prayer for their own healing every day, without excuses of "I didn't have time". Make this clear and obtain their agreement before proceeding. The Receiver must exercise this responsibility.

8. Explain that the speed of healing will be at the pace that the Receiver will allow. Also explain that at times it will be hard work; they will need to push through, but during the sessions you are there to encourage that to happen.

9. Encourage the Receiver to pursue their healing between sessions, reading and meditating on Scripture. They may be encouraged by reading a book with some exercises to follow, such as my book *Let the Healing Begin*. If they are not great readers, give them a single sheet with a short summary of simple exercises to follow. Chapter 18 contains some useful resources.

10. Explain that this first session is about identifying the underlying problems, and the ministry will not begin until the next session. Keep your manner friendly, humorous, and informal, to set them at ease, because they may feel nervous.

11. Ask if the Receiver is seeing a doctor, and discover details of any medication, counselling, or therapy ongoing or in the past. Be wary of ministering to someone who is paranoid or psychotic. They need professional help first. Explain what pastoral prayer ministry is.

12. Encourage the Receiver to tell you what they perceive is the presenting problem, describe their past history, and say what they would like Jesus to do for them.

13. Be open: observe the person and listen to them; notice body language; ask for clarification if anything isn't clear; reflect back what you are told to make sure that you have understood and that the Receiver feels heard and affirmed.

At this point of gathering information, be aware that prayer ministry may not be the right thing at this time. If you decide to go ahead, wait until you have seen how the person responds to ministry in the second session before making a firm commitment to proceed.

14. If the Receiver seems to be suicidal or depressed, refer them to their doctor immediately and encourage them to seek counselling.

15. If the Receiver is suffering a recent bereavement they may benefit from bereavement counselling. Give them the contact details of an organisation that provides this.

16. When the person has left after their first session, make notes of any main areas for ministry, such as:
- angry with mother
- absent father
- low self-image
- negative thoughts
- rejection issues
- needs to forgive...
- needs...
  – anything at all that has stood out as a possible issue.

17. At end of the initial time of chatting, once you are satisfied that you have a clear picture of the Receiver's situation, finish with a closing prayer inviting the Holy Spirit to bring healing.

18. In this time of prayer at the end, you may want to include a simple "visual rooms" exercise (see Chapter 11). Ask the Receiver to see themselves at home somewhere.

Ask where this is and then continue with the exercise. Explain that today you will not be addressing any of the main issues, only taking them through visualising Jesus coming to meet with them in some safe and comfortable area of their home. It can be very revealing to notice the Receiver's experience and responses in welcoming Jesus into the familiar territory of their home. It provides an opportunity for you to see how responsive they are to visualisation. The Receiver may have been very anxious at coming to the first session, and not overloading it means they can go home without feeling exhausted.

19. Once the Receiver has left discuss the area of need and anything you both noticed with your ministry partner. If there was anything of a disturbing nature disclosed by the Receiver, pray for each other.

SESSIONS 2–6

At the second session, explain that from now on the sessions will consist of prayer ministry. You will be inviting the Holy Spirit to come and surface the root cause of what the Receiver is suffering.

Ask if they have been having any memorable dreams in recent times. The feelings accompanying the dreams are often significant. Encourage the Receiver to keep pen and pad by the bed to record anything significant on waking.

The Receiver may start to tell you about their emotional or mental state during the week. Listen, but don't get into any counselling mode. Be directive that the session this time will consist of prayer ministry.

If appropriate explain that the Bible says our body is the temple (house) of the Holy Spirit. Ask "How many rooms of the house have you invited the Holy Spirit to enter into?" Suggest the Receiver open up all the rooms to Him. Suggest they do this out loud. Encourage the Receiver to take time welcoming Him. This can be helpful to people who find it difficult to receive.

1. Encourage the person to relax.

2. Invite the Holy Spirit to come – placing your hand gently on the Receiver's head.

3. Ask the person to surrender their intellect to Him – our mind gets in the way. Encourage them to surrender their mind and memories to Him.

4. Invite the Holy Spirit into:
    *   mind
    *   body
    *   spirit
    *   will
    *   emotions
    *   memories
    *   past hurts.

5. Now **wait** and observe. Give Jesus space and time.

6. Ask the Holy Spirit to surface anything He wants to heal today.

7. **Wait** (pray in the Spirit).

8. Reassure – "It's okay; don't strive."

9. **Wait**. Sometimes people may start to move their eyes under their eyelids as if seeing something. If so, ask what they are seeing – are they remembering something?

10. Sometimes a tear may fall. Ask "What feelings are surfacing?" Don't worry if there are none at this stage.

11. Ask Jesus to surface anything **key** that He wants to deal with. We don't have to remember everything – only the key things that need healing.

12. Ask the Receiver to invite Jesus into their memories, or ask Jesus to show the Receiver the root cause underlying their suffering – whatever seems right, as the Spirit leads you. Encourage the Receiver not to strive but to allow the Holy Spirit to show them anything from the

past still affecting present experience.

13. Ask the Receiver if they are experiencing any emotions or if they are recalling any memories. Often the Receiver will say, "This sounds silly but..." Reassure them that nothing that happens is silly, and encourage them to share what is happening.

14. Watch the person's body language. If the body starts reacting, ask what is happening.

15. Take direction from the Holy Spirit on how to proceed.

If the Receiver discloses occult activity or it is manifesting, bind it in Jesus' name and speak with someone in leadership in the church about it later.

Some people think or fear they have an evil spirit when often they haven't. As always, listen to the Holy Spirit and track what He is doing.

Only rarely would I conclude that someone has a demon, and I would certainly not tell anyone they were demonised. If I had been mistaken, I would have created a serious pastoral problem needing careful follow up.

Sometimes people come for help convinced they have a demon because they have habits of sin hard to shake off – they think it must be a demon, when in reality they have an undisciplined "old nature" which is responsible for the sins they commit (see Romans 7:21–23).

This needs to be resisted but it cannot be cast out. When under the power of the Holy Spirit people may cry out and thrash around, but this is not necessarily a symptom of demonisation. Often it is a person's response to past hurts that have been repressed. As the Holy Spirit brings these to the surface, they may first feel the pain before the Holy Spirit heals it.

If you receive a prophetic word or picture, be sensitive about when and how to share it. Minister it to the person by turning it into a prayer,[1] rather than just telling the Receiver you have a picture, as that can distract them or bring them out of the place they are in with Jesus. The attention is suddenly on you and your picture! If the Receiver responds in any way to the prayer you can then offer the picture. Timing is important.

Reassure them: "You are safe – Jesus is here."

If nothing seems to be happening, the person may feel peaceful even though nothing significant is manifesting. Sometimes the Lord works quietly with people; we don't need to rush the ministry.

This may be the moment to do one of the "room" exercises as a child (see Chapter 11).

1. Encourage the child to go and open the door.
2. Encourage the Receiver to tell Jesus anything they want to.
3. DON'T SUGGEST ANYTHING: LET THE HOLY SPIRIT DO IT.
4. Ask Jesus to do what He wants to do.
5. Ask Him to comfort the child and give them safety and security.
6. You could say, "Let that little girl/little boy receive the love of Jesus" or, "Let that girl/boy tell Jesus what is hurting her/him."

It's amazing what this can lead to.

ANGER

A great book on this subject is *Healing Life's Hurts: Make Your Anger Work for You* by Graham Bretherick.

Many Christians seem to think anger is wrong, so those who have grown up in a Christian home may have had parents who suppressed their own anger, or punished a child who displayed anger. But in reality, anger is an emotion given to us by God as a release valve. It is part of the "fight or flight" response that keeps us safe if we are in danger. A whole host of automatic responses occur in our body when we get angry:

- Adrenalin epinephrine is pumped into the body. It increases the heart rate, enlarges pupils and increases mental accuracy.
- Cortisol is given out into the body, activating the immune system and increasing blood flow.
- Glucagon is released into the body, releasing sugar (energy) from the liver into the blood stream.
- Thyroxin is freed into the body. It regulates our metabolism to keep things in balance during the stress period.
- The pituitary gland is activated, releasing hormones that trigger the other hormones to energise us.

Wow! That is incredible, isn't it? Anger is a powerful energy that can strengthen us to move quickly when danger is imminent.

Of course we get angry when we are not in danger but may feel threatened in some way, or get angry when things are not going our own way. Hopefully we can all improve in how we express ourselves when this happens.

A healthy way of expressing anger is to let out a noise such as "AAAAARRRRGGGGHHHH!!!". This is a great release, and though it may make people jump, it doesn't verbally attack them or physically harm them.

By contrast, for some the pattern of anger displayed when growing up may have been violent or frightening. The sight of a parent out of control can terrify and distress a child. As a result, the child may react by vowing never to be out of control like that, choosing instead to suppress their anger. This creates a ticking time bomb.

Those who have been abused may have pushed down their anger, powerless to react, and it may be festering inside, turning bitter and growing into hatred. This is like poison in the body.

The complication, if this has been the case, is that as the child has matured, the adult may have judged the child within who is angry. This may silence the child within so that the anger/

bitterness/hatred is never allowed to surface. This can then lead into destructive behaviour (towards the self or towards others) and/or emotional or spiritual deadness.

We can see an example of festering anger in the Bible story of the life of King Saul. He saw David being more successful than he was in battle. He became jealous and angry. The anger festered into bitterness. We see that eventually the Lord allowed an evil spirit to torment him. This led to him attempting to kill his own son and David. Many times King Saul sent soldiers to kill David but every time he eluded him (1 Samuel 19).

If anger is modelled in the home in a good way, a child will grow up with a healthy attitude in how to display it. Many of us have grown up with unhealthy management of anger, and many are encouraged to believe anger is wrong and must be suppressed. I didn't used to show anger. I used to get upset instead. I wasn't shown a healthy model of anger. Because of her mental illness, my mother would retire to bed when she was angry, removing herself from her children as a punishment. When I was summoned to her bedside she would chastise me but when I apologised for making her angry she didn't restore the relationship by saying that she forgave me. She stayed in bed, causing me to believe that saying sorry didn't have any effect. As an adult I now realise that my mother had no idea that she was portraying unforgiveness. Her illness crippled her emotionally and mentally.

When I was a teenager my quiet, mild-tempered dad became mentally ill too. This caused him to shout in anger at least a couple of times every day. I came to the conclusion that anger was a bad thing that should not be expressed.

Only when I was writing my first book, for which I had to study anger in depth, did I become aware that I rarely showed anger. I discussed it with my daughters, who both said, "At last you have realised! It was really annoying when we were young. You used to get tearful when we did something wrong. That was much worse than if you'd got angry." I was amazed that they had never mentioned it before. I have to say that these days I have no problem whatsoever in expressing anger! After giving myself (and my inner child) permission to display anger, I had to learn what it was, and how to express it appropriately. At first it would course through my body and I would feel flushed with it. Then I learnt to give it a voice by using the energy to make a loud noise. I found I was very good at using my body by shaking my arms or stomping up the stairs.

Paul says, "In your anger do not sin" (Ephesians 4:26), which should offer us a clue that being angry is not sinful, but how we handle it can be.

Righteous indignation is appropriate; fits of rage are not (Galatians 5:20). We may feel righteous anger when we hear of children being abused in some way or become aware of gross injustice.

Self-control is a Christian virtue and a fruit of the Spirit: this then should be our aim, although for me I know I have more than the occasional lapse!

BODY LANGUAGE

When ministering to someone, watch their body language. The Receiver may start to form a fist or their body may go stiff all over when pain is surfacing. Some feel tension or pain in their stomach. Ask the Receiver if they feel angry. Ask them where they feel it in their body. Do not assume you know where that is.

Encourage them to let the anger surface. Reassure them that they are in a safe place. Let them know it doesn't matter what they say (some may be worried in case they swear and you will judge them). You will notice their body fighting to keep it in. Their breathing will become laboured.

Try not to get in the way. Grab some cushions or make some space, so the Receiver doesn't hurt themselves. Large seat cushions from a sofa are helpful. Encourage the Receiver to use their voice or body to release anger.

If the person struggles, finding it difficult to display their emotions, reassure them that it's safe to let go – it's okay. If they begin to make noises and feel embarrassed about that, encourage them to release the sound – it's safe to let go; it's okay.

Place the cushion or piled cushions in front of them. Get the Receiver to kneel or sit on the floor and encourage them if appropriate to hit out the anger onto the cushions.

At first their expression of anger may be tentative. Keep praying release and freedom. Keep encouraging them to let rip. For some it may help to think of the cushions as the people who have hurt them. The person is expressing anger without hurting anyone.

Often the Receiver has huge pent-up feelings and emotions about certain people. They may hate someone who abused them. Their suppressed anger is like a festering internal boil oozing pus.

Sometimes, rather than hitting out the Receiver needs to vocalise their feelings to precipitate release of the suppressed anger.

Some may prefer to kick or even strangle a cushion. Others may contain their anger in their body, and need to push it out by making a noise. Take your lead from what you see in the Receiver and from the Holy Spirit as you decide how to proceed.

Afterwards the Receiver often feels exhausted. Proceed as follows in your ministry:

1. Lead the Receiver to ask for forgiveness for bitterness or hatred or anything else that applies.

2. Help them receive forgiveness. Pronounce it over them in Jesus' name.

3. Lead them to extend to the perpetrator the forgiveness that they have received.

4. Explain that this is a rational choice they need to make even when their feelings may not want to comply, because it is a command of Jesus that will be part of their healing, and they need to make a start (Matthew 18:21–35).

5. As the Receiver starts to forgive the perpetrator, there may be lots of tears, and more pain may surface, especially as they vocalise "I forgive you for...", listing what has been done to them. This is part of owning the pain, so that it can be released.

6. For others it is helpful to imagine the perpetrator sitting opposite in a chair as the Receiver audibly forgives them. Place a chair opposite the Receiver as they are forgiving.

7. Encourage the Receiver to speak out their anger.

Throughout the whole process, keep checking with the Lord, asking Him what to do next, what He wants.

VENTING ANGER STORY

A few years ago I was ministering to a woman who had been repeatedly abused by her father; I used the exercise of placing a chair opposite her.

I sensed I should put an object on the chair for her to relate to. There was nothing in the bare room we were using except for a roll of loo paper that I had ready for her tears (I must explain that we were at a conference abroad and tissues were in short supply!). As we had nothing else, I placed the loo roll on the chair.

I said, "Here he is... This is your dad. What would you like to say to him?... Say anything you want to." Suddenly this quietly spoken woman started to laugh hysterically, shouting, "Yes... that's about right... just right... now I can wipe my **** on you. It is what you deserve. You have ruined my life... you disgust me. I hate you!"

She ranted on and on and then got hold of the toilet roll and threw it across the large empty room. She then took hold of the metal chair and threw that across the room, screaming out her pain. Fortunately the chair remained in one piece!

Afterwards she said she felt amazing. Poison inside her had been released.

I find it very satisfying seeing someone feel safe enough to let go of their suppressed feelings. Please do not feel worried about doing this. As long as you are following the direction of the Holy Spirit, everything will be okay.

RELINQUISHING A CHILD

I prayed for a woman called Jackie who was very distressed and sobbing deeply. She said she felt as if she were behind bars. Jackie told me that her son had experienced growth problems from three months old and now, aged six years, he still looked and acted like a three-month-old. In addition to this, her husband had left her a couple of years previously, after he'd had an affair. Jackie said she was always comparing her son with other children the same age and it upset her; she felt he had been robbed of his childhood. When I asked her about anger, she said she didn't think she should be angry. We spoke for a while – about everything that had happened and ways of displaying anger in a safe place. She said her feelings about her son were the biggest issue at that time.

Suddenly it struck me that Jackie needed to grieve the son who seemed to die when he was three months old – the death of dreams and aspirations for her son, the life she had projected for him that would no longer take place. I explained that she would need to bring that three-month-old son to Jesus at the cross, to see herself handing him over to Jesus. Jackie sobbed and sobbed as she said goodbye to all her plans that would never happen. She said goodbye to the child she had dreamed he could be. In her mind's eye Jackie handed over her baby son bodily to Jesus, placing him into Jesus' arms. I said, "He is safe with Jesus. He will never let him go."

She opened her eyes and looked at peace.

I knew Jackie was still on a journey with her healing and wholeness and would have other issues still to be dealt with, but I felt privileged to be part of her journey and see this part of the Lord's work in her life.

FEAR, FIGHT, FLIGHT, AND FREEZE

During a time of prayer ministry the Receiver may remember a time when they suffered terror. As well as the body's automatic response of fight or flight, our protection in danger, some may experience FREEZE. This is well demonstrated by certain animals in the wild. You may have seen on a TV wildlife documentary the phenomenon of an impala chased by a lion suddenly falling down as if dead. The lion goes up to the impala and walks away. The lion wants fresh meat it has killed and seems confused, perhaps because of the lack of the smell of fresh blood. Once the lion has gone the impala will stand up, shake itself, and off it goes. It seems as if it is shaking the fear and terror out of its body. It had almost become the lion's dinner!

As humans we experience this to a small extent in a state of shock. Our teeth may chatter, and our body tremor or shake.

STORY OF TERROR AND FREEZE

I was ministering to someone who had almost died in childbirth. She had had an emergency dash to the hospital from a home birth that hit problems – a journey of terror and shock. I realised that the mother was still holding the shock within her body. As I was ministering, I noticed her hand shake once or twice. I encouraged her to shake off the shock and terror of what she had experienced. She stood up and started to shake it off herself, from the inside out.

Although this started mildly, her breathing soon accelerated as she began releasing all the terror and trauma of what had happened. She started coughing and retching as she let go of those pent-up emotions. All the while I was encouraging her to be free of all that traumatic birth experience.

She looked completely different by now. We went on to work through some other issues – her fear of death, and her anxiety about her other child. A few weeks afterwards she sent me a note saying that from that day she had been given her life back.

A HELPFUL EXERCISE

The idea for this exercise came from the thought that we are usually relaxed when we are in bed and covered over.

Sometimes at the third or fourth session I will ask the Receiver if they are willing to try something different. I usually keep in the room a full-length pad from a garden recliner, a couple of throws, and a cushion. I will ask the Receiver if they want to lie on the small mattress on the floor with one throw under their body and the other as a cover. I explain that for about fifteen minutes I will just pray in the Spirit using my prayer language, and we will see at the end what Jesus has done. This will often relax the Receiver so that Jesus can come and do what He wants. If you don't pray in tongues, just think about Jesus and worship in the Spirit. Place your hand lightly on the person's shoulder. It is useful to sit on a small padded footstool as you do this, or you might end up with cramp or pins-and-needles from kneeling or sitting uncomfortably on the floor.

I have had some dramatic results with this exercise. It is interesting to observe the Receiver's body language. Some put the throw over their head. Others wrap it tightly around them like a bandage. Yet others leave it loose and sometimes only partly cover themselves. It is important that the Receiver is comfortable. Some people find it takes them a few minutes to get still. A lot of us are not familiar with silence.

The first time you try this, it will seem like a long time. At times I have seen the Receiver find amazing healing and release. At other times they have heard the Lord speak to them, showing them several connecting memories to a root cause of inner pain. Sometimes I see the Receiver place a hand on their stomach as they cry. I will then gently place my hand on top and continue to pray in the Spirit.

Only once have I had someone say they found the exercise difficult. One Receiver spent ten minutes struggling to relax before she finally felt peaceful. She was suffering from the results of chemotherapy.

One lady, from a group where I had shared about pastoral prayer ministry, put the exercise into practice on her way home. She visited a friend with cancer. During the exercise her friend felt that something had left her, and felt amazing afterwards.

This is also a practical exercise for those times when you have to minister to a lot of people one after the other. They can make appointments fifteen minutes apart. I have used this exercise with a large group of youth leaders – once for a total of four hours non-stop, with two five-minute comfort breaks! The first hour seemed endless! Then the time sped by. It was an awesome experience.

After the prayer ministry the youth leaders could go into another dedicated quiet room to continue receiving and "soaking" in His presence.

You may like to have music playing in the background as people sit quietly like this, but if so it should be instrumental music avoiding recognisable songs, as the familiarity and the words will claim attention, turning the songs into a distraction.

HOLDING

Although we don't need to hug people, occasionally the Lord may prompt us to do a ministry of "holding". This can precipitate massive healing. Some people have never been held. It is often a big need inside. It must be done in a sensitive and respectful way, having explained and sought permission beforehand. I have tried this on a number of occasions. Here are some of my observations:

1. Say to the Receiver: "I really sense that Father God wants to hold you in His arms. Would you like that? I sense that He wants to use me to demonstrate this by holding you in my arms. Are you comfortable with that? It is different from hugging. I hold you in my arms while I pray over you, and you can stop at any time."

2. Sit on the floor side by side and place an arm around the person. Sometimes they snuggle in.

3.   If a married couple is ministering and everyone is in agreement it can be very healing for a man to do the holding for either gender.

4.   While holding, pray in the Spirit or connect to the Holy Spirit, interceding for the person.

5.   This can be a very moving experience. Have tissues ready for all involved!

6.   Some people have been starved of touch.

7.   There will be a natural conclusion when you sense that it has come to an end. Just say "Amen", so the Receiver can come back from the ministry.

BASICS IN SHORTHAND

Here is a list in brief of some of the things that come up time and time again in PPM:

- confess
- repent
- receive forgiveness
- extend forgiveness
- surface... inner pain, unresolved anger
- declare ... who God is... who they are in Him... irrational beliefs are wrong
- choose... positive thoughts (countering habitual negative patterns), ways, beliefs
- proclaim... what Jesus has done and is still doing
- renounce... evil, vows
- release... give permission to inner child
- embrace... inner child, good things from past
- devour... healing Scriptures
- arm... with two-edged sword, armour of God
- deny access... to enemy
- voice... let the inner child and adult have a voice
- break... soul-ties, power of lies.

PERSONAL HEALING OF A HORRIFIC MEMORY

I believe Jesus heals the effects of painful memories. We don't necessarily have to recall a memory for Jesus to heal its effect, but I have known Jesus visit a bad memory and bring healing into it. He once healed me of a horrific memory, at the same time releasing me from unforgiveness and judgment.

I have already mentioned that our two-year-old daughter Joanna drowned in our garden swimming pool. The memory that I never wanted to recall was when doctors were trying to save her life in the resuscitation room. They wanted me to remember something that had happened during the last week and speak to Joanna about it in an attempt to stimulate her brain, and kick start it back to life. As you can imagine, the responsibility of trying to come up with the right words to bring life was terrible. The sight of her lying there naked with tubes in her was one of my last memories of her.

There were two occasions a couple of years later when I visited young children in hospital. On both visits I saw a child naked with tubes in them. I nearly fainted and had to leave the hospital. I realised this was connected to my memory of Joanna in that resuscitation room.

I mentioned this to my friend Mary, and we met up at the end of the church service with a group of others for prayer ministry. As soon as the group started praying I fell to the floor under the power of the Holy Spirit. As soon as I hit the deck everything went blank. I had disassociated from the memory. Everyone seemed to be in the full swing of prayer and I didn't want to spoil their fun so I tugged on Mary's clothes to let her know I wasn't connecting with the ministry. Mary brought everything to a halt, explaining that I wasn't ready yet. She told me to ring her when the memory had surfaced and I felt ready.

The next day was terrible. All day long I kept thinking about my mum and how much I hated her for letting me down throughout my life. I felt bombarded with these memories. I became more and more angry with her. My head felt as if it would burst and I felt such hatred and loathing.

That evening I met up with Mary and another friend Margaret. I told them what had been happening during the day. As they asked the Holy Spirit to come upon me, I started to vocalise my feelings against my mother. I was crying and letting out my anger. When I had nothing left and felt quite limp, Mary said I needed to say sorry to Jesus for all my hatred, loathing, and bitterness concerning my mother, and receive His forgiveness. This I did. Then she said, "Now extend to your mother the forgiveness you have just received." Through gritted teeth, I did it. I felt the relief one feels after vomiting. I was exhausted but free.

Then I said thank you to my two friends, and was about to leave when they asked if there was anything else I wanted prayer for. Suddenly it clicked. I realised that I had judged my mother for letting me down, but I also felt that I had let Joanna down, by allowing her to fall into the swimming pool and then not finding words to bring her back as she lay in that resuscitation room.

I explained this, and agreed to let Jesus come and bring healing to that memory.

As they started to pray I saw a thick blackness engulfing me. It was horrible. I knew I had to push through this to get into the memory I feared, because it was blocking my freedom. I used my will to push through the fear of that memory and suddenly it cleared as I let out an ear-piercing scream (I believe I may have received deliverance then from a spirit of fear). Suddenly the memory returned and I opened the door into the resuscitation room. It was as vivid as if I was there in real time.

I saw Joanna lying there naked with the tubes in her. I explained to Mary and Margaret what was happening. Mary said, "Look for Jesus there. Ask for Him to be there."

At first I just tried to conjure Jesus up out of my mind, but that wasn't working. I started to feel a bit panicky and scared. I said out loud, "Jesus, please come and be here with me in this memory; I need You!" Suddenly I sensed the presence of Jesus there, and the whole scene changed. Instead of standing near Joanna's head I was seeing the room from the ceiling looking down. Then everything spun around and now I could see Joanna from the feet up, lying there. I saw two hands, just from the wrist down, dipping into a large jar of beautifully fragrant ointment, the pure nard mentioned in the Bible (John 12:13) when the woman anointed Jesus. As the hands came out of the big jar they spread the ointment all over Joanna's body. At the same time I heard the words, "I am preparing her for her burial." As I heard and saw this I started to cry again, saying, "I didn't know You would do that for her; I thought this was for You." I found myself repeating this over and over, crying. Later, Mary said this went on for half an hour! I felt so overwhelmed by the beauty of what I had just seen and experienced.

I was overcome by the most incredible joy at what I had witnessed. That my Jesus, who had been anointed by a woman with pure nard, should do the same thing for my child to bring me healing and to get her ready to be with Him, was the most beautiful thing.

Something else that amazed me was that the hands I saw spreading the ointment were the same ones I had seen before I became a Christian. For many months, when I shut my eyes I would see two hands leading me somewhere. With my eyes closed I had an impression of these same hands. I believe this was the Holy Spirit drawing me to Jesus.

It would be blasphemous to me to make up a story like this, as I knew that this same thing happened to Jesus. What I didn't know, until I looked the story up later (Matthew 26:12), was that it was *in preparation for **His** burial* that the woman anointed Jesus. These were exactly the same words He said to me about Joanna! For a few years I often revisited this place of healing; each time it brought me joy.

This new memory and these images have stayed with me as clearly as when this first happened over thirty years ago. It still moves me to tears; but tears of joy. How amazing is our Jesus, who can change something so horrific into something so precious and beautiful.

Jesus said, "Let the little children come to me and do not hinder them, for the kingdom of heaven belongs to such as these."

Matthew 19:14

Then Mary took about a pint of pure nard, an expensive perfume; she poured it on Jesus' feet and wiped his feet with her hair. And the house was filled with the fragrance of the perfume.

John 12:3

[Jesus said,] "When she poured this perfume on my body, she did it to prepare me for burial."

Matthew 26:12

[Jesus also said,] "Wherever this gospel is preached throughout the world, what she has done will also be told, in memory of her."

Matthew 26:13

Notes

1. Turning a picture into a prayer could be as simple as seeing a picture of a dark cloud over the Receiver and praying, "Jesus, please come to anything hanging over [name] that they dread or any foreboding or expectation of evil."

Chapter 14

IDENTITY AND LOSS

WHAT IS OUR IDENTITY?

Am I what the media or culture says I am?
Am I who my parents say I am?
Am I what others say about me?
Am I what I look like?
Am I what my abuser said I am?
Am I who God says I am?
Am I what I do as a job?
Am I the names I am called or my nicknames?

Our identity, the sense of who we are in relation to the world around us, comes from our parents and siblings, our teachers and friends – and maybe from our enemies too.

My birth name is Jean, but I have never liked it because *seven* other girls had the same name as me in my class at primary school! My dad called me a special name but it wasn't the sort of name I wanted others to call me. When I became a Christian at the age of thirty, I sensed Jesus say that He was giving me a new name – Jeannie. This meant so much to me. I felt like a new person. It seemed to sum up who I really was.

Human beings feel a deep need to belong. In a young person the search for identity will be displayed by the way they dress and what music they like to listen to. In adult life, the status conferred by our job may supply our identity. Then, if we are made redundant, or when we reach retirement age, we can feel devastated, lost. Or we may derive our identity from our marriage and parenthood – only to find we don't know who we are any more when our children grow up and leave home, or if we lose our partner through death or divorce. We need to have a surer foundation to our identity than our occupation or the other people in our life. If we grew up in a Christian family, we may have been taught who God is, and who we are in relation to Him. This is the foundation that will never let us down. It will affect our self-worth and self-esteem. Those who have grown up without this secure identity may have to work through the false identities projected onto them by how others see them – sometimes in formation from a very early age. Those who have suffered abuse may especially easily form a mistaken view of who they are, seen through the eyes and attitudes of the perpetrator.

Children need affirmation in their sexuality, their character, their sense of where they belong, and the knowledge that (right or wrong) they will always be loved. They must be free to fail as well as succeed. This gives them the confidence to explore new things, to develop and grow, so that one day when they leave the family home they will be ready to embark on a fulfilled life of their own.

MAKING A CHOICE

Choice is involved in establishing true identity. Some may have to reject false identities projected onto them by others before who they truly are can emerge. Others may have been stunted by circumstances, never able to fulfil their true potential: in Jesus they find the courage and faith to grow into who they were really meant to be.

The Holy Spirit affirms our identity: "The Spirit himself testifies with our spirit that we are God's children" (Romans 8:16).

During prayer ministry, ask Jesus to show the Receiver how their siblings, parents, carers, friends, teachers, or bullies may have shaped aspects of their identity by speaking negatively. Suggest they have the choice not to live this out any more – to throw it off; to jump up and walk towards Jesus, to receive what He is giving them. As always, proceed as the Holy Spirit directs: memories may surface at this time.

TAKING OFF THE GRAVE CLOTHES

Lazarus was buried in a cave (John 11). Jesus didn't go in and get him when he raised him from the dead. He called out to him in a loud voice: "Lazarus! Come out!" Still all tangled up in the linen wrappings of a corpse and with a cloth over his face, Lazarus came stumbling out of the cave. Then Jesus drew others into His miracle, saying, "Take off the grave clothes, and let him go free!" This is what we are doing in pastoral prayer ministry. At times I have sensed the prompting of the Holy Spirit to call someone from "out of a cave", either somewhere they have retreated deep inside or a place that is death for them – a safe, familiar place maybe; but a dead place nonetheless. Either they have chosen to go there or they have been pushed there through the abuse of others. For some it is as if they have given up on life. Just like Lazarus they are dead inside their cave.

When calling someone from out of this place you may have to speak it out more than once, encouraging the person to put their will behind what they are doing. To begin with, assess the response in their body language. Communicate with the Receiver who has been struggling with the experience of being almost buried alive.

A SPACIOUS PLACE

The Bible tells us, "He brought me out into a spacious place" (Psalm 18:19). In ministry I sometimes use these words, saying, "Jesus wants to call you out into a spacious place – listen for His voice!"

Often after a pause in the prayer ministry the Receiver may say, "Just before you started saying that, I heard Jesus calling my name. It was really strong and I could feel something inside me responding, but in my mind I was resisting. He called out again; and this time I chose to go where He was calling me."

It would be good for the Receiver to go home from the ministry with some Scriptures to read through, about who God is and who we are in Him. They will grow spiritually by proclaiming out loud these Scriptures. A wonderful verse affirming our identity is: "See what great love the Father has lavished on us, that we should be called children of God! And that is what we are! The reason the world does not know us is that it did not know him" (1 John 3:1). Chapter 18 contains a list of additional Scriptures.

MINISTRY RECAP

Pastoral prayer ministry may include any of the following, not necessarily in this order:

1. Pray-er to invite Holy Spirit to come, and wait.
2. Receiver to make choice and walk towards Jesus.
3. Receiver to throw off whatever hinders them from receiving healing.
4. Pray-er to ask Holy Spirit to surface any root memories/feelings relating to identity.
5. Pray-er to ask Jesus to come and minister to memories (if appropriate).
6. Receiver to make a choice aloud to become the person Jesus intended.
7. Receiver to declare who they are not.
8. Receiver to affirm who they are.

During this time these areas may need to be dealt with:

- Receiver to renounce any false identity resulting from abuse.
- Pray-er/Receiver to identify any irrational beliefs and deal with them by Receiver renouncing them out loud as untrue.
- Receiver/Pray-er to identify any vows made and renounce.
- Receiver/Pray-er to identify and deal with any lies believed.

- Pray-er to identify any guilt and shame, and minister accordingly.
- Pray-er to identify and address low self-worth and self-esteem via root memories.
- Pray-er to call Receiver out of cave (if appropriate).
- Receiver to receive from Jesus their identity.
- Pray-er to give appropriate worksheets and Scriptures.

Refer to contents page for the various areas of ministry.

SELF-WORTH/SELF-ESTEEM

As well as identity issues some may have a lack of self-worth, with the associated low self-esteem and problems of self-image. This can take a while for a person to work through. If the Receiver finds background reading helpful, I can recommend either Mary Pytches' book *Who Am I?* or my book *Let the Healing Begin* (with exercises after every chapter). If out of print, they are available second-hand online. See also Chapter 18.

As the Receiver is working through one of these books, it will help the prayer ministry if you work together with them, focusing especially on exercises where they are stuck and ministering into areas with which they strongly identify.

So many different life experiences can damage self-worth, self-esteem and self-image. Ask Jesus to show the root causes and memories, and to surface the pain relating to them. Ask the Holy Spirit if any vows, lies, irrational beliefs, or bereavements need addressing. There could also be areas of guilt and shame from abuse.

As well as receiving ministry into these areas, in between sessions it would be good for the Receiver to do the following:

- Pray for their own healing daily.
- Read Scriptures from worksheets, and declare who God is and who they are in relationship to Him. (The emotionally absent parents worksheet in Chapter 18 is of particular relevance.)

- Worship Jesus for a short time every day.
- Read the Bible every day, even just a few verses.
- If they are unable to do this for some reason, then at least regularly invite the Holy Spirit and welcome in the presence of Jesus.
- Every day between sessions, work through some part of the worksheet you have given them, relevant to their need and situation.

EMOTIONALLY ABSENT PARENTS

The parent who is physically present but ignores or neglects their child can make the child feel invisible, of no account. The child can feel that everything and anything else is more important to the parent. I have heard Receivers say, "I felt as if I melted into the wallpaper", "I didn't feel as if I existed." They are left with the impression that their parent's career, their social life, their hobby, even the TV or the newspaper, was far more important than the child in their parent's life. It is a huge loss. Not only does the child suffer deep bereavement, but because a child usually believes in their parents uncritically, they often feel they must be to blame, thinking there must be something severely wrong with them to deserve this neglect and rejection. This sense of inferiority inevitably affects a child's identity – it alters their sense of who they are and where they belong. The good news is that healing can take place in all these areas.

Healing of the damage done by emotionally absent parents may include (in no particular order):

- receiving healing in root memories
- repenting of bitterness/hatred
- receiving forgiveness
- extending forgiveness to parent/s
- healing roots of rejection and inferiority
- surrendering of guilt and shame
- surfacing of any suppressed anger

- receiving the Father's love
- receiving the mothering of Father God
- receiving affirmation from Father God.

HEALING STORY: ABSENT PARENT AND IDENTITY

At an overseas conference, Ken and I met Dave, who had been on medication to control Obsessive Compulsive Disorder for more than ten years. This disorder was encroaching more and more into his life, and he wanted prayer ministry for it.

As my husband and I laid hands on him, the word "grief" came into my head. I asked Dave whether he was grieving over something in his life. He told us his story. His mother, a Christian, had an affair with a married man – the pastor of her church. She conceived a child, Dave. When the pastor heard that his mistress was pregnant, he abandoned her, the child, his wife, his church, and left the area, never to be seen again. His dad the pastor not only sinned against his wife, his mistress, and his son, he also sinned against his church and the Lord.

Dave grew up never meeting or knowing his dad. As Dave told us this story, into my head came the Bible story of the man born blind. He was accused by the Pharisees, "You were steeped in sin at your birth." I realised that Dave was carrying the guilt of both parents' sin. He felt *he* was steeped in sin at his birth! I asked him if this was so. He agreed. Dave was carrying a massive amount of false guilt and shame. This had become his identity. He had been the child whose conception caused a marriage to break up, his mother to be abandoned to the struggle of single parenthood, and a pastor to leave the church and community in disgrace. As the psalmist said, "Surely I was sinful at birth, sinful from the time my mother conceived me" (Psalm 51:5). This was how Dave felt about himself. He needed to give up this false identity to find out who he really was. It was a real battle for him. He said, "If I give it up, I won't know who I am."

We asked Dave to bring that guilt and shame to Jesus at the cross, where it belonged, and surrender it. It wasn't his sin

– he had done no wrong. It was his parents who had acted in sin. When he did this, he found great relief.

Then I noticed his hands forming a fist as his whole body stiffened. I asked him whom he was angry with. He replied, "My dad."

Dave had been carrying all that guilt and shame, as well as anger that had affected not only his identity but his temperament – he was an extremely anxious person. His compulsive disorder was his attempt to lessen and control his anxiety. It was a coping strategy. Having a compulsive disorder also made him anxious and ashamed.

Dave struggled a while to release his anger. He didn't want to let his dad off the hook. Also his anger made him feel more powerful instead of weak. But at last Dave was able let go of his anger. All the while my husband and I had our hands laid on his lower back, encouraging him to let any pain surface, and let it go. We were speaking words of release and freedom.

After this we realised Dave longed for a father. His heavenly Father had His arms open wide to Dave, but Dave's arms were already full. Dave needed to let go of his longing for an earthly father so that his empty arms could receive what his Father God wanted to give him. Dave's arms were also full of his victim identity, resulting in blame. I asked him to bring all this stuff and lay it down at the feet of Jesus.

This touched another part of Dave's identity. He said, "What would I be left with? I wouldn't know who I was." I answered, "Yes, you would. You would know that you belonged to your heavenly Father. The thing is, you haven't met Him yet." For a while Dave struggled over this challenge. Then in a loud groan he chose to give it all up in Jesus' name. He confessed all his big feelings against his dad and received forgiveness. Then, after receiving forgiveness himself, he released forgiveness to his earthly father for sinning against Dave and leaving him.

Bit by bit he got rid of the stuff that filled his arms. Then I said, "Dave, take Jesus' hand and ask Him to take you to meet your heavenly Father." We watched (me with tears in my eyes) as Dave called out, "Father!" What happened next was extraordinary. Only God Himself could have orchestrated it. As Dave had his arms outstretched meeting his heavenly Father, the worship song "The Father's Song" was being sung by Matt Redman from inside the marquee where the conference was continuing without us. It was a wonderful moment. Dave's tears were streaming down his face, as with a mixture of crying and laughing he continued to receive freedom and healing. At that moment my husband Ken gave Dave his hanky (fortunately it was clean!) saying, "As a father would give to his son, take this as if from your heavenly Father." Dave took the hanky, and wiped his eyes, face, and nose. I was so touched by this typical gesture from a father to his son. We had some tissues but Ken felt his action was symbolic, and felt a prompting from the Lord that it would bring some healing – which it did!

Dave laundered the hanky and a couple of months later emailed me to say that he treasured it as a reminder of the healing he received that day. Three months later, he emailed to say that he had seen his doctor and been taken off his medication, as all his OCD symptoms had stopped. A year later, when we saw Dave again, he was still free of all his symptoms.

Thank You, Father God, that we are Your children!

LOSS

Bereavement and loss can arise through a wide variety of circumstances – anything from the disappointment of plans that fail to materialise, through to a robbery or the traumatic losses of rape, disability, or death. There are a whole host of situations that involve loss, such as never knowing your biological parents or growing up in the home of an alcoholic. This loss can leave a gaping hole within.

Some try to fill up this space with something such as excessive spending, excessive sex in and outside of marriage, recreational drugs, or addictions to alcohol, gambling, and food. Some under-eat or over-eat; some binge-eat and vomit it back up.

GRIEVING

Grieving a loss is significant. It is genuine acceptance that we have lost something we can never have again. Sometimes even giving permission to the Receiver to grieve is helpful. For those who have suffered the death of someone they love, or who have a loved one with dementia or Alzheimer's, bereavement counselling would be beneficial.

Grieving can involve the following stages: shock, trauma, denial, anger, guilt, shame, excessive sorrow, depression. The grieving person can go in and out of these stages in no particular order at no particular time. They can keep visiting these stages: they are not necessarily progressive. Usually the person needs to come to the point where they accept their loss and say goodbye before they can come out the other side sufficiently to enjoy life to the full again. The stage of depression can be the time when acceptance of the loss begins, though anyone stuck in this stage needs to see their doctor.

It would benefit the grieving person to read either a book about the subject of loss and grief or a book written by someone who has had several bereavements and come out the other side more whole: *Growing Through Loss and Grief*, by Althea Pearson, and *When Heaven is Silent*, by Ronald Dunn.

If a person gets stuck in an aspect of grief, they may find prayer ministry helpful, especially the comfort and counsel of the Holy Spirit. Some of the exercises already mentioned may be useful; for example, through visualising, the grieving person can take the person who has died to Jesus at the cross so that they can say goodbye to them, relinquishing them to Jesus. Also, saying out loud the things they never said to the person might be helpful. Look through the contents page for suitable headings that might apply.

When someone we love dies it can knock open other wounds or scars that we thought were healed. Sometimes it is because they were only part-healed. Often this can be an opportunity to receive healing into the current loss as well as the past one. I have ministered to those who are grieving the death of a parent and this loss has surfaced some other grief that had never been addressed – for instance some abuse that had happened in childhood at the hands of another family member.

Although no one would choose to suffer grief and bereavement, if we allow it to, growth can come from our losses.

Think of a beautiful flower: when the petals fall and it dies it exposes the seeds as they fall into the ground. Just one seed from that plant, the following year, will produce a flower that has many seeds.

> **Very truly I tell you, unless a kernel of wheat falls to the ground and dies, it remains only a single seed. But if it dies, it produces many seeds.**
>
> John 12:24

Suffering a deep loss and then receiving healing from God can also give us something to give away to others:

> **... who comforts us in all our troubles, so that we can comfort those in any trouble with the comfort we ourselves receive from God.**
>
> 2 Corinthians 1:4

> **A Man of sorrows acquainted with grief... surely He has borne our griefs and carried our sorrows.**
>
> Isaiah 53:3–4 NKJV

HANNAH'S STORY OF LOSS AND IDENTITY

Hannah had been sexually abused repeatedly as a baby by her father, while others molested her and abused her emotionally. Her father was imprisoned for the abuse, and her parents divorced.

As you can imagine Hannah's self-worth and self-esteem were very low when I met her; she felt disgusted at herself. After several sessions Hannah started to get healed up. Her desire was to articulate her feelings, but this seemed to elude her. She struggled to make sense of what had happened to her. All she had suffered had a huge impact on her identity. She didn't know who she was.

Hannah was also tortured by guilt (as most people who have been abused usually are). All she had ever wanted was to be loved, and this was something that she had never experienced. She had a good relationship with Jesus but didn't really know her heavenly Father. Hannah realised the child within her had suffered such a lack of affection that she never felt as if she belonged anywhere.

One day during a prayer time she allowed these feelings to surface, and invited Jesus to come and heal her deep-rooted sense of abandonment. Jesus came to her and showed her a house full of little children. She went into the house and joined them, playing and belonging. I had no idea what she was seeing, but at that same moment I quoted a verse from Scripture: "'My Father's house has many rooms... I am going there to prepare a place for you' – my Father's house, your Father's house" (John 14:2). I suddenly thought that this sounded like a funeral, like a death. I sensed Jesus saying, "Yes, a death to what was." I waited and prayed in silence allowing Jesus to do what He wanted to do. Tears flowed down my face as I sensed His healing presence and His love and compassion for that little girl within her. After a while I shared a picture I had seen. At the doorway stood a man with Hannah as a little girl, dressed beautifully as if at a royal ceremony. The man announced in a very loud voice, "Here is Hannah – she belongs to Jesus, she belongs to Father God." Then I saw her dressed as a princess. Again the man announced to everyone present, "Here is Hannah, daughter of the King!"

Jesus stamped His identity into the depths of her suffering. No words could do that – only the powerful love of the one who called her to Himself.

Hannah cried and cried as she received her very identity from the King Himself. He acknowledged her as belonging to Him. It was as if the Holy Spirit were announcing Hannah's identity in the spiritual realm as well as the earthly one (Romans 8:16). It was a holy moment.

She belongs to the King, she belongs to Jesus, and she is HIS. She held her hands on her chest as this realisation sank in, as she received it into the depths of her being. It was beautiful to watch such a healing.

Afterwards she said that she realised she would never be the same again – it was a life-changing event for her. Hannah knew that God had given her a place to visit again and again, a place of belonging. She said she knew that when she got into bed every night she could surrender herself to the One who would comfort her – who would visit her to say goodnight. She would have all the things she had never experienced as that little girl. Thank You, Jesus, for healing that part of Hannah.

MINISTRY TO LOSS

Ministry to loss may contain the following, in no particular order:

1. Receiver to bring the person or circumstance and surrender it to Jesus.

2. Pray-er to ask the Holy Spirit into areas where the Receiver is "stuck".

3. Pray-er to use "visual rooms" exercise to receive Jesus and speak to Him, and receive healing (see Chapter 11).

4. Pray-er to ask Holy Spirit to surface any root memories that may need healing.

5. Pray-er to help Receiver deal with areas or guilt and shame (see Chapter 8).

6. Pray-er to invite Jesus to come and share sorrow, and weep and grieve with person.

7. Pray-er to invite Jesus to come and hold Receiver in His arms.

8. Pray-er to invite Jesus into the "gaping hole" inside, to fill it with His love.

9. Pray-er to ask Jesus to take the inner child to meet our heavenly Father (if appropriate).

10. Pray-er to ask Jesus to restore what has been lost.

Be open to other areas into which the Holy Spirit may lead you.

REJECTION AND SELF-REJECTION

The loss and emotional wounding of rejection from childhood can cut deep within, especially for those who have been adopted. Even with love and security in their life with non-biological parents, such feelings persist for some. It is common for those suffering rejection in their turn to reject others. Both areas need addressing. There may also be a sense of abandonment, accompanied by issues of anger, resentment, and rebellion. God is love, and His love can reach the deepest, darkest place. Therapy or counselling could be very helpful before prayer ministry for those who were abandoned as children, or who carry a sense of abandonment because they know their birth mother gave them up for adoption or fostering. For some, feelings of rejection are constant; others experience different intensities depending on their history. Often people who have a strong sense of rejection find friends with similar issues.

Rejection undermines the capacity to give and receive love and acceptance. Often there is a need for healing of the spirit through releasing forgiveness to those who caused the original pain. The grief is for what has been lost – and that can be an imagined past as well as a real past; people often idealise what they did not experience. The Receiver will have a need to feel significant. One of the "visual rooms" exercises could help with this (see Chapter 11). From just one occasion of significant rejection, further moments of rejection can accumulate. It is as if the Receiver has "reject me" written on their forehead. The Receiver may have lots of memories of rejection in their mind, but ask Jesus to show them the root times. This is the area to minister into. Those with deep issues of rejection may also suffer bouts of depression. It would be good for the Receiver to surrender all words and labels such as "reject", "failure", "worthless", and "victim" to Jesus.

A sense of rejection can grow within from the seed-thought of an off-the-cuff remark by a parent mentioning that their birth was not planned. Some more insensitive parents may have even described the child as a "mistake".

Some children grow up with a sense of rejection because they believe their sibling to have been favoured by their parents.

But healing begins when we take hold of the Bible's teaching that our parents didn't give us life – God Himself did!

> **The Spirit of God has made me; the breath of the Almighty gives me life.**
>
> Job 33:4

> **Rather, he himself gives everyone life and breath and everything else.**
>
> Acts 17:25

> **... all the days ordained for me were written in your book before one of them came to be.**
>
> Psalm 139:16

Self-rejection can result from perceived rejection by others. This seems to push the person even deeper, and will need to be addressed separately. Usually the person will have low self-worth, low self-esteem, inferiority, and identity issues. They may also need to grieve their loss of feeling accepted.

> **For everything God created is good, and nothing is to be rejected if it is received with thanksgiving, because it is consecrated by the word of God and prayer.**
>
> 1 Timothy 4:4–5

The Receiver needs to admit and own the pain of rejection. Then they need to grieve and release the pain of both rejection and perceived rejection. The perpetrator/s of rejection will need to be forgiven also. This will have to be done repeatedly until all the pain has gone. There may also be need for deliverance.

Self-rejection is often linked with self-hatred. Both these bonds can be broken by the person; it's their choice. The enemy loves keeping people tied up to these huge destructive thoughts and actions. The outcome of self-rejection and self-hatred can be symptomised by self-abuse, including eating disorders, self-harm, drug abuse, alcohol abuse and promiscuity. For more on this, see the section on self-hatred in Chapter 15.

MINISTRY FOR THOSE SUFFERING REJECTION

1. Invite the Holy Spirit on the whole person, including mind, emotions, and memories. The Receiver needs to give Jesus permission to come into their memories. **Wait**. *Then either*:
*   Ask Jesus to surface their inner pain. If appropriate, identify any strong feelings towards the person/s who did the rejecting.
*   Release suppressed anger in Jesus' name. If the Receiver is crying, place a hand on their stomach or the small of their back and speak release with Jesus' authority.
*   Receiver may need to be vocal in saying things never previously expressed. Encourage them that they can say anything they like.

and/or:

*   Ask the Lord to show them any root cause of rejection.
2. At some point break the power of rejection. The Receiver will also need to ask for forgiveness for any bitterness and/or hatred or other sin. Then the forgiveness they have received should be extended to the perpetrator of rejection.
3. When appropriate, ask Jesus to bring His healing to the inner child/adult.

When someone has been damaged by someone else, strong emotions are often buried or suppressed in the subconscious. Christians frequently harbour buried, unresolved, unexpressed anger which can fester into bitterness, hatred, loathing, revenge, and a desire to bring harm to the other person to the extent of ultimate retaliation: physical attack. The sooner *that* lot is released the better for all concerned!

Rejection and self-rejection may create an entry point for the enemy to bind the person, so they may also need deliverance. For help with this, see Chapter 15. If the Receiver has issues of rebellion and hatred, these will need to be confessed and repented of.

ABUSE

There are many forms of abuse – physical, emotional, mental, sexual, and neglect; and these may be of varying levels. From the very first experience of abuse, it is as though the person has been branded with an invitation to further abuse – it creates a re-evaluation of self-worth. Since that first time there may have been many subsequent experiences of abuse. The Receiver may point to one instance, but the Lord may reveal a much earlier occasion. Sometimes the Receiver may think that the earliest time is not the most significant until the pain starts surfacing. Sometimes it is like peeling off layers. Usually the root and memories of abuse are the ones to aim for. When the pain is very acute the Receiver may initially refuse to let these memories surface. This can be the mind's way of protecting itself when it is too painful. Alternatively they may be disassociating from it. Either way, it is important to go gently, with all sensitivity and close reliance on the Holy Spirit's leading.

There may be an awareness by the Pray-er that something terrible has happened to the Receiver, but the Receiver will need to build up more trust in the Pray-er before allowing the pain to surface and the abuse to be remembered. Never suggest to someone that they have been abused. If they have been abused the pain will surface sooner or later, at the speed the Receiver can bear.

Be very careful with people who are having flashbacks (fragments of memory) of their abuse. This can be very frightening for them, as some abused people have never remembered it before, and flashbacks can keep recurring randomly during the day at the most unlikely times. People suffering in this way would be wise to seek specialist counselling or therapy.

Some who have been abused develop a victim mentality. To receive a full healing they will need to let this go and bring it to Jesus. Others may have adopted lots of coping strategies that get in the way of real healing and will need to be surrendered to Jesus.

Some live in denial and will need a process of gently peeling away protective layers before discovering the truth and receiving their healing from Jesus.

There is probably no way that our four to six sessions offered will be enough for cases of severe abuse, but prayer ministry is only part of their journey; it need not take them all the way. We minister to the presenting issues in someone's life, and this gives them the help they need to take things on at their own pace. Some may need professional therapy or specialist counselling, and it may be the prayer ministry that gives them courage to embark on getting professional help. Others may come for the four to six sessions then return a couple of months later for more. All healing comes from God (Exodus 15:26) whether it be through a doctor, a counsellor, or by prayer.

I have seen survivors of abuse receive the most amazing healing from Jesus through the ministry of prayer. Personally my aim is to ensure that the Receiver has the best possible help for what they are suffering. The Lord will guide you in whom to suggest if the person needs counselling (this is usually apparent at the first session), or if they should continue with the prayer ministry route.

It is important not to feel overwhelmed by someone's story. We need to keep a balance. Jesus knows all things; He is more than able to handle anything any one of us has ever suffered. I believe that if we are willing to be engaged in this ministry,

He will take us on a journey of learning. He is the Teacher, Counsellor, and Comforter. He knows what He is doing. He will show us what to do every step of the way.

Above all, the Receiver needs to know this is a "safe place" for them. Often, during a time of ministry, I reassure them, "You are safe", as they are remembering something painful; or I tell them, "You can let that go or let it out; this is a safe place."

Ask Jesus to surface anything He wants to heal today. Say to the Receiver, "As far as you are able, just allow Jesus to surface something He wants to heal." This gives the person assurance that it is okay; things are not going to get out of control. It is at their pace. After one or two sessions, the Receiver will start to feel more confident about even deeper ministry. Observe the Receiver's body language for any signs of discomfort or unease.

Possible areas of ministry include:

- grief/loss/deep sorrow
- betrayal
- rejection/self-rejection
- hatred/self-hatred
- suppressed anger
- guilt
- deep shame/remorse
- irrational beliefs
- lies
- vows
- revenge
- bitterness
- fear
- forgiveness
- absentee parents
- lack of self-worth/self-esteem
- inferiority
- disassociation

- separation from inner child
- judgment of inner child
- anger/hatred of inner child
- denial
- need to control.

Any of the above may manifest in the following illnesses and disorders:

- Obsessive Compulsive Disorder
- eating disorders
- sexual disorders
- addictions
- depression
- severe anxiety
- panic attacks
- suicidal thoughts
- personality disorders
- skin disorders
- mental illness
- physical ailments of various types.

This list may make the task seem overwhelming, but it doesn't all need addressing at once. Some people may simply need to talk through things they have never told anyone before. That is when it can be most helpful to seek out specialist counselling *before* prayer ministry. Then, when the Receiver comes for PPM there is less need to keep talking things over, and ministry can progress at a fast rate. Some may need long-term professional help, and should ask their doctor for referral to a specialist.

Areas covered by the prayer ministry may include:

- encouraging the grieving process
- surfacing inner pain and anger
- healing memories (they don't have to be recalled)
- finding their voice – the inner child

- experiencing safety and security through Jesus
- affirmation of heavenly Father
- receiving forgiveness for strong feelings against the perpetrator
- encouraging process of forgiving the perpetrator
- receiving the healing touch of Jesus
- surrendering a victim identity
- letting Jesus remove labels
- taking off labels themselves
- renouncing lies
- renouncing vows
- surrendering irrational beliefs
- letting go of self-hatred
- loving themselves
- letting go of fear and receiving God's perfect love
- taking off shame
- surrendering guilt
- receiving cleansing (if appropriate)
- surrendering the body to Jesus
- healing of the spirit
- healing of the soul
- renewing of the mind: conscious, unconscious, and imagination
- giving up a fantasy world
- embracing what it is to be male or female
- celebrating womanhood or manhood
- integrating adult and child within
- cutting soul-ties
- surrendering control to Jesus.

A very useful book to read in preparation for helping survivors of sexual abuse is Paula Sandford's *Healing Victims of Sexual Abuse*.

STILLBIRTH AND MISCARRIAGE

Our first child was stillborn. It happened forty years ago in the days when doctors and nurses tried to help the loss by taking the baby away immediately after it was born. Parents had no time to grieve. People were unaware of the damage this caused the parents. I never saw our stillborn little girl. To this day I don't know whether she was incinerated or buried in some unmarked grave. We never had any ceremony to mark her life and death. We didn't know we could have one and we were not encouraged to have one either. Grieving a child you have never seen is excruciating. There are no memories to grieve other than those in the womb.

During the pregnancy the mother will have imagined her child's life, thinking of names, of showing off the baby to family and friends, planning games and toys and happy times, considering where her child might go to school, and thinking of her baby playing together with her friends' babies. Suddenly all the plans stop. They are not to be.

Feelings of failure, guilt, shame, and anger pile on top of the already unbearable pain of loss and bereavement. It can feel like being run over by a truck. Some just feel numb with the shock.

It is difficult for the mother to feel that she fits in anywhere now. The parents of the child are a mother and father still, but no one relates to them as such if it is their firstborn. For me it felt as if I didn't fit in with those who had children and I didn't fit in with my friends who didn't have children. I was the oddity in the middle. The uncomfortable social embarrassment of friends not knowing what to say – even crossing the street to avoid me – added to the distress. This immense loss can become the unacknowledged elephant in the room.

During the time I was going through the awful grief following the death of our two-year-old, Joanna, I wrote about the terrible pain of grief and loss – not of Joanna, but of Sarah, my baby stillborn. As I went through some files in preparing this section, there it was, after all these years. What was true for me then remains true now: Jesus does not wave a magic wand and take all pain away leaving nothing but sunshine and smiles: He offers something deeper than that. He is with us in the very depths of our pain, as raw and agonising as it can be; and it is that (and only that) which can heal us.

A Loss So Deep

The cutting edge of loss
Cuts deeper every day.
A blunt blade getting sharper
As the wound is on display.
A raw erupting boil,
Oozing pus and splitting deeper.
As anger and resentment
Unwinds, making deeper.

The slimy pit with no escape
The numbness of the mind
Churning empty stomach,
Nothingness left behind.
The world moving on with speed,
I'm trapped going round and round.
I'm silently screaming:
Out of my mouth, comes no sound.

People speak in whispers,
A smile is on their lips.
"Are you getting over it now?"
Words making senseless drips.
No one seems to understand.
The nightmare is still here.
Everything inside is broken up.
Nothing at all seems clear.

Pointless parties are offered.
"You must come, it'll cheer you up."
Why am I not allowed to grieve?
My baby's dead – isn't that enough?
The baby isn't mentioned,
Glances are nervous when others don't know.
In come old friends who haven't a clue.
They glance away, and then glance below.

Now they're embarrassed,
Shall they risk it and ask?
How easy I could make it?
I think, "But why should I?"
I want to break their mask!
Everyone says, have another baby,
It's not like having a mug of tea!
I want **THAT** baby – the one that died,
That's the only answer for me!

I'm crying but no one can hear me.
My arms are wide, ready, and free.
They lay by my side empty,
By the breasts that are ready to feed.
Empty arms, empty womb,
I am a mother – but no baby
Ready to cuddle and caress.
All the clothes but nothing to dress!

I didn't see her lifeless body,
Eyes shut – never seeing the world
All she saw: the inside of my womb,
Untouched she died – untouched in her tomb.

She'll never be late for school,
She'll never have a friend,
She'll never plan any parties.

In the womb the beginning was the end.
She died where she was loved,
Inside the body that fed her.
Dear Jesus, my friend, draw me closer,
And let's face this pain together.

You know my pain,
You share it too.
YOU know the beginning and the end.
To the "why?" there is no answer,
But there's hope in your living and dying.
I put my trust in you now.
I let go of my baby to you.
We are all but on a journey,
She just got there far too soon...

I KNOW SHE IS ALIVE IN YOU

It may help a person facing a similar bereavement to contact one of the organisations that support parents:

SANDS Stillbirth and Neonatal Death Society:
www.uk-sands.org

The Birth Trauma Association:
www.birthtraumaassociation.org.uk

The Miscarriage Association:
www.miscarriageassociation.org.uk

Also bereavement counselling could help.

GRIEVING MOTHERS

Ministry needs to allow the person to get in touch with their grief and loss. Using the "room exercise" could be helpful. Sometimes the Receiver's grief may be cut off. Their mind may no longer be connecting with their emotions. This is why, for some, prayer ministry is often better after some counselling.

If the Receiver had a stillborn baby many years ago, the baby may never have been named. It can be a really powerful and moving ministry to be part of such a personal time for the Receiver. Just ask the Receiver what name they have for the baby and get them to speak it out, naming their child. This is very helpful to do if someone has had a miscarriage too. For some the gender of the baby was unknown; the Receiver can ask Jesus to tell them. It is very healing to picture bringing the baby to Jesus and handing the child over to Him. This may well be a hard thing for them to do, but encourage the Receiver to pursue this.

It is good to also encourage the Receiver to make a memory box (if it is a current bereavement), putting in anything and everything about their child. Every memory is precious. It could also be helpful for one or both parents to write a card to their child expressing their feelings, hopes, parental aspirations, and plans that will now never come to pass.

GRIEVING FATHERS

Fathers can feel a strong sense of failure and inadequacy, as well as grief and loss. They may find it difficult to talk about their loss with friends. Many internalise it. It can be helpful for men to do some sport or exercise that involves whacking the life out of something. This can help them get out pent-up strong feelings. Some may be helped by writing, drawing, or painting something to express how they feel.

Some men may need support when their wife is pregnant again. Some feel as if they want to run away in case of another failure. Men do not always deal with feelings and personal trauma before things become acute, especially if this is compounded with other losses they have never dealt with. The shock of the loss of their child may touch on other unresolved grief and loss. It may come as a shock when past pain surfaces. It can compound their grief into being unbearable, and some choose to run away rather than face it. For some this can be an opportune time to let past pain surface as well as the current loss.

Chapter 15

DELIVERANCE AND CLEANSING

This chapter covers the ministry of deliverance in a pastoral prayer session, which may involve inner healing.

INTRODUCING DELIVERANCE

As this is a big subject, it can be helpful to study some of the work done on this area of ministry. The following materials give a sound biblical basis:

Spiritual Warfare DVDs box set or audio CDs, by John Wimber

Deliverance from Evil Spirits, by Francis MacNutt

Demolishing Strongholds, by David Devenish

Come Holy Spirit, by David Pytches

Deliverance ministry typically either fascinates or frightens people, but there is no need to be worried about it. Deliverance is simply the Kingdom of Light overcoming the kingdom of darkness in a person's life, releasing them into freedom.

> **... God anointed Jesus of Nazareth with the Holy Spirit and power... he went around doing good and healing all who were under the power of the devil, because God was with him.**

Acts 10:38

Deliverance is like "foot washing": not always very pleasant, but the end result is a clean foot! It is part of setting captives free and releasing prisoners from darkness. We can't pick and choose which bits we do. However, where possible we should undertake deliverance ministry in partnership with an experienced minister, both for guidance and our own instruction.

Usually deliverance is required for people involved in habitual sin or who have suffered severe trauma. These evil spirits are easier and quicker to dispel. The Lord equips us with whatever we need for each situation. Some people may need deliverance because they have worshipped the devil, been involved in the occult, or been dedicated to other gods.

At conferences, the deliverance of people who have been involved in the occult is much quicker, because usually the person has recently become a Christian, and the people all around have been worshipping the Lord. Evil spirits hate prayer and the worship of Jesus. Deliverance is usually less speedy when someone makes an appointment outside the worshipping environment.

If during the ministry time it appears that a person has a strong infestation of demons (this will be seen by the person speaking in a strange voice, excessive contortions of the body, and their facial expression will distort and take on an evil form), then bind any spirits contrary to the Holy Spirit, and contact your team leader. Even when you feel out of your depth, always remember:

> ... the one who is in you is greater than the one who is in the world.

1 John 4:4

And know this:

> ... every spirit that does not acknowledge Jesus is not from God. This is the spirit of the antichrist, which you have heard is coming and even now is already in the world.

1 John 4:3

PERSPECTIVE

It is believed that Satan was a beautiful angel God appointed to be in charge of other angels. In the following verse he is called the "morning star", translated from the word "Lucifer":

> How you have fallen from heaven, morning star, son of the dawn! You have been cast down to the earth, you who once laid low the nations! You said in your heart, "I will ascend to the heavens; I will raise my throne above the stars of God; I will sit enthroned on the mount of assembly, on the utmost heights of Mount Zaphon. I will ascend above the tops of the clouds; I will make myself like the Most High." But you are brought down to the realm of the dead, to the depths of the pit.

Isaiah 14:12–15

At some point, Satan became proud and decided he wanted the other angels to worship him instead of God. Some of them did and were cast out of heaven by God. These fallen angels are referred to as demons or evil spirits, often unclean spirits. Other passages about this are found in Ezekiel 28:12–17 and 2 Corinthians 11:14.

The Corinthians verse speaks of Satan masquerading as an "angel of light". It refers to the devil as a "prowling lion waiting to devour". He is a deceiver, a liar, and an accuser. He is subtle and cunning.

In the Bible Satan is often referred to as the devil or the enemy. He is allowed to pass in and out of God's presence until the day when he will be ultimately banished. That day will be when Jesus returns to earth in all His glory to establish His Kingdom here forever.

The Bible teaches that the devil is limited in what he can do. As we see in Job 1:6–12 and Job 2:1–7, the devil has to ask God for permission before doing anything specifically involving God's people.

The Lord said to Satan, "Very well, then, everything
he has is in your hands, but on the man himself [Job]
do not lay a finger." Then Satan went out from the
presence of the Lord.

Job 1:12

"Simon, Simon, Satan has asked to sift you as wheat."

Luke 22:31

Deliverance is ministry of the church that has been ordained
by God. Discernment and sensitivity are needed. It is important
that the Receiver is loved and not made to feel that they are bad
or untouchable. We need to separate in our minds the demonic
activity from the person.

It is important that we do not engage in this ministry unless
we have been authorised to do so by the leaders of our church.
This is our covering. We all need to be under authority and
submit to it.

OUR PROTECTION AND ARMOUR

Sometimes people can be afraid of ministering deliverance
because they fear they will not know what to do. Though it is
wise to have done some background study and beginners should
partner with experienced ministers, nonetheless *all* believers
have received power and authority in Jesus' name to preach the
good news about Jesus and His Kingdom, heal the sick, cast out
demons, and, when He says so, raise the dead.

Knowing this, we have no need to fear. The devil and
evil spirits know too. We don't have to tell them we have this
authority. They sense it even when we are just standing next to
the person.

So make sure you have received this authority before
embarking on any deliverance ministry. Ask the Lord for it and
receive it.

> **Calling the Twelve to him, he sent them out two by two
> and gave them authority over evil spirits.**
>
> Mark 6:7

> **They drove out many demons** and anointed sick
> people with oil and healed them.
>
> Mark 6:13

If you have an opportunity before ministering deliverance, confess any of your own sin; this protects and empowers us against attacks of the enemy. The enemy loves to accuse us of being sinful, but if we have repented and confessed it to Jesus he has no hold to latch onto. It is important for us to be regularly confessing our sin, receiving forgiveness and praising the Lord for who He is, as well as studying the Bible and staying close to Jesus. We never know when we may be required to be involved in deliverance ministry.

If you realise in advance that you are about to enter into a deliverance situation, put on the whole armour of God (Ephesians 6:11–17) so that you can stand against the enemy's schemes. We need to be sure that we have put this on. That is why it is described as armour. At times I also ask for the blood of Jesus to cover me and my family. Sometimes this might be a hurried prayer if I suddenly find myself in this situation, but it is important to do it. This is not a superstitious act; it is part of the counsel of God.

RECEIVER'S RESPONSIBILITY

The Receiver needs to take active responsibility too during this ministry, cooperating in wanting and telling the spirit to go. The Receiver will need to confess their sin and repent, and they may need to give up an object, activity, attitude, or habit; but they may find this too hard to contemplate at first. They may feel victimised, and justified in keeping such sin as bitterness or hatred; but it must all be renounced. Even if the person seems to be overcome by the evil spirit we can still talk to the Receiver's spirit by using their name when we speak to them.

SOME PRACTICAL THINGS TO KNOW

Sometimes deliverance takes place without us ever referencing it as such. Some inner healing can bring the freedom of deliverance. When a person believes lies, or makes a vow, they are binding themselves. The enemy takes advantage of this, and an evil spirit can attach itself to the lie or the vow. When the person chooses to break the vow or lie, or renounce it, making this choice deliberately, the spirit can no longer stay there. There is nothing to attach to. Then a simple word breaking the power of it in Jesus' name has the effect of expelling any evil spirit.

WORDS TO SAY

When deliverance is required in the course of prayer ministry, I would say, "In Jesus' name, I break the power of darkness and tell it to go." I do not call it a spirit, as the spirit knows what it is. I know I am coming against it, and it cannot stay, as it has nothing to cling or attach to.

We may often choose to speak the words that Jesus did: "Be quiet", "Come out", "Be free". He addressed the victim, and He rebuked the demon, telling it to come out and never enter again.

We do not need to tell the evil spirit to go anywhere other than where Jesus designates. He can tell them where to go. We can just say, "Go to where Jesus tells you."

It is unnecessary to tell someone they have an evil spirit. This can be very frightening. Sometimes after deliverance the person has been completely unaware of what was happening. It doesn't help to frighten them by explaining what happened. They are now free; that's all they need to know.

In some cases it is obvious that someone needs deliverance. They might tell you that they are experiencing evil in all sorts of ways. They might feel compelled to do things that they would not ordinarily do. At other times it manifests during a time of prayer ministry by the Receiver doing strange contortions of their body; their voice may suddenly change completely, or they may start growling, and their facial expression takes on an evil form. Sometimes the Receiver may be gripped with intense pain in part of their body. The person may suddenly arch their spine backwards almost touching the floor. The Receiver's eyes may suddenly fill with hatred. Sometimes the eyes roll up so that you see the whites of the Receiver's eyes. They may also writhe like a snake on the floor. These manifestations seem dramatic, but this is what is seen when there is a strong demonisation of the person. Often it is less dramatic.

People can often scream out as they are releasing inner pain, but this should not be assumed to mean demonisation. The Holy Spirit's gift of discernment will show us.

If demons are showing off and making a lot of noise, just say, "In Jesus' name, I tell you to be quiet." You can also tell a demon to go quietly in Jesus' name.

Another way of addressing a manifesting demon is to say, "I bind anything contrary to the Holy Spirit in the name of Jesus Christ." If ministering in this area is beyond your experience, find a couple of experienced people confident and authorised to minister and cast it out. The demonised person will not feel troubled if they have to wait.

People may get scared because they remember the verse in the Bible where someone has an evil spirit being cast out and the evil spirit starts to beat up the people ministering! In this instance the people ministering were not followers of Jesus; they were not using the imparted power or authority of Jesus (Acts 19:13–16). But we are clothed with Christ, we bear His name, and we have His authority. We must remember that Jesus is upon us and inside us, and nothing can harm us if we are not deliberately sinning.

> **When Jesus had called the Twelve together, he gave them power and authority to drive out all demons and to cure diseases...**
>
> Luke 9:1

The power of Jesus terrifies demons but it doesn't stop them trying to frighten us. They may try to say they will do all sorts of things to us. They threaten and lie. But as you stand up to them and persist by saying they are to come out of the person, they eventually flee. They may try to wear us out, but they too can get worn out.

Some people may need deliverance before, during, or after receiving prayer ministry for past hurts. This will be discerned by receiving direction from the Holy Spirit.

BIBLICAL ACCOUNTS OF DEMONS

There is no need to make a case for the existence of demons. Jesus would not have given the command to His disciples to "cast out demons" if they didn't exist! In the New Testament Jesus is sometimes shown casting out demons at the same time as bringing the same person healing. Examples include:

- the epileptic boy (Matthew 17:14–21; Mark 9:17–29; Luke 9:37–43)
- the crippled woman (Luke 13:12)
- a man in the synagogue (Mark 1:23–28; Luke 4:31–37)
- two demon-possessed men (Matthew 8:28–34)
- Legion (Mark 5:1–20)
- a woman's daughter (Matthew 15:22–28)
- people demon-possessed (Matthew 8:16; Mark 1:32–34; Luke 4:41)
- Peter's afflicted mother-in-law (Luke 4:39).

You don't have to look very far in the New Testament to see Jesus casting out demons.

An evil spirit entered Judas – a follower and disciple of Jesus, called by Jesus, anointed by Jesus, performing healing in His name just like all the others. Judas sinned. We are told that he was a habitual thief who often stole from the money bag that he was in charge of. At the Last Supper an evil spirit entered him. He betrayed Jesus for money, and the end result was that Judas committed suicide.

Ananias and his wife were believers, meeting with the apostles; they were part of the first and one and only church in the world. This church was moving in power and showing care to everyone around them. Yet they sinned by deceiving everyone in keeping back some of the money they had announced as their gift to God, instead of giving it all to the apostles. In a word of knowledge, Peter said, "How is it that Satan has so filled your heart that you are lying to the Holy Spirit? **You have not lied to men but you have lied to God**." At hearing this Ananias fell down dead. Three hours later his wife Sapphira also lied and she too fell down dead (Acts 5:1–11).

Christians who – like Judas, Ananias, and his wife – have unresolved sin can be troubled by demons, which can attach to fear, sin of any sort ingrained by habit, hatred, bitterness, greed, pride, rebellion, and many other sins. When these things take place, the demon perceives a right to stay there permanently. When the sin is confessed, repented of, and healed up, the demon can no longer stay there. It has to go. It has lost its foothold.

In my personal experience of this ministry, I have seen that a person often needs deliverance of several evil spirits. Sometimes one or two are expelled, but as the prayer ministry develops it is like peeling off layers. More evil spirits are exposed and are dealt with. We don't have to go looking for them; as mentioned earlier it is usually obvious.

Sometimes I have been called on to minister deliverance at conferences with thousands of people in attendance. The power of the Lord has been present to heal, with everyone in a heightened state of expectancy of receiving from Him. Sometimes during these times I have received a different "tongue" to my usual prayer language from the Lord, and the person has become free in a matter of minutes. This "tongue" sounds more commanding and authoritative than the one with which I usually minister. I have no idea when it will come. It usually occurs if someone has been worshipping the devil and they have been a Christian a short while. As I utter it the Receiver usually has a strong reaction, contorting their body – it seems to loosen the demon/s. Usually the Receiver has no recollection of the ministry afterwards. At other times I have bound the evil that is manifesting, then addressed the person's human spirit directly by speaking their name and talking of things that are normal everyday things. Dialling down like this makes it easier for the person to cooperate, giving me a chance to discover some of their story before proceeding with inner healing and deliverance.

Occasionally the person was dedicated to other gods or spirits by their parents when they were a baby or small child. The Receiver knows the name of the god or spirit and renounces it. At other times the person has recently made a commitment to Jesus but not yet fully surrendered all aspects of their life to Him. They may have been involved in worshipping the devil or asking evil spirits to empower them. Some youths do this when they are engaged in "cage fighting" (illegal at the time of writing). Youths and adults may engage in role-play games online or on gaming machines where they take on a character inviting power to enter them. Involvement may start innocently but they become ensnared, spending longer periods of time engaged in "gaming". At other times the person has wanted to be empowered by evil because they feel scared of being powerless. I would never tackle this type of ministry on my own but partner with someone else in ministering to the person. As previously mentioned it is always preferable to pray in pairs, although if there was no one else about it wouldn't prevent me doing other types of prayer ministry such as physical or emotional healing.

It is always important to find out the underlying cause of how the person became demonised in the first place. This needs to be addressed or the individual may return to their former state or a worse state. As well as receiving inner healing (where appropriate), the person will also need to receive an infilling of the Holy Spirit. Some take-home sheets would be helpful, and if possible a follow-up session.

MY FIRST ENCOUNTER

The first time I (with another woman) was engaged in casting out a demon was in my early days of prayer ministry.

We had met in the evening at the church to pray for a woman. It gave me a great shock when the meek and mild-faced woman in front of me suddenly started manifesting. Her face changed. It contorted into a hate-filled manifestation of something really evil, and she began to speak in a deep growling voice. As this was a first experience, it took about an hour to cast out this demon. Eventually she was free, leaving us both very exhausted. By this time it was about 11 p.m.

I learned my first lesson – never pray for deliverance after 9 p.m.! The enemy loves us to get tired. He takes advantage of it.

The next day I spoke to our vicar, who was very kind and gave us some tips for future reference. I thought he was going to tell us off!

After this I read up a bit about deliverance. I haven't got a good memory and was worried that I wouldn't remember anything. I needn't have worried: I learned to let the Holy Spirit lead me and I just followed!

KEY ACTIONS FOR THE RECEIVER

Key things for the Receiver to do in deliverance are:
- engage in confession and repentance
- receive and extend forgiveness
- renounce evil or evil spirits by name if known (either the Receiver or Pray-er knows the name of the evil spirit as revealed by the Holy Spirit, or the Receiver was dedicated to an evil spirit or god by their parents as a child and discovered the name at a later date, or the Receiver dedicated themselves to a god or evil spirit with full knowledge of its name)
- use their will when choosing to renounce evil, bondages, lies, etc.

- surrender their will to Jesus
- cooperate and share what the demon may be saying or doing in their life
- cooperate in cleansing prayer
- if appropriate, dedicate their body to Jesus.

Apart from what has already been mentioned the Pray-er should:

- use oil (if appropriate)
- fill with the Holy Spirit
- give glory to God.

> **Submit yourselves, then, to God. Resist the devil, and he will flee from you.**
>
> James 4:7

DELIVERANCE AND YOUNG PEOPLE

Evil spirits are not deaf, we do not have to shout at them, and we do need to be pastorally sensitive to the person. They may be receiving some inner healing and their friends are joining in praying. Very quietly under my breath, I whisper, "I bind you in the name of Jesus, and tell you now to go where He directs." After this I may say so the Receiver can hear me, "Be free now; just let that go. You don't need it any more." Many times the young person has coughed or shown signs of a demon being expelled, without their friends realising. Then I just ask the Holy Spirit to come to them with the love and light of Jesus. If they start crying or moving about after this, I will enter into an inner healing prayer where they will have to make some choices, or there may be a need to repent and ask Jesus for forgiveness.

We don't need to tell the evil spirit to go to any special place. Just be firm.

DELIVERANCE AND INNER HEALING

The model of ministry we were taught under the leadership of David and Mary Pytches at St Andrew's Church Chorleywood was to first take the inner healing route. We don't need to go looking for demons in people. Obviously if something starts to manifest, we would usually deal with it and cast it out. If it took a little while, then we would stop and go back on the inner healing route. There is no point in casting out a demon without cleaning "the rest of the house", and if the house is clean the demon will usually go.

If we cast the demon out and don't deal with the cleaning up, the person will probably get another demon doing a similar thing to them, or in some cases other demons could come with it and the Receiver ends up being in a worse state than before.

> When an impure spirit comes out of a person, it goes through arid places seeking rest and does not find it. Then it says, "**I will return to the house I have left.**" When **it arrives, it finds the house unoccupied, swept clean and put in order.** Then it goes and takes with it seven other spirits more wicked than itself, and they go in and live there. And the final condition of the person is worse than the first.
>
> Matthew 12:43–45

In addition to the demonic activity, we must always address the inner hurts beneath it or to which it has become attached.

Sometimes it is unclear which ministry has priority. That is why it is important to have no preconceived ideas but follow the direction of the Holy Spirit. He may give a word of knowledge or prophetic word, or an insight that will go directly to the point of access.

If I were ministering to someone who was not a Christian and they were manifesting demonisation I would bind the evil spirit/s in Jesus' name, but for the reasons given above I would not cast it out. I would then give the Receiver the opportunity to give their life to Jesus before proceeding with their cooperation in casting out the demon or starting some inner healing ministry.

GOING ON A JOURNEY

I wouldn't bother to ask the demon its name, as they lie; the devil is the father of lies. I recently heard John Wimber saying on a DVD that he asks the demon how it gained entry and what activity it does in the victim and what it causes the victim to do. Demons do like showing off and boasting so I suppose they would readily answer this. I have never done this personally but I may try this if the Lord directed me to do it.

Sometimes just asking the "light of the love of Jesus into any darkness" or asking Jesus "to dispel any darkness with light" is sufficient when someone is being troubled by an evil spirit. This can be prayed into the mind (conscious and unconscious as well as the imagination), body, or soul.

SPIRITUAL TIES

This can be a spiritual bonding between two souls, usually involving manipulation and/or sex. Some people call these soul-ties.

If someone has been in a sexual relationship outside of marriage or an adulterous one, the Receiver can have a spiritual binding to that person or persons that will need to be broken, otherwise it will form a foothold for the enemy. Women who have been beaten by their husbands but keep returning to them can also be affected by this spiritual tie or soul-tie that binds the person's mind, emotions, and will. In the Bible it says:

> **For this reason a man will leave his father and mother and be united to his wife, and the two will become one flesh.**
> Mark 10:7–8; see also Genesis 2:24 and Ephesians 5:31

This is such a cementing together that they are as one.

In adultery the bond that has been cemented together by marriage is torn by both parties (if they were both married). This can have a deep effect.

Manipulative parents can also be spiritually tied to their children with unhealthy relationships of manipulation or bullying. Sometimes an adult male or female can be overly dependent on their mother or father. Neither has ever cut the cord tying them together.

Young people may have a spiritual bonding to a very manipulative friend, causing the Receiver distress.

The Bible tells us that we can loose this bonding.

> "Truly I tell you, whatever you bind on earth will be bound in heaven, and whatever you loose on earth will be loosed in heaven..."
>
> Matthew 18:18

This spiritual binding needs to be broken by the person who has done the cementing (i.e. the Receiver). The Receiver needs to choose to surrender the person to Jesus and also be willing to have that bond broken in Jesus' name by the Pray-er, setting them free (loosing) spiritually, emotionally, and mentally.

People can also receive something passed down from their relatives. This can be from hereditary illnesses that are in the family. Sometimes this is received through the unwitting curse of a parent saying something like, "You will always have [name of illness] because I have it and your grandma had it", etc. This should be renounced by the Receiver, broken in Jesus' name, and cleansed by the Pray-er.

CLEANSING

Cleansing is a simple prayer asking Jesus to come and make the Receiver clean both inside and outside. We can ask Jesus to cleanse us by His blood that was shed on the cross. It is also good to announce the cleansing: "In the name of Jesus be clean."

Cleansing is sometimes referred to in connection with physical healing in the Bible. Leprosy made a person ritually unclean under the Jewish law and ostracised the leper from society, making them an outcast. When Jesus healed lepers, He said, "Be clean," making it clear that the healing He offered was physical, spiritual, and relational.

> **Heal the sick, raise the dead, cleanse those who have leprosy, drive out demons. Freely you have received; freely give.**
>
> Matthew 10:7–8

Part of pastoral prayer ministry is restoring every aspect of the whole person. Deliverance cleanses people from the taint of bondage.

SEX OUTSIDE OF MARRIAGE

Sometimes people will come to be cleansed from the sin of sexual immorality. After the Receiver has repented, and asked for and received forgiveness, speak cleansing, and in Jesus' name cut the bonding between the couple, naming them. Encourage the Receiver to dedicate their own body to Jesus.

> **Flee from sexual immorality.[1] All other sins a person commits are outside the body, but whoever sins sexually, sins against their own body.**
>
> 1 Corinthians 6:18

PORNOGRAPHY

After the Receiver has repented and confessed their sin to Jesus and received forgiveness, they will need to renounce pornography. Break the power of anything contrary to the Holy Spirit – anything unclean. Ask the Receiver to open their eyes, look deeply into them, and speak the cleansing of Jesus Christ. Bind and break the power of pornography and lust in Jesus' name. Speak the cleansing blood of Jesus into their imagination and any fantasy. The Receiver will need to destroy any pornographic images on any technology, including movies, photos, or publications. There may also be unclean spirits. These too will need to be bound and cast out.

A helpful book for both Pray-er and Receiver is *Captured by a Better Vision – Living Porn Free*, by Tim Chester.

SELF-HATRED

Self-hatred is usually binding. Usually someone has had terrible things done to them, but instead of hating the one who has done these things the person turns the hatred inwards. I have seen people clawing at their face, pinching, punching, or slapping themselves or trying to gouge out their own eyes during a power encounter with the Holy Spirit. If they are wearing a necklace they may twist it around trying to choke themselves.

Speaking the person's name and dialling down the ministry means it can proceed without such destructive manifestations. This deliverance needs the Receiver's full cooperation.

Explain that in the account of God creating the world with all the animals, trees, and plants, He saw that it was good and it pleased Him. Then when He made mankind in His own image, He saw that it was "*very* good" (Genesis 1:31). It really pleased Him. If we are saying that we hate something God made, it is like saying that God made a mistake when He made us. God doesn't make mistakes; He makes people He loves. He is perfect (Psalm 18:30). We need to repent and ask God's forgiveness for not liking or loving what He has made.

MINISTRY FOR THOSE WITH SELF-HATRED

Key things for the Receiver to do during prayer ministry:
- repent and confess their sin of hating themselves to Jesus
- receive forgiveness from Jesus
- renounce self-hatred: "I renounce hating/loathing myself"
- declare, "I choose to like what Jesus made"
- declare, "I choose to love what Jesus loves"
- declare, "I choose to love myself" (putting his/her will behind this choice).

The Pray-er could say aloud, "In Jesus' name I break the power of self-hatred" (the same might need to be done for self-rejection).

This may lead on to the healing of memories causing shame, or this may have taken place earlier. Also ask Jesus to surface anything else related.

As always when engaged in prayer ministry, it is as if we are going on a journey with the Holy Spirit leading us. I usually have no idea what we will see or do on the journey, but I do know that with Jesus in charge, something good will happen. In the end we will get to the place that this individual is able to reach at this stage of their journey towards healing and wholeness.

Notes

1. This used to be referred to in the Bible as "fornication". Nowadays it is listed as "sexual immorality".

Chapter 16

STORIES OF DELIVERANCE AND FREEDOM

MICHELLE: FREEDOM FROM DEPRESSION

In South Africa I met Michelle, so ill with depression that she hadn't worked for three months.

Every week for six months she had been going for prayer ministry, and a couple from her church had cast demons out of her on each occasion! This seemed to be common practice in the area she lived in. It had caused her to sink into depression. I asked Michelle what was troubling her. She explained. As she spoke, I realised that far from being demonised, Michelle was simply burdened by old-fashioned sin. As she was single and longed to be married, once she had confessed her sin, repented of it, and received forgiveness, I also prayed about her future and her desire for a husband. She told me she felt as if a black cloud had lifted from her mind. The following year I met her again and heard that three months after we had prayed, she met a man and fell in love; they were now engaged, due to marry in a couple of months' time. Praise God!

ED: FREEDOM FROM HATRED

I was called over to a young man who looked about twenty years old who was lying on the floor. His body was rigid and twisted, his hands were clenched tight, and his legs were crossed. Ed looked very scared, with terrified open eyes. He was emitting some loud painful cries intermittently. A couple of young men had been praying for him for some time.

I asked Ed where his pain was; he pointed to his head and chest. He said that he was trying to get the pain out of his body. I asked one of the men praying to place their hands on Ed's chest and head, and I placed my hands on top of his.

As we continued to pray Ed became more and more vocal. His pain was increasing. My thought was to get Ed to sit up and come out of the ministry so that I could talk with him. After chatting to Ed about this, he said that although the pain was increasing he was also receiving comfort from Jesus at the same time. We decided to continue with the ministry at his request.

Suddenly Ed made some loud gasping noises and he seemed to have some release and relief from his pain. He said that he felt he was finally getting somewhere. We gave Ed some water. From time to time I encouraged Ed that he was doing a good job, as well as directing him to give voice to the pain. It was as if he were pushing it out of his body.

After another big surge of release where Ed let rip with some big noises, I asked him how he was feeling. He said that his chest and stomach felt free but the pain had intensified in his head.

From a word of knowledge I was sure that Ed had suffered physical abuse. I asked him whether he had violent images relaying in his mind. He said, "yes".

I asked Jesus to cleanse his mind of the images and asked Ed to look me in the eyes. Every time he tried to do this he kept shutting his eyes or looking away. I realised that there were two things going on: Ed was pushing out pain that had been unexpressed and seemed to be trapped in his body, and he was also troubled by an evil spirit, as he couldn't maintain eye contact.

I sensed the Holy Spirit indicating that the root cause was a spirit of hatred. Also I had a knowing (this may have been a word of knowledge) that Ed had fed off this to make himself feel strong instead of powerless, unable to stop the abuse.

I asked Ed if this was true. He agreed it was. At first Ed tried to ask Jesus to take away the hatred, but I interrupted and said that he needed to confess this to Jesus, receive His forgiveness, and then tell the hatred to go. He did this. Then I asked him to tell the violent images to go too, as he had also fed off these to fuel his hatred. After Ed had done this, in Jesus' name I broke the power of hatred and violence and told it to leave Ed.

At this point Ed let out one final cry of pain. Suddenly he shouted out, "Peace at last... I am free... in my head, my body. For the first time in eighteen years my whole body feels peaceful." My heart filled with such compassion for this young man. I asked Ed how old he was. He said, "I am twenty years old."

After all those years of pain Ed was finally free, resting in the arms of Jesus; exhausted but finally peaceful.

My God, how great You are and how wonderful Your love is that sets us free.

BILL: FREEDOM FROM REJECTION

At a conference, a man lying on his back said he had something inside him that needed to come out. He didn't know what it was but it didn't feel good.

His name was Bill. I asked him to put his hand on his stomach, and I placed my hand on top of his. I commanded anything contrary to Jesus Christ to go. Bill started to contort his face into something nasty. He prayed a demonic tongue and started to roar. I told it to be quiet in Jesus' name and to go – leave. Then I said three times "Let go." I didn't shout or raise my voice, but spoke firmly and with authority. Bill let out another roar and I told it to be quiet again. Suddenly his body went rigid. I asked him what was happening, and he said his legs felt really stiff and his body tight all over. As I prayed, he continued manifesting but nothing was budging. I ignored the evil spirit, asking Bill by name what had happened to him that was so painful. He said he had been engaged to be married but his fiancée had broken off their engagement. I asked him what feelings this had given him. He said, "Betrayal, hatred and self-rejection." He said he felt angry with everyone around him all the time. I told him he needed to confess this vengeful anger and rejection to Jesus. He did, and received forgiveness.

I told hatred, self-rejection, and betrayal to be gone in Jesus' name.

Bill started to cough and retch, expelling the demons. We turned him on his side so he didn't choke. Sticky phlegm-type mucus was expelled from his mouth. He was free!

We prayed for healing and release from his pain. He started to cry with deep sobs. After a while, I asked him to release forgiveness to his fiancée, to extend to her what Jesus had done for him on the cross. He was able to do this. We asked the Holy Spirit to fill up the empty space he now had.

We prayed in tongues for him for a while as he lay there looking peaceful. Afterwards he said he felt lighter and completely free. Praise God!

As you will see from that story, at first I went for the deliverance of the evil spirit because that was what I first saw manifesting. I don't usually spend too long doing this if it is resisting. It didn't go because the demon felt it had a right to be there. It was attached to the sin and the pain of betrayal. Once those problems were dealt with, the demon had no more foothold and left as a matter of course.

MAX: DELIVERED OF A SPIRIT OF DEATH AND FEAR

During a time of prayer ministry at a conference I was called over to a young man who couldn't move his jaw. His jaw and teeth were clenched so tight it made his face look a strange shape. His eyes were open very wide, like a rabbit caught in the headlights; he looked terrified.

I asked him if he was frightened. He nodded. I looked deep into his eyes as I said, "You are safe with Jesus; don't be afraid." I prayed, "Jesus, please come and stand between Max and his fear; put Your cross there, Jesus." I bound anything contrary to the Holy Spirit, in Jesus' name. I asked Jesus to show Max what his fear related to. Max's jaw loosened, and his eyes returned to normal. I asked him what Jesus was showing him. He said his mum and dad had been missionaries in Africa when he was young. Jesus showed him a time when, as a young boy, he heard gunshots through the window, and saw his dad hit with bullets, covered in blood and badly injured. His mum had suddenly clamped her hand over Max's mouth, throwing him and herself under a table. Of course she had done this for his protection, but to the little boy it had added to the terror.

Immediately I started to pray for the child who had suffered so much trauma. I asked Jesus to draw it out of that little boy. Max started shaking violently as he got free of this. I then invited Jesus to come and hold Max, and heal that frightened little boy; to bring him safety and security. In Jesus' name I also broke the power of death, as it had come close to him. I felt a powerful surge of the compassion of Jesus for Max. I knew that Jesus was bringing a deep healing to him. After a little while, Max opened his eyes and smiled. He said he felt really different inside. Jesus then gave me an encouraging prophetic word for Max about his future.

CHARLIE: FREEDOM FROM CONFUSION

A young man came up to my husband and me and said that everyone thought he was gay and he wasn't sure of his sexuality. I asked a few questions and Charlie said that when he was four years old a teenager had sexually abused him.

As he grew up and became fully aware of his sexuality, he felt that in some way he seemed to be different from the rest of his friends. He was often taken to be gay. But Charlie said he didn't want to be gay; he felt as though he was somehow being pushed into it.

I explained to Charlie that four years old is a crucial time for a boy. It is the age when he begins to look beyond his close relationship with his mum as a baby, to his dad as a masculine role model. This is part of a boy understanding who he is and learning what it means to be male. The mother must allow the strong tie between herself and her son to ease off so that crucial development can take place.

I asked Charlie to see himself in a room as a four-year-old, and then asked him to invite Jesus into the room with him.

I broke the power of lies and accusation in Jesus' name. I asked Jesus to free Charlie's mind of confusion. He reacted and manifested, and started coughing as he was delivered. I then asked the adult Charlie to visit that little boy within him. I asked him what he wanted to do, and Charlie said, "I want to hold him." This he did. Then I asked Jesus to remove any labels that other people had put on him. Afterwards Charlie said he felt really different and free. Charlie asked me what he should do if people kept saying he was gay. I said that he needed to start declaring who he was and who he wasn't.

KYLE: CLEANSING FROM PORNOGRAPHY

I ministered to a young man in his early twenties after a church service. Kyle said he had had acute anxiety for four years and was taking medication for Obsessive Compulsive Disorder. I asked him to think of himself as a child in a place he liked going to. He said he loved being in the woods near his home. As he pictured himself there in the woods, I asked him to invite Jesus to be there with him. After a little while, Kyle said he couldn't believe it – Jesus was playing with him on a slope and they were swinging on a rope together! Kyle said he had never thought of Jesus in those terms before – as his friend – and of himself as a friend of Jesus.

Next I asked Kyle to see himself as a teenager. He said he could see himself as a young man in the woods; now Jesus was wrestling with him playfully and had him in a headlock!

I spoke freedom to him in the name of Jesus. Kyle started to cough and retch. I asked him to look me in the eyes, but as I spoke more freedom and cleansing in Jesus' name, Kyle couldn't keep eye contact. I asked him whether he had seen any violent or pornographic films. He said he had watched porn throughout his teenage years. He said sorry to Jesus, repented of it, and renounced it. He received forgiveness and then forgave himself. I looked into his eyes again and spoke cleansing deep down into his soul. Afterwards he said he felt really peaceful and very different. Thank You, Jesus!

Chapter 17

NOTES FOR LEADERS: PASTORAL PRAYER MINISTRY

GATHERING THE PASTORAL PRAYER MINISTRY TEAM

A team needs to be hand-picked by the church leader, as the members must be trustworthy, teachable men and women with a heart for people. They must be open to their own on-going wholeness, and should be able to listen to the Holy Spirit's leading without feeling the need to help Him in their own strength with their own wordy prayers!

Training and equipping times should take place before embarking on pastoral prayer ministry. Everyone has to be clear about the model and practice. After this time a regular get-together every couple of months is beneficial to the team and leader. The team can share what they have seen the Lord do in the preceding weeks during prayer ministry in the church and the PPM sessions (confidentiality being maintained), for the encouragement of all. This could offer an opportunity for discussing difficulties experienced, as well as times of teaching and laying hands on one another for refreshment and wholeness.

It is good for the pairs on the team to take a break of two to three weeks after seeing someone for four to six sessions, so they don't feel overstretched. If people continue to do in-depth prayer ministry every week, they may get overloaded and wish to discontinue. It is best to avoid that, so the team can grow in numbers.

PRACTICAL POINTS

Pastors/Ministers or leaders of the church may wish to refer individuals that they counsel to seek pastoral prayer ministry as part of the healing process. If members of the congregation repeatedly come up for prayer ministry after the church service then someone on the leadership team may suggest that the person may benefit from some sessions of PPM.

Posters and leaflets are helpful, explaining what PPM is, when it is available, and how to obtain it.

A co-ordinator is advisable, to take calls at the church from those wishing to book an appointment. The co-ordinator can then pass this information on either to the designated person from the next pair on the list, or to a designated team member.

A room big enough for three chairs and a small table (for tissues, water, a Bible, notes to pass on, a pen and notepad, etc.) should be set aside at the church.

A record needs to be kept by one person, of the name and contact details of the Receiver, as well as contact details of everyone on the PPM team. It is best for people to be seen at church in a neutral setting. It is helpful for the co-ordinator to keep a record of who is being seen by whom, as the Receiver may return for more sessions at a future date and continuity is desirable.

To avoid people coming for PPM with the wrong expectations, give details in an email or leaflet in advance of the first session, explaining what to expect on their first and subsequent sessions. It would also be good to spell out details of any commitments expected in between sessions. This could include:

- taking responsibility for their own wholeness and healing
- praying daily for their own healing and pursuing it
- doing any homework offered on worksheets
- informing PPM pair in advance if they are ill and cannot attend.

Here is an example of that sheet:

PASTORAL PRAYER MINISTRY – "WHAT TO EXPECT" SHEET

Please inform the people ministering to you if you are currently having, or have in the past received, any counselling or therapy.

Please inform the couple praying with you if you are on medication for emotional or mental health issues.

Two people on the pastoral prayer team will meet with you for 4–6 sessions.

Sessions will take place at church in a small room.

Everything you say is confidential, except in the case where another person's life is in danger or a young person/teenager is being abused.

Sessions will last for 60–90 minutes.

At the first session most of the time is available for you to talk about what issues you want to work through. There will be a short prayer ministry at the end. The next 3–5 sessions will be spent in prayer ministry.

The couple praying will invite the Holy Spirit to come, and ask Him to surface any root cause of inner pain. Then they will follow the lead of the Holy Spirit.

> **... continue to work out your salvation [wholeness]
> with fear and trembling, for it is God who works in you
> to will and to act in order to fulfil his good purpose.**
>
> Philippians 2:12–13

Our healing is part of our salvation. We are told in Scripture that salvation is worked in us but we have to work it out. The word "salvation" in this verse means wholeness. This means that we have to take responsibility in receiving and working out what the Lord is doing in us during these sessions.

Part of that responsibility is to keep on seeking healing from Jesus in between the sessions, completing any worksheet/s you are given.

If you are ill and cannot make the session, please let the people ministering to you know as soon as possible.

It is natural to feel very tired after the sessions.

It is helpful for the co-ordinator to send out a response sheet so the team can use feedback received to improve the PPM. On the next page there is a sample response sheet:

PASTORAL PRAYER MINISTRY – "RESPONSE" SHEET

Your comments help us to continually learn and improve the prayer ministry we offer. Please could you fill this form out and email/send it back to.................................
This will remain confidential. Many thanks.

How many sessions did you have?

Is this the first time you have had PPM?

Was PPM explained clearly at the start?

What did you find helpful?

_____

What did you find unhelpful?

_____

Did it meet your expectations?

_____

Did it meet your need at that time?

_____

Did any of the exercises make you uncomfortable?

_____

Do you have appropriate support for the future?

_____

On the basis of your own experience, would you recommend PPM to someone else?

_____

Any other comments?

_____

Chapter 18

WORKSHEETS AND SCRIPTURES

These worksheets and Scripture sheets may be photocopied. The Pray-er may want to give an appropriate worksheet to the Receiver to work on between sessions. These worksheets and other resources are also available in an easy-to-print format on my website www.ourhandshishealing.co.uk

GUILT

Ask yourself the following questions:
- Is it guilt? – awareness of something I have done wrong
- Or is it false guilt? – something someone else has done to me but I have believed a lie that it was my fault (abusive people often retain power by making those they prey on carry a sense of guilt)

Some questions to answer:
- What are the things in your life that cause you to feel guilty?
- How have you dealt in the past with your guilty feelings?
- What were your parents' expectations about right and wrong?
- What happened when you failed?
- Were blame, criticism, and punishment frequent?
- What stops you receiving forgiveness and letting go?
- What do you blame yourself for?
- Is there anything you blame God for?

If the problem is guilt

Ask the Lord to come upon you. Come to Jesus, confess the sin (whatever it is), repent of it (choose to turn away), and receive forgiveness. Say "thank You" to Jesus. If we don't really receive His forgiveness, it is as if we are saying what Jesus did on the cross wasn't enough. We then just go round in circles. Some people find it helpful to see Jesus on the cross. Some like to visualise bringing their guilt as a labelled parcel, handing it to Jesus and then walking away. If you are not a visual person, just say out loud:

> *Jesus, I'm bringing this guilt to You. I am sorry I did not receive the forgiveness You offer. I bring this guilt to You now and choose to turn away from it. Thank*

You that You said in Your word that if I confess my sin You will forgive me and cleanse me. I receive that cleansing now with thanks that You do not keep a record of wrongs. THANK YOU THAT ON THE CROSS YOU SAID, "IT IS FINISHED." Amen.

If we confess our sins, he is faithful and just and will forgive us our sins and purify us from all unrighteousness.

1 John 1:9

Also, if appropriate:

Jesus, I ask now that You will cut off everything that I have received from my family [insert father, mother, or ....?] to do with guilt, punishment, or shame. Break now the cycle of guilt and self-blame. I choose to receive Your forgiveness and the abundant life You offer. I lay down at Your feet the opinions of others.

It may help you at this point to think of your family members at the foot of the cross with Jesus and yourself – you on one side of Jesus, they on the other side of Him – then walk away, leaving them with Jesus. If you cannot visualise it, just say it: "I am now bringing..."

If the problem is false guilt

Put the blame of the sin where it belongs. The sin was committed by the person that hurt you. You are not responsible for it. Again come to Jesus, standing at the cross in your mind's eye. Say aloud, "Jesus, it wasn't my fault." Name the person who did it and what was done to make you feel guilty. "I choose now to let go of false guilt and blaming myself. Amen."

If you have blamed Jesus for them hurting you, ask for His forgiveness. Then receive it.

Scriptures

If we confess our sins, he is faithful and righteous
to forgive us our sins, and to cleanse us from all
unrighteousness.

1 John 1:9 KJV

You can proclaim the promise of forgiveness in this Scripture for
yourself by saying it aloud (*I* instead of *we*): "If I confess my sins,
He is faithful and righteous to forgive me my sins, and to cleanse
me from all unrighteousness."

... let us draw near to God with a sincere heart and
with the full assurance that faith brings, having
our hearts sprinkled to cleanse us from a guilty
conscience and having our bodies washed with pure
water.

Hebrews 10:22

But with you there is forgiveness.

Psalm 130:4

I want you to know that the Son of Man has authority
on earth to forgive sins.

Luke 5:24

Then he took a cup, and when he had given thanks, he
gave it to them, saying, "Drink from it, all of you. This
is my blood of the covenant, which is poured out for
many for the forgiveness of sins."

Matthew 26:27–28

There is now no condemnation for those who are in
Christ Jesus...

Romans 8:1

"Then neither do I condemn you," Jesus declared.

John 8:11

SHAME

Look at the Scriptures on this sheet and ask the Holy Spirit to feed you with the truth.

If you feel dirty or ashamed, invite the Lord to cleanse you:

> **"Take off his filthy clothes... I have taken away your sin and I will put fine garments on you."**
>
> Zechariah 3:4

Visualise it if you can, or just say out loud, "Jesus, I am taking off the shame..." – do this as if it were a garment. Put on clean clothes – be "clothed with Christ". Acknowledge that Jesus now lives in you – receive His purity. Offer your body as worship to Him:

> **Therefore, I urge you, brothers and sisters, in view of God's mercy, to offer your bodies as a living sacrifice, holy and pleasing to God – this is your true and proper worship.**
>
> Romans 12:1

> **Do not offer any part of yourself to sin as an instrument of wickedness, but rather offer yourselves to God as those who have been brought from death to life; and offer every part of yourself to him as an instrument of righteousness.**
>
> Romans 6:13

Choose from now on to live in the healing you have received. When we receive healing, we sometimes retain the habit of living the old way. We have received freedom, but we need to discipline ourselves to walk in it (Galatians 5:1).

Forgiving others is a necessary part of the healing process. We come to Jesus and confess our deep feelings against others who have hurt us; we then need to extend the same forgiveness to others and cancel their debt to us.

Surrender to Jesus any feeling of being a victim. See Him standing at the foot of the cross and bring it to Him. What happened to you is no longer your identity.

The worksheets on identity and loss may also be helpful.

Scriptures

In you, Lord my God, I put my trust. I trust in you;
do not let me be put to shame, nor let my enemies
triumph over me. No one whose hope is in you will
ever be put to shame, but shame will come on those
who are treacherous without cause.

Psalm 25:1–3

In you, Lord, I have taken refuge; let me never be put
to shame; deliver me in your righteousness.

Psalm 31:1

I sought the Lord, and he answered me; he delivered
me from all my fears. Those who look to him are
radiant; their faces are never covered with shame.

Psalm 34:4–5

And we eagerly await a Saviour from there, the Lord
Jesus Christ, who, by the power that enables him to
bring everything under his control, will transform our
lowly bodies so that they will be like his glorious body.

Philippians 3:20–21

Do you not know that your bodies are temples of the
Holy Spirit, who is in you, whom you have received
from God? You are not your own; you were bought at a
price. Therefore honour God with your bodies.

1 Corinthians 6:19–20

FEAR

We can have spontaneous negative thoughts that confront us with the worst case scenario and flood us with instant fear. We need to act immediately on these thoughts and say "NO" to them. Or there may be demoralising thoughts that go round and round in our heads, accusing us: "You can't do that", "You will mess that up", etc. The Bible says, "Take captive every thought to make it obedient to Christ" (2 Corinthians 10:5).

Some of us have been taken in by a belief system based on lies. Look at the following exercise:

1.   Make a list of all your fears.

2.   See if any of them are connected to each other.

3.   When did this fear first start?

4.   See if any of the fears you have listed are based on lies. For example, "You will be all alone", "No one will like you or love you", etc. See from the list below the promises of Jesus that counteract those lies.

5.   Choose not to live out of those lies any longer.

6.   Do any of these lies, when you uncover them, come down to the three most common fears:

•   fear of death

•   fear of being alone

•   fear of not being in control or powerless?

If so, look at the truth in the Bible:

•   Jesus defeated death on the cross and we have eternal life (Romans 6:4–11; John 3:16).

•   Jesus said He will be with us always to the very end of the age (Matthew 28:20).

•   We need to surrender control to Jesus: all power and authority belong to Him but He allows us to use it in His name. We need to receive it (Matthew 28:18–20; Luke 9:1).

Examine the statements above. What do you think? Are they true?

If we believe they are true, then we need to stand by that belief and live with that truth inside us to replace the fear. Jesus didn't just *speak* the truth: HE IS THE TRUTH. He said of Himself, "I am the way and the truth and the life" (John 14:6).

Pray the following Bible verses (right now, and on a regular basis) to receive, and to live out of, this truth:

> The Lord is my light and my salvation – whom shall
>   I fear?
> The Lord is the stronghold of my life – of whom shall
>   I be afraid?

Psalm 27:1

> "So do not fear, for I am with you; do not be dismayed,
> for I am your God. I will strengthen you and help you;
> I will uphold you with my righteous right hand. All
> who rage against you will surely be ashamed and
> disgraced... For I am the Lord your God who takes hold
> of your right hand and says to you, Do not fear; I will
> help you."

Isaiah 41:10–11, 13

> The Spirit you received does not make you slaves,
> so that you live in fear again; rather, the Spirit you
> received brought about your adoption to sonship. And
> by him we cry, "Abba, Father."

Romans 8:15

Turn some of the following verses into prayers. Select others to declare – proclaim – out loud. Declaring is powerful. You are declaring things to yourself, acknowledging who God is and giving the enemy a kick up the backside!

Promises of God from the Bible:

> "Never will I leave you; never will I forsake you."

Hebrews 13:5

... fear not for I am with you; be not dismayed for I am your God...

Isaiah 41:1 ESV

"... surely I am with you always, to the very end of the age."

Matthew 28:20

Do not be anxious about anything...

Philippians 4:6

"Do not be afraid, little flock, for your Father has been pleased to give you the kingdom."

Luke 12:32

"For we know that since Christ was raised from the dead, he cannot die again; death no longer has mastery over him."

Romans 6:9

"My grace is sufficient for you..."

2 Corinthians 12:9

There is no fear in love. But perfect love drives out fear, because fear has to do with punishment. The one who fears is not made perfect in love.

1 John 4:18

The Lord is with me; I will not be afraid. What can mere mortals do to me?

Psalm 118:6

But as for me, it is good to be near God. I have made the sovereign Lord my refuge. I must tell of all your deeds.

Psalm 73:28

Come near to God and he will come near to you.

James 4:8

Even the very hairs of your head are all numbered.
So don't be afraid; you are worth more than many
sparrows.

Matthew 10:30–31

"He will wipe away every tear from their eyes. There
will be no more death or mourning or crying or pain,
for the old order of things has passed away."

Revelation 21:4

When you pass through the waters, I will be with you;
and when you pass through the rivers, they will not
sweep over you. When you walk through the fire, you
will not be burned; the flames will not set you ablaze.

Isaiah 43:2

Having disarmed the powers and authorities, he made
a public spectacle of them, triumphing over them by
the cross.

Colossians 2:15

For God so loved the world that He gave His only
begotten Son, that whoever believes in Him should not
perish but have everlasting life.

John 3:16 NKJV

There is no fear in love. But perfect love drives out
fear, because fear has to do with punishment. The one
who fears is not made perfect in love.

1 John 4:18

It would also be beneficial to read the whole of Psalm 139 and
Psalm 91.

(Let go of fear, confess it, and grasp hold of love – choose love.)

USE THE WORD OF GOD AS STRENGTH – DEVOUR IT!

Take the following Scripture passage apart. Choose a part every day for five days, meditating on it and choosing to live by its message.

> **Trust in the Lord**
> **with all your heart**
> **and lean not on your own understanding;**
> **in all your ways submit to him**
> **and he will make your paths straight.**
>
> Proverbs 3:5–6

Day 1: TRUST IN THE LORD: I will trust in You, Lord... I choose to trust in You... remind me when I forget to trust You... Trust in the Lord.

Day 2: WITH ALL YOUR HEART: I choose to trust You, Lord, with all my heart... with all my heart, not just part of it... as far as I am able I will trust You with all my heart... I am sorry when I have trusted You with just part of me... in Jesus' name I choose to trust You, Lord, with all my heart...

Continue in the same way until all the verses have been done.

Another way is to emphasise one word at a time. It is a good way to learn and digest the verse. It can be very empowering to say it aloud. Try this with the following verse as well as the one above.

> **Even though I walk through the valley of the shadow of**
> **death I will fear no evil, for you are with me; your rod**
> **and your staff, they comfort me.**
>
> Psalm 23:4

<u>Even</u> *though I walk through*
Even **<u>though</u>** *I walk through*

*Even though **I** walk through*
*Even though I **walk** through...*

Start at the beginning of this verse using this idea throughout.

Here is another verse of Scripture that you can use in the same way:

> **When I am afraid, I put my trust in you. In God, whose word I praise – in God I trust and am not afraid. [Out loud choose not to be afraid] What can mere mortals do to me?**
>
> Psalm 56:3–4

ANGER

Surely there is not a single person in the whole world who does not sometimes struggle with anger. By itself anger is not wrong – sometimes it is justified; sometimes it's just the way we feel. The important thing is that its strong energy does not overwhelm us. Part of our discipleship is learning how to handle strong emotions like anger gracefully, so that through the power of Jesus in us we are always bigger than our anger and know how to find a way through to peace – that's self-control.

The exercises below are to help you identify how anger was modelled to you as you grew up. This might help to surface memories that may need healing during times of prayer ministry.

> "In your anger do not sin": Do not let the sun go down while you are still angry, and do not give the devil a foothold.
>
> Ephesians 4:26–27

> Get rid of all bitterness, rage and anger, brawling and slander, along with every form of malice. Be kind and compassionate to one another, forgiving each other, just as in Christ God forgave you.
>
> Ephesians 4:31–32

> Refrain from anger and turn from wrath; do not fret – it leads only to evil.
>
> Psalm 37:8

Exercises

1. How was anger expressed as you grew up?
   By your parents? Your siblings/friends? Teachers?

2. Did anyone have rages? What happened? How did that make you feel?

3. Some people who feel anger is wrong try to cover it up, but it leaks out in passive aggression. Here are some ways they may display this. Do any sound familiar?

- non-communication
- obstructing
- sulking
- chronic lateness
- not fully engaging in conversation
- self-pity
- blaming others
- withholding
- manipulative helplessness.

All the behaviours on the list are ways of displaying anger that has been suppressed. This is not a healthy way to express anger. There will be pain from growing up with a passive aggressive parent.

My parents expressed anger by

_____

When I was a child I displayed anger by

_____

Now I am an adult I express anger by

_____

How do you display anger? Here are some examples of negative ways of displaying anger:

- withdrawing
- getting upset and crying
- punishing others
- shouting
- hitting
- swearing
- swallowing it
- abusive language.

Here are some healthier ways to diffuse the emotion of anger:

- making a noise
- releasing the energy by going for a run
- hitting a pillow
- running on the spot
- writing it out and ripping up what you have written
- praying out loud in your prayer language
- digging the garden or weeding
- using the energy created by anger to do something with your body, such as kicking a ball
- ripping to shreds an old newspaper.

Ask Jesus to free you from the roots of any unhealthy display of anger, such as rage or passive aggression.

Make a list of those against whom you have harboured anger and rage, especially those who have hurt you mentally, emotionally, physically, or sexually.

If appropriate write a letter (DO NOT SEND IT) expressing your emotions and spelling out how anger has hurt you, then shred it. If anger rises in you while doing this and you feel tension in your body, hit out the strength of the anger in a safe way by striking big pillows or cushions.

Realise the immensity of your feelings and confess to Jesus any rage, bitterness, resentment, vengefulness, or hatred. Receive forgiveness and pass it on to those who have hurt you.

A helpful book to read is *Healing Life's Hurts: Let Your Anger Work for You*, by Graham Bretherick.

IDENTITY

God calls Himself "I Am that I Am" and makes us in His image. This means our identity is very important to our spiritual health: we must know who God really is and who we ourselves really are. There are many wonderful Bible verses to help us. When you have looked up the Scriptures in these two lists, write out one Scripture from each list every week, digest it, and proclaim it. Let them become part of you and strengthen your new identity in Christ.

Who God really is

God is King of the universe. This means that all circumstances are ultimately in His hands. He is in control of my life (Psalm 24:1; 1 Chronicles 29:11–12; Job 12:10; Romans 8:38–39).

God is righteous. He cannot sin against me (Psalms 119:137, 142; Psalm 36:6; Psalm 103:6).

God is just. He will always be fair with me (Deuteronomy 32:4).

God is love. He wants to help me to get the most out of life (1 John 4:8).

God is eternal. The plan He is working out for me is everlasting (Deuteronomy 33:27).

God is all knowing. He knows all about me and my situation and how to work it out for good (2 Chronicles 16:9; Psalm 139:1–6).

God is everywhere. There is nowhere I can go that He won't take care of me (Psalm 139:7–10).

God is all powerful. There is nothing He can't do on my behalf (Job 42:2).

God is truth. He cannot lie to me (Hebrews 6:18; Titus 1:2).

God is unchangeable. I can depend on Him (Malachi 3:6).

God is faithful. I can trust Him to do what He promises (2 Peter 1:3-4; Jeremiah 29:11-13).

God is holy. He will be holy in all His acts (Revelation 15).

Who I am in Christ

I am a new creation (2 Corinthians 5:16-19).

I belong to God (Romans 14:7-8).

I am the apple of His eye (Psalm 17:8).

I am His treasured possession (Deuteronomy 7:6).

The Holy Spirit lives in me (John 14:26; 1 Corinthians 3:16).

I am a child of God (1 John 5:18-19).

I am the aroma of Christ (2 Corinthians 2:15).

I am written on His hands (Isaiah 49:16).

He took my guilt and shame on the cross (Hebrews 12:2; Romans 8:1-17).

He died for me (1 Peter 2:24; Romans 6:23; 2 Corinthians 5:21).

He bought me with a price – His life (1 Corinthians 6:19-20).

I will be with Him for eternity (Matthew 28:20; John 3:16).

I am tenderly loved (Jeremiah 31:3).

Nothing can separate me from His love (Romans 8:39).

God is my Father (Isaiah 64:8; John 14:23; John 20:17).

As you get used to doing this on a regular basis you will no longer have to look at the sheet, because these truths will become part of you as you **"let the word of Christ dwell in you richly"** (Colossians 3:16 NKJV).

As you read the Bible every day, notice other truths about who you are in Him; treasure them and write them down. Make up a promise box with cards in and fill with Scriptures that affirm who He is and affirm you in Him. Read them often until those truths sink in and become part of you.

Go through Scripture, seeing the truth, and start declaring it. For example, look at the text below:

> **So God created mankind in his own image, in the image of God he created them; male and female he created them.**
>
> Genesis 1:27

Then declare the truth aloud: "I am created in the image of God."

Find more verses that you can start declaring aloud. This will not only build you up with truth but it keeps the enemy at bay. Fill your mind with truth and you will be able to recognise and refute the enemy's deceit and lies.

As you pray, speak to God as your:

- Creator
- Father
- Provider
- Brother
- Friend
- Shepherd
- Healer
- Saviour
- King
- Lord.

He is Father   I am_____   He is my_____

He is King   I am_____   He is my_____

He is Brother   I am_____   He is my_____

He is Saviour   I am_____   He is my_____

He is Teacher   I am_____   He is my_____

He is Friend   I am_____   He is my_____

He is Healer   I am_____   He is my_____

He is Comforter   I am_____   He is my_____

He is Counsellor   I am_____   He is my_____

He is Shepherd   I am_____   He is my_____

Because of Jesus I am my Father's daughter/son; therefore I am a daughter/son of the King!

LOSS

With any type of loss we may feel empty inside. Meditating on Scripture can fill that space with truth. In Scripture we are told that Jesus has many names. One of them He called Himself is "the Truth". He said, "I am the way and the truth and the life" (John 14:6). We may know Him as our friend or our Lord. We can also get to know many more of His names. Jesus is the bread of life and that means we can feed on Him and His word. He is also the good shepherd who laid down His life for us, His sheep. He carries us when we are hurt, as a shepherd carries a lamb. Below are some Scriptures that will help fill that space as you read them and digest them, as you would good food.

With the following exercise take just one line of Scripture a day.

Look at Psalm 23 and meditate on it.

Take each word and take it in turns to emphasise it. It is a good way to learn and digest the verse. It can be very empowering.

> **The** *Lord is my shepherd*
> *The* **Lord** *is my shepherd*
> *The Lord* **is** *my shepherd*
> *The Lord is* **my** *shepherd*
> *The Lord is my* **shepherd**

Continue through the whole psalm, saying it out loud. It is very comforting and has the effect of going inside you. The Lord can use Scripture in many different ways to bring healing and freedom. Jesus doesn't just speak the word; the Bible tells us that He *is* the Word.

Scriptures

...all the days ordained for me were written in your book before one of them came to be.

Psalm 139:16

"Blessed are those who mourn, for they shall be comforted."

Matthew 5:4

"He will wipe every tear from their eyes. There will be no more death or mourning or crying or pain, for the old order of things has passed away."

Revelation 21:4

Humble yourselves, therefore, under God's mighty hand, that he may lift you up in due time. Cast all your anxiety on him because he cares for you.

1 Peter 5:6–7

My flesh and my heart may fail, but God is the strength of my heart and my portion forever.

Psalm 73:26

EMOTIONALLY ABSENT PARENTS

Write a letter to your mother and then to your father (do not give it to them). Put in the letter all the things that you are thankful for in what they gave you as you grew up. Then describe in detail how they may have let you down or failed you. After re-reading your letters, pray and thank God for your parents – make a start and forgive them their failings. Keep on working through your detailed list of the ways they failed you, forgiving them for their failings. You might need to do this several times before it doesn't hurt any more.

Look at the character and personality of your parents:

- What do you see in yourself that comes from them?
- Where have you judged aspects of them negatively and rejected them in yourself?

Confess that judgment, of them and of yourself, to Jesus and ask His forgiveness.

Accept the good traits you have inherited. Thank God for them, embrace them, and celebrate them.

Identify those traits you share with your mother or father that you despise. Ask the Lord to help you change.

If appropriate, forgive yourself for failing your own children in those or other areas.

If appropriate, ask the Lord to make you a good parent (when the time comes, if you are not yet a parent). If you didn't have a good role model of parenting, ask Father God to teach you and mould you.

Get rid of any lies you have believed about your heavenly Father, and affirm the truth of who He is. Look at the table below. If your parent was like any of the things on the left-hand list, you may have transferred that onto how you see your heavenly Father. Out loud renounce the lies and out loud speak out the truth from the right-hand list. Look up the Scripture references. Feed on them to give you what you didn't have.

Lies	Truth
Not interested and distant	Up close, personal, and involved (Psalm 139:1–8)
Uncaring	Kind and compassionate and loving (Psalm 103:8–18)
Cold-hearted	Affectionate (Isaiah 40:11)
Strict and demanding	Accepting and filled with love (Zephaniah 3:17)
Impatient and angry	Slow to anger, abounding in love (Exodus 34:6; 2 Peter 3:9)
Cruel or abusive	Protective of me, gentle, my shield (Psalm 18:2; Isaiah 42:3)

Scriptures

"Can a mother forget the baby at her breast and have no compassion on the child she has borne? Though she may forget, I will not forget you! See, I have engraved you on the palms of my hands; your walls are ever before me."

Isaiah 49:15–16

"I will be his father and he will be my son."

1 Chronicles 17:13

A father to the fatherless, a defender of widows...

Psalm 68:5

... the Spirit you received brought about your adoption to sonship. And by him we cry, "Abba, Father."

Romans 8:15

We are all "children of God."

John 1:12

REJECTION

Jesus understands rejection (Isaiah 53:3). He was rejected by His own people when they were given the choice of Barabbas or Jesus to be crucified. They rejected Jesus.

On the cross Jesus felt the separation from His Father as He took the sin of the whole world on Himself, all the sin that ever was or will be committed. He cried out, "My God, my God, why have you forsaken me?" (Matthew 27:46).

> **He was despised and rejected by mankind, a man of suffering, and familiar with pain.**
>
> Isaiah 53:3

> **He heals the broken-hearted and binds up their wounds.**
>
> Psalm 147:3

The first step is to acknowledge and release the pain of rejection. Then go on to grieve what you have lost. Give yourself permission. Then release the person/people who rejected you, by forgiving them. You will need to keep doing this until it doesn't hurt any more. The next step is accepting what has happened to you, every day asking Jesus to bring His healing.

Receive your full acceptance from Jesus. You are significant to Him.

> **Therefore if any man be in Christ, he is a new creature: old things are passed away; behold, all things are become new.**
>
> 2 Corinthians 5:17 KJV

Let the truth sink in:

> **Though my father and mother forsake me, the Lord will receive me.**
>
> Psalm 27:10

I am convinced that neither death nor life, neither angels nor demons, neither the present nor the future, nor any powers, neither height nor depth, nor anything else in all creation, will be able to separate us from the love of God that is in Christ Jesus our Lord.

Romans 8:38–39

God's promises and words of comfort:

Whoever dwells in the shelter of the Most High will rest in the shadow of the Almighty. I will say of the Lord, "He is my refuge and my fortress, my God, in whom I trust."

Psalm 91:1–2

HELPFUL BOOKS, RESOURCES, AND ORGANISATIONS

Go to www.ourhandshishealing.co.uk for worksheets and other useful resources.

BOOKS

The Holy Spirit & Gifts

Jeannie Morgan, *Encounter The Holy Spirit*, Monarch Books/Elevation, 2011.
David Pytches, *Come Holy Spirit*, Hodder & Stoughton, 1985.*

Physical & Emotional Healing

Francis MacNutt, *Healing*, Ave Maria Press, 1999.
Francis MacNutt, *The Prayer that Heals*, Ave Maria Press, 1980.

Inner Healing

Frank & Catherine Fabio, *Healing the Past, Releasing Your Future*, Sovereign World, 2006.
Jim Glennon, *Your Healing is Within You*, Bridge Publishing, 1991.
Dennis & Mathew Linn, *Healing Life's Hurts*, Paulist Press, 1997.
Tom Marshall, *Healing from the Inside Out*, Sovereign World Ltd, 2000.
Josh McDowell, *His Image, My Image*, Thomas Nelson Inc., 1993.
Jeannie Morgan, *Let The Healing Begin*, David C. Cook/Kingsway, 2007.
Russ Parker, *Free to Fail*, Triangle Books, 1998.
Leanne Payne, *The Broken Image*, Baker Books, 1995.
Leanne Payne, *Restoring the Christian Soul Through Healing Prayer*, Baker Books, 1996.
Mary Pytches, *A Child No More*, Hodder & Stoughton, 1996.*
Mary Pytches, *Who Am I?*, Hodder & Stoughton, 1999.*
Mary Pytches, *Yesterday's Child*, Hodder & Stoughton, 1996.*
David Seamands, *Healing for Damaged Emotions*, David C. Cook, 1991.

Spiritual Healing

Marc Dupont, *Walking Out of Spiritual Abuse*, Renew, 1997.
R. T. Kendall, *Total Forgiveness*, Hodder & Stoughton, 2003.

Abuse

Nancy Alcorn, *Violated – Mercy for Sexual Abuse*, Winepress Publishing, 2008.
Tori Dante, *Our Little Secret*, Hodder & Stoughton, 2006.*
Marc Dupont, *Walking Out of Spiritual Abuse*, Renew, 1997.
Paula Sandford, *Healing Victims of Sexual Abuse*, Charisma House, 2009.

Self-Abuse

Nancy Alcorn, *Cut – Mercy for Self Harm*, Winepress Publishing, 2007.
Dr Kate Middleton, *Eating Disorders: The Path To Recovery*, Lion Books, 2007.

Deliverance

David Devenish, *Demolishing Strongholds*, Authentic Media, 2000.
Francis MacNutt, *Deliverance from Evil Spirits*, Chosen Books, 2009.

Bereavement

Ron Dunn, *When Heaven is Silent*, Authentic Media, 2008.

Addictions

Nancy Alcorn, *Trapped – Mercy for Addictions*, Winepress Publishing, 2008.
Don Williams, *Jesus and Addiction*, RPI Publishing, 1993.

Anger

Dr Dan B. Allender, *The Wounded Heart*, Navpress, 2008.
Dr Dan B. Allender, *The Wounded Heart Workbook*, Navpress, 2008.
Graham Bretherick, *Healing Life's Hurts: Make Your Anger Work for You*, Monarch Books, 2008.

Sexual Sin

John White, *Eros Defiled*, InterVarsity Press, 1977.
John White, *Eros Redeemed*, InterVarsity Press, 1993.

Mental Illness

Cathy Wield, *A Thorn in My Mind: Mental Illness, Stigma and the Church*, Instant Apostle, 2012.

Stillbirth, Miscarriage & Abortion

Pam Vredevelt, *Empty Arms*, Multnomah, 2001.
Jack Hayford, *I'll Hold You in Heaven*, Regal, 2009.

Pornography Addiction

Tim Chester, *Captured By A Better Vision: Living Porn Free*, InterVarsity Press, 2010.

(*May be out of print, but can be found second-hand online.)

DVDS

Mary Pytches *(6-week courses with workbooks, available at www.new-wine.org)*:

Road to Maturity

The Marks of Maturity

John Wimber *(available at www.vineyardresources.com)*:

Kingdom of God

The Cross

Spiritual Warfare

Signs & Wonders

Spiritual Gifts

Teach Us to Pray

Darren Wilson *(Inspirational material for small groups or congregations, available at www.wpfilm.com)*:

Finger of God

Furious Love

Father of Lights

COURSES

Holy Trinity Brompton run the following courses *(www.htb.org.uk)*:

The Bereavement Journey

Dealing with Depression

New ID for Eating Disorders

The Recovery Course (for those with various addictions)

Restored Lives (for those separated or divorced)

The Post Abortion Healing Course

The Well Course (for those who have experienced rape or sexual abuse)

TRAINING

Deep Release *(www.deeprelease.org.uk)* – Training Courses and one day training for counsellors and church pastoral workers from psychotherapist Pauline Andrew and team.

OTHER RESOURCES

Poems by Marilyn Hulland: www.godsparpoems.com

ORGANISATIONS

Acorn Christian Foundation – training and support, www.acornchristian.org, 01420 478122.

Alcoholics Anonymous – www.alcoholics-anonymous.org.uk, helpline: 0845 769 7555.

Anorexia and Bulimia Care – www.anorexiabulimiacare.org.uk, 0300 011 1213.

Association of Christian Counsellors, www.acc-uk.org, 0845 124 9569.

Beacon Foundation – helpline for survivors of satanic cult/ritual abuse, 01745 343600

BEAT (previously the Eating Disorders Association) – information, help, support groups, resources, www.b-eat.co.uk, 0845 634 1414.

Bespoke – counselling, coaching, prayer ministry, marriage enrichment. Support for church leaders, groups, teams, organisations. www.bespokepollards.com, 01392 882209.

British Association for Counselling and Psychotherapy, www.bacp.co.uk, 0145 588 3300.

Burrswood – Christian Centre for Healthcare and Ministry, www.burrswood.org.uk, 0189 286 3637.

Care for the Family & Bereaved Parents Network, www.care.org.uk, 0292 081 0800.

Child Death Helpline, www.childdeathhelpline.org.uk, Freephone 0800 282 986; freephone for mobiles: 0808 800 6019.

Christian Healing Mission, www.healingmission.org, 0207 603 8118.

Churches' Child Protection Advisory Service, www.ccpas.co.uk, 0845 120 455.

Cruse Bereavement Care, www.crusebereavementcare.org.uk, helpline: 0844 477 9400.

CWR Education and training in counselling, 01252 784700.

Deep Release – courses around the UK, publications, and counsellors, www.deeprelease.org.uk, 01277 226121.

Freedom from Torture – centres in England and Scotland, www.freedomfromtorture.org, 020 7697 7777.

Harnhill Centre of Christian Healing, prayer ministry, and training, www.harnhillcentre.org.uk, 01285 850283.

Kainos Trust (eating disorders) – teaching and counselling, 01594 516284.

Kaleidoscope Project – education, training, counselling in drug-related issues, 0845 4506507.

Life for the World Trust – training and support for churches and community projects to set people free from addictions, www.lftw.org.

Mildmay Mission Hospital, London – Christian hospital providing care for those living with or affected by HIV or AIDS, www.mildmay.org, 0207 613 6300.

Mind and Soul – training and facilitating networks for churches. Conferences to inform and engage leaders and individuals about the needs of those with mental health issues, www.mindandsoul.info.

The National Association for People Abused in Childhood, www.napac.org.uk, 0800 085 330.

Nationwide Christian Trust – helpline: 0044 844 576 (international), 0844 576 8876 (UK).

Rape Crisis and Sexual Abuse, www.rapecrisis.org.uk, Freephone helpline: 0808 802 9999.

S.A.N.D.S. Stillbirth and Neonatal Death Society – www.uk-sands.org. Excellent website offering information and help to bereaved parents and relatives. Helpline offering a listening ear or help to parents or relatives: 0207 436 5881.

Self-Harm – a charity providing training for individuals or organisations (part of Youthscape), www.selfharm.co.uk.

United Kingdom Narcotics Anonymous – www.ukna.org, helpline: 0300 999 1212.

The WAY Foundation (for men and women who have been widowed) – www.wayfoundation.org.uk, 0300 012 4929.

Young Minds – booklets about mental health and young people, including bullying, depression, eating disorders etc., www.youngminds.org.uk, 0207 089 5074.